P9-DWZ-886

Wine *for* Every Day *and* Every Occasion

Other books by
Dorothy J. Gaiter and John Brecher

Love by the Glass: Tasting Notes from a Marriage
The Wall Street Journal Guide to Wine: New and Improved

Wine *for* Every Day *and* Every Occasion

red, white, and

bubbly to celebrate

the joy of living

Dorothy J. Gaiter *and*
John Brecher

WILLIAM MORROW
An Imprint of HarperCollins*Publishers*

WINE FOR EVERY DAY AND EVERY OCCASION. Copyright © 2004 by Dorothy J. Gaiter and John Brecher. All rights reserved. Printed in the United States of America. No part of this book may be used or reproduced in any manner whatsoever without written permission except in the case of brief quotations embodied in critical articles and reviews. For information address HarperCollins Publishers Inc., 10 East 53rd Street, New York, NY 10022.

HarperCollins books may be purchased for educational, business, or sales promotional use. For information please write: Special Markets Department, HarperCollins Publishers Inc., 10 East 53rd Street, New York, NY 10022.

FIRST EDITION

Designed by Leah Carlson-Stanisic

THE WALL STREET JOURNAL® is a trademark and service mark of Dow Jones & Company, Inc.

Printed on acid-free paper

Library of Congress Cataloging-in-Publication Data

Gaiter, Dorothy J.
    Wine for every day and every occasion: red, white, and bubbly to celebrate the joy of living / Dorothy J. Gaiter and John Brecher. — 1st ed.
        p. cm.
    Includes index.
    ISBN 0-06-054817-7
    1. Wine and winemaking.   I. Title: Wine for every day and every occasion.   II. Brecher, John.   III. Title.

TP548.G1755 2004
641.2'2—dc22   2004042429

04 05 06 07 08 WBC/RRD 10 9 8 7 6 5 4 3

To Zoë and Media

Contents

Introduction

"The Most Delicious Wine"

"I'm not very interested in wine, but as you've pointed out, you mostly write about the good things in life, with a wine column as the vehicle. Along the way, I've accidentally learned a bunch about wine." —**JOHN MARTIN, STAMFORD, CONNECTICUT**

"I think that the service you provide is to nudge Americans ever so gently toward a real culture of wine drinking, stripped of the status seeking and pretentious one-upmanship that so often comes into this field." —**TERRY HUGHES, NEW YORK CITY**

What's the most memorable wine you have ever had? If you're like most people, your answer isn't something like "Ah, yes. It was the '59 Latour. It had marvelous hints of brambles and a finish like a blushing nymph." Nope, if you're like most people, the most memorable bottle of wine you ever drank was that simple white wine at the taverna while you were on vacation in Greece or the rustic red you shared in Tuscany or the Champagne on your wedding day or even that carafe of cheap red you sipped on your first date at that little Italian joint on the corner with the red-and-white-checked tablecloths. Sharing with friends, remembering, and making life a celebration—that's what wine is really all about. That's what this book is about, too.

When our daughter Media was born in 1989, she was five weeks premature, so the doctor immediately placed her in an incubator in a bright white room. There she was, all by herself, right in the middle of the room, with lights shining on her. We think wine, which isn't nearly as precious as Media, is too often presented the same way: as something sitting on a pedestal in the middle of a room, alone, in a vacuum. It's sad that this image of wine, as a thing apart, has become prevalent in the United States, because that's not how wine was meant to be enjoyed—and, indeed, is not the way to enjoy wine. We couldn't wait to spring Media from that lonely, sterile room, to hold her close, coo at her, and introduce her to her adoring grandparents. Wine, too, should be brought down to eye level, passed around to people you care about, and enjoyed.

We have been drinking, studying, and—mostly—enjoying wine almost since the day we met and fell in love, June 4, 1973. We were both twenty-one at the time, starting work on the same day at the *Miami Herald*. For more than a quarter-century, we were prominent "hard news" journalists— Dottie was a reporter, editor, and editorial writer at the *Miami Herald*, the *Miami News*, the *New York Times*, and the *Wall Street Journal*; John was a reporter and editor at the *Miami Herald, Newsweek*, and the *Wall Street Journal*. During all that time, wine was our refuge, our private passion. We tried wines from all over the world, and, whenever we could, we traveled to try wines at the source. What always attracted us, however, was not the wine itself but the total experience of having the wine, the memories associated with it. Truth is, we really did have the '59 Latour, and it really was remarkable, one of the greatest wines we've ever tasted, but what we remember best about it was that we shared it with John's brother Jim, the first time he visited us in New York. We remember what the wine tasted like, but we also remember sitting around the dining room table laughing so hard as Jim told more and more outrageous stories about John's boyhood while the wine slowly disappeared.

Wine is such an important part of our life and our memories that, early on, we began to save labels (see "Saving the Memories") and keep notes. We remember occasions, restaurant meals, and holidays by the wines we drank. We look at the old labels, and we might recall what the wine tasted like, but we most certainly recall what we were doing when we drank it, what was going on in our lives. To us, that's what wine is all about. To this day, we're bored when people want to discuss with us whether the 2004 vintage in Bordeaux will match the 2002, but if you want to tell us about a great Chardonnay you shared with the winemaker while visiting wineries, we're all ears.

We became wine writers by accident. In 1998, John was page one editor of the *Wall Street Journal* and Dottie was the *Journal*'s news editor in charge of urban-affairs coverage. A friend of ours, Joanne Lipman, was named editor of the new section of the *Journal* called *Weekend Journal* and asked if we'd be interested in writing a column about wine in our spare time. We figured we'd do her a favor, so we agreed. Heck, how long could a column about wine take? Well, it ate up our lives. From the first column, "Tastings" was enormously popular. We began receiving hundreds of letters from readers. Wine stores across the country reported that they sold out of our recommendations within hours of the column's publication. All day we worked at our "real" jobs; all night, every night, we worked on the column, conducting our own blind tastings. Of course, this did not amuse Media or her younger sister, Zoë. Plus, we were getting fried.

By early 2000 we couldn't take it anymore. We went to our boss, Paul Steiger, the managing editor, a terrific journalist and an even better person. We told him we simply couldn't do both jobs anymore. He paused for a moment, leaned back, and finally said, "Well, which job would you rather do?" It took us about, oh, a nanosecond to tell him we'd like to do the column full time, and he said we could. It's a good thing, because the column's popularity has only grown since then. We now appear on television and radio, make speeches, and write books in addition to the column. And—this is our favorite part of the job—we get letters. Lots and lots of letters. Over the years we have received, and we have personally answered, more than twenty-five thousand letters and e-mails from readers. These letters have given us a unique perspective on what people really want to know about wine.

What we have learned is that people simply want to enjoy wine, especially as part of celebrations and holidays. What wine should I lay down for my newborn? What wine is best with Thanksgiving turkey? What wine do I give my wine-loving friend for Christmas? What wine do I serve at a wedding? Readers also want to know how to have more fun with wine: How do I hold a wine tasting? How do I get the most from a visit to wine country?

We try to answer all of these questions and many more. The book is arranged somewhat chronologically, so that it is a kind of month-by-month guide to making life fuller with wine, both enriching rituals and creating new ones. In many chapters we also have listed a number of specific wines you might look for when celebrating a certain occasion. We do this a little reluctantly because we believe you should always try something new. There are new wines on the shelves all the time, from new vintages, new regions, new winemakers. New is fun; different is fun; and no one, including us, can tell you what you will like. One thing we've learned as wine writers is that people want some specific guidance, especially when it comes to important occasions. So we have tried to answer that call with lists of specific wines. In every case these are wines that have been our favorites in blind tastings or are wines that we have found consistent year after year in our "real life." Our advice is impartial. We accept no free wine, don't meet privately with winemakers when they visit New York, and do not attend any event that is not open to the public. We buy all of our wines from retail shelves. We believe the wines speak for themselves.

We have tried to list enough specific wines so that you might be able to find one, but it is impossible to know what's available where you live. A wine that's as common as water in one state is rare in another. One wine store might have dozens of French wines, and another might have few. It's important to find a wine store you like and trust (see "Wine Shopping"), because no column or book will be able to tell you what's available in your neighborhood. And don't obsess about vintages. We have listed vintages for some of the wines based on our tastings, because the notes relate to that vintage (vintage is listed in parentheses after the wine notes). But good wineries tend to be consistent. If you liked Geyser Peak Sauvignon Blanc 2003, you will probably like the 2004 as well. We have also listed prices as a general guide. If we say one wine costs $10 and another costs $30, at least you'll get a general sense of where they fit on the price scale.

We have organized the book so that you can get targeted, practical advice, such as what Champagne to drink on New Year's Eve, but we don't mean this as a how-to book. Our hope is that you will read it from front to back and grasp our true meaning: wine is part of a full life and can make your days a little better in many ways. Ultimately, the subtext of this book is about something far more important than wine. It's about community. *You* are the wine community. Throughout this book you will meet scores of people just like you—regular people who see wine as something to be shared and savored with friends and loved ones. These are the people who are the real experts at overseas wine travel, at tasting groups, and at tailgate parties. To truly understand love and wine, meet John Watson, who once broke our hearts and then taught us that romance knows no age (see "Open That Bottle Night").

It is clear to us that the wine community is growing. That's not showing up very much in statistics yet, but look closely and you can see that America has finally turned the corner. As we shopped for holiday presents over the past couple of years, we were amazed by how many more wine-related gifts are available in all sorts of general-interest catalogs. There are more television shows about wine, both regional and national. Wine bars were one of the hottest trends of the past couple of years. Our own column runs in newspapers all over the United States. Something important is happening—and that's great, because wine, to us, is really about something more, something deeper. Wine is universal, linking people, places, and times in a more special way than even we could have imagined. During the war in Iraq in 2003, our colleague Helene Cooper, who was embedded with the troops in Kuwait, wrote a story about Warrant Officer La'Quitta Joseph, one of the few women on the front lines. This was in Helene's original draft: "She fantasizes about things at home to help get herself through the days—preparing a spaghetti dinner with Italian herbs or soaking in her bathtub with a glass of white Zinfandel wine. The last is mentioned shame-faced; she said she's been trying hard to like the more highbrow Merlots, especially those recommended by her heroes, *Wall Street Journal* wine critics John Brecher and Dorothy Gaiter, who she reads every week. But so far, she hasn't managed to acquire a taste for much beyond white Zinfandel." While this didn't make it into the newspaper—damn editors!—we were so touched that we told our readers about Ms. Joseph and conducted a blind tasting of white Zinfandel on her behalf (for our favorites, see "The Fourth of July"). That brought a note from Irv Hamilton of Alameda, California, who wrote that the column "created images of the kinds of positive things that go through the minds of people who are coping with difficult situations. Thank you for noting and endorsing the white Zinfandel–based fantasies of an army officer on duty now. Thanks also for causing me to recall a special moment with a glass of wine as a soldier a long time ago." We asked Mr. Hamilton to tell us more. His letter, in so many ways, sums up everything we love about wine and everything we find important about it.

> *I signed up to go into the army right out of college, and I was on active duty from July 1957 to July 1959. I was assigned to the 2nd Armored Cavalry Regiment and sent to Nürnberg, Germany. Our unit patrolled the border between what was then West Germany and Czechoslovakia. While in college (Northwestern), I was familiar with German wines, because they were inexpensive and readily available. Moselbluemchen and Liebfraumilch sold for 99 cents a bottle or less. These were obviously pretty ordinary wines and not particularly good examples of what German winemakers can do. But I liked them even so. A friend of mine in the regiment also liked wine, and one evening we happened to meet a German World War II veteran. He had been a POW in the U.S. and had been well treated, so he liked Americans. Particularly soldiers.*
>
> *When we talked about our interest in wine, he invited us to meet him and his wife at a* weinstube *called La Boheme. We had been to a number of* bierstuben, *but we had no idea what a weinstube was. On that first visit to La Boheme, and other times we met them there, he introduced us to German wines. Doing so, we shared some wonderful evenings learning about the wine-producing regions and the grapes. We became fascinated by German wines and decided to make a pilgrimage to one of the places from which they came. We had jointly bought an old Volkswagen, and one weekend we got a pass and went to the wine country. I had thought that first trip had been to the Mosel district. But my army buddy, John, who I called this week, corrected me, saying that it was on the Rhine. As we recalled the trip, I realized he was right.*
>
> *"Do you remember that place overlooking the river, where we sat in an outside patio under a gazebo with grapevines?" I asked.*
>
> *"Of course," he answered without hesitation.*
>
> *"And the big bowl-shaped wineglasses," I recalled.*
>
> *"With the green base," he added.*

We talked about it, recalling the event in detail, especially the color and taste of the well-chilled wine. We decided that it was the most delicious wine we had ever tasted. We tried to recall what we were drinking. But with all the years that have passed, we don't remember the name. We do remember the day, the sun coming through the overhead grapevines, the view of the river, and the taste of the wine.

I said, "That was one of those truly memorable moments." And we agreed there was no question about that.

Since then, I've continued to drink German wines, particularly for special occasions, because for some reason fine German wines seem festive. I also drink wines made from the Riesling grape here in the U.S. And when I drink them, I always recall that day overlooking the river and relishing that very special wine.

This morning, I logged onto the Internet and found an on-line phone book for Nürnberg, Germany. I looked up the name of the man who had started all this at La Boheme weinstube and found a phone number. The man who answered the phone was our German friend's son. I explained that I was calling on the chance that I would be able to talk to the man who had befriended two wine-drinking GIs. Sadly, he died a number of years ago. But his son was obviously pleased when I told him of his father's hospitality and how I still think about his father today. He invited me to visit him should I travel to Germany. And if I do, he said we would drink some good German wine.

With all these pleasant thoughts rattling around in my brain, today at lunch I went for a walk. I visited my favorite nearby wine shop and bought a bottle of 2000 Bacharacher Hahn Riesling Kabinett. I will chill it, bring together some friends, and share all of this with them. And, yes, all of this— the very pleasant recollections, the phone calls, and the visit to the wine shop—happened as a result of your column last week about an army warrant officer dreaming of drinking white Zinfandel.

Wine-Tasting Parties | The Nouveau Thing

"I would love some recommendations for a home wine-tasting party. We want to get a total of about ten people and just try some wines that ordinarily we would not try back to back. I was wondering if you had any overarching advice. New glasses with each bottle? Salty treats between wines? Make sure everyone has a cab ride home?" —DAN PIETTE, HOUSTON

Some people say that Beaujolais Nouveau, which arrives with great fanfare on the third Thursday of every November, is nothing more than an excuse for a party. To which we say: "Yeah, what's your point?" To us, Nouveau is such a great excuse for a party that our Nouveau party is the only one we throw all year. It's also the perfect way to prove to yourself that a wine-tasting party can be far more fun than you ever imagined.

Our party-giving days began badly. Many years ago we threw one to welcome an old friend to New York. Dottie's famous dip didn't set, the record player (yes, this was a long time ago) broke midway, and it seemed as though everyone stayed for five minutes and then said they had to go home to put the kids to bed—although none of our friends had kids back then. The party was so notoriously bad that we're sure it's still studied at hospitality schools all over the world. Our parties have improved since then, and we give all the credit to the Nouveau.

Beaujolais, which is made from the Gamay grape, is one of the greatest wine bargains in the world. There is plain Beaujolais, then the slightly better Beaujolais-Villages, and then the even better Beaujolais with names like

Fleurie and Moulin-à-Vent. All of them are fruity, fun, and reasonably priced. They go with a wide variety of food, from hamburgers to salmon, and can be served at a variety of temperatures. Gosh, what more could anyone want in a wine? These Beaujolais show up several months or a year after the harvest, so, for example, the 2004 vintage will be on shelves sometime around the middle of 2005. Nouveau, though, is picked, fermented very quickly, and released right away, just weeks after harvest. Our parties celebrate the fact that it's the first wine of the new harvest in France. A serious wine? No. But it is serious about being fun. It's meant to be drunk young, when it's filled with fruit and exuberance. By tradition, it should never be consumed after the end of the year in which it was produced.

Because it is such an unpretentious, fun, gulpable wine—and because it's inexpensive—it's just the right place to start if you're thinking about a wine-tasting party. Now, we're not talking here about a serious wine tasting for a group of serious wine tasters; for more on that, see "Wine-Tasting Groups," which is about how to form a wine-tasting group. Those are fun, too, but here we're talking about un-self-conscious, unrestrained, informal fun. Not only does the exuberant wine help create an exuberant party, but the tasting itself gives people who may never have met each other something to talk about. Here's how we do our party.

    ᐷ **Buying the Wine.** If you are going to hold a Nouveau party on the actual day that the wine is released and is therefore available for purchase—and it's always the same day all over the world—you need to leave your morning free to buy it. Call a few days before to see which store is expecting the wine—you can never be sure. If you're lucky, one store will have three or four different ones. For a good wine-tasting party experience, you should have at least three different wines, and four is better. More than that begins to get cumbersome for a casual party, though we have served as many as six.

    ᐷ **Which Ones to Buy.** It really doesn't matter—the fun here, after all, is deciding on the favorite among them—but there are a few we've found consistent year after year. See the list at the end of this section.

℀ **Number of Bottles.** For our sixty friends, we buy six bottles of each wine. There are usually six glasses of wine in a bottle, but this is a tasting, not a frat party, so we figure ten glasses per bottle.

℀ **Chill Out.** These are better slightly cool, so if your house or apartment is warm—and ours is always overheated in late November—you should put the bottles in the refrigerator for a little while, even a couple of hours, before the party if you have the time.

℀ **To Bag or Not to Bag.** We put all the wines on a table with a big number in front of each one, and we don't hide the labels by putting the bottles in bags. For an informal party like this, that's too complex.

℀ **What Food to Serve.** Because Nouveau is young and fresh, we think vibrant tastes go best with it. We serve flavorful finger food and plenty of it, such as fried shrimp with ginger garlic sauce, asparagus wrapped in smoked salmon, sesame chicken with brandy apricot sauce, beef tenderloin on puff pastry, foie gras mousse, sweet potato tartlettes, and bourbon pecan bread pudding. For many years, we did all of this ourselves, but it just got to be too much. We realized we were working so hard that we weren't enjoying the party. So now we hire a caterer to prepare the food and to move around the crowd serving it. (Before we hired a caterer, we certainly never made foie gras mousse.)

℀ **One Glass or Many?** When our friends arrive, we hand them a glass of No. 1 and tell them that they should ultimately taste all of the wines. One glass is just fine. This is informal, after all (and more than one makes cleanup a real chore). Be sure to have some buckets around so that people can pour out wine they don't want to drink (though they won't) before moving on to the next one. Have extra glasses available (plastic glasses are okay in a pinch), because some people will inevitably put down their glasses and lose them. Trust us on this.

℀ **Keep Pouring.** This is really important. It's critical for both you and your caterers always to have a bottle in hand and move among the guests with different bottles, asking "Are you ready for No. 2?" It has been our experience that if we don't circulate with bottles, guests won't help themselves. We number the wines because few people remember the names, but everyone remembers tasting No. 3 or whichever.

ᏫᏫ **Don't Forget to Vote.** We don't have a formal vote. We just occasionally ask people, "So, what's your favorite?" It becomes obvious which wine is the favorite—not just because everybody is talking about it, but because more bottles of that one are empty. Sometimes it's fun to put a little ballot box in the corner with slips of paper and ask people to write down their favorite. Then announce the winner. Sure, one will be the favorite, but all of them will get some votes, proving that this is very much a matter of personal taste.

ᏫᏫ **Give Them the Slip.** Write down the names and prices of the wines on a piece of paper and have copies ready for everyone to take (and maybe even the name of the stores where you bought them). We've found that many people like one of the wines so much that they want to be sure to look for it the next day—and we can't tell you how many calls we've fielded from people the next day saying, "Ummm, I already forgot. What was the name of my favorite, the one with the red label?"

ᏫᏫ **Arrive Home Alive.** Make sure everyone has a way to get home safely. You want to make sure they're around for the next Nouveau party.

We guarantee you that everyone will have a good time at this party. They will even linger longer than they expected because they want to taste all of the wines. This is something that will stay with them: they will be amazed that they really could taste the difference among the wines. Many experts, for instance, sniff that all Nouveau tastes alike, but your friends will know that's not true—and they'll know that they can tell the difference, which can be a pretty eye-opening experience when it comes to wine. Some Beaujolais seems to have hints of salt, and quite a few smell like bananas (that's a function of certain yeasts that are used in the fermentation process). Your guests will walk in saying they don't know the difference between one wine and another but leave with a definite preference.

This type of party doesn't have to focus on Nouveau, of course. The wine can be Chardonnay, Merlot, or whatever. We would urge you to keep it simple, though, with the same type of wine, so this remains a party with wine tasting instead of a wine-tasting seminar.

Some Beaujolais Nouveaux

These have been among our favorite Beaujolais Nouveaux year after year. The notes here are from the 2003 vintage, but they are consistent with our notes from several years. Keep in mind that there are all sorts of Nouveau-type wines in stores in November, soon after the traditional harvest season, such as Novello from Italy. (Other regions, such as New Zealand and Australia, have harvest seasons earlier in the year.) Wine is also made in every one of the United States—yep, all fifty—and many local wineries have Nouveau-type wines that might be fun to try. Some wineries in California, including Beringer, make Nouveaux—sometimes from the same grape as Beaujolais—so you might think about including one of those in your tasting. These Beaujolais Nouveaux might cost up to $10 when they are first released—that's supposedly because of the airfare, but it's probably really because of demand—and then prices slowly slip over the next couple of weeks, usually to around $6 or so.

> ***Paul Durdilly.*** Our perennial favorite. Seriously blue-purple, with a vibrant, youthful nose. A winning combination of depth and spirit. It's exuberant and pure, with such clean, fresh-fruit tastes that it's like standing in a vineyard.

> ***Georges Duboeuf.*** The old standby is reliable as always, filled with raspberries and some richness. Nicely jammy. Its slightly heavy tastes are un-Nouveau-like and always a little disturbing to us, but there's no way to deny that this is consistently tasty.

> ***J. Arthaud.*** Vibrant fruit nose, filled with blackberries and raspberries. Clean and easy to drink, with excellent acids for food. Light on its feet, but still with a hint of earth that gives it a sense of place.

> ***Michel Picard.*** Jammy, almost chewy tastes. Fun, like a peanut butter and jelly sandwich. Simple and pleasant.

Mommessin. Bright, zesty, and fun. Nouveau is meant to be a celebratory wine, something to drink, not to sip. This is a great example
of that. A glassful of smiles.

Tasting Parties for Large Groups

It is possible to hold a really big tasting party, whether for Nouveau or
for any other kind of wine. We have organized blind wine-tasting parties for groups up to six hundred for our employer, Dow Jones & Co. We
have hosted doctors in Washington, technology executives in San Diego,
and advertising honchos in Miami, all for our employer. A mass tasting like
this takes a great deal of planning and costs real money, but this is a terrific
way to break the ice at a large gathering. Here is the memo we send to
event organizers when we are going to do a tasting. You will see that some
of these overlap with our advice for a small party, but here it is, step by
step, so you can use it as a blueprint for any large tasting:

1. You will need a large, open room. No chairs. We find that the event is
more fun and less formal when people walk around.

2. Choose four to six wines of a certain type—say, American Chardonnay
under $20. While it's possible to do this many ways—Chardonnay from
around the world or expensive versus inexpensive wines or Chardonnay
versus Riesling—we find that simple head-to-head tastings are easiest
and best in large groups.

3. Figure ten tastes per bottle. So, if you're expecting a hundred people,
get ten bottles of each wine. (Remember that this is a tasting, not a bar,
so the pourers need to understand to pour a taste, not a full glass.) Keep
tabs on how many guests are actually going to show up. You may need
to send someone out to get more wine, or, if it appears that you may
have some no-shows, you might want to hold back on opening all of the
wine beforehand. Some stores will take back unopened bottles.

4. Have one table for each different wine and one pourer at each table
(more pourers if the group is really large, of course).

5. Before the event, put all the wines in bags (plain old brown lunch bags are fine, but anything that covers the bottle to the top is good) and take out all the corks. By the time the guests show up, the bagged wines should be on the tables, and it shouldn't be possible to tell what they are. (If these are whites, keep them in the refrigerator until they're brought out and then don't worry about keeping them cold. They'll be fine as they warm up.) It's very important that all pourers understand that wine boxes, labels, and corks—anything with a winery's name on it—must be hidden so guests have no clue which wines are being served.

6. On each table, have a "spit bucket" for people to pour out their wine and a pitcher of water in case they want to rinse their glasses or their palates.

7. When people enter the room, give them a single glass. They will use that glass throughout. Have extra glasses available.

8. Have some sort of box in the room where people can place their "ballots" at the end of the event. All you really need are pieces of paper, the size of business cards, that people can write a number on, and maybe some pencils. You also need someone assigned to count the votes; if it's a large group, that person should keep a running count so the tabulating doesn't take forever at the end.

9. Schedule one hour for the event and tell everyone to be on time (because it's a tasting, they might think they can wander in anytime). With everyone there, the host can stand up and explain what this is about and how it works. Welcome them, talk a little bit about wine—what type of wine it is, why you chose that type—and then talk about how the tasting works. Explain to guests that they should taste all the wines, but they don't need to taste them in order from No. 1 to No. 6. Inform them that they will vote on their favorite wine at the end.

10. Tell people to start tasting and that they now have twenty minutes to taste all the wines and mark their ballots. We find that one hour is plenty for this whole event because people are eager to taste the wines and then eager to vote and see the "winner," so it's best to move quickly.

11. Leave everybody alone to taste and talk. In a matter of minutes, everyone will be having a grand time. In twenty minutes, remind people to taste all the wines and to mark their ballots (you will need a microphone; you can't imagine how loud this crowd will get). Then, five minutes later, remind them again to vote and tell them they have two minutes to do so. Five minutes after that, get the vote from the counter and announce the results, from least liked to favorite, including the prices. This is always greeted with moans and cheers and surprise. At this point most people will want to retaste some of the wines. Now that they know that their favorite was the cheapest, for instance, they'll want to make sure they're not crazy; and they'll want to retaste that more-expensive one that they hated. People will start changing their minds once they know the prices and the labels, which is why a blind tasting is good.

12. As people leave, give them a list of the wines they tasted and how much they cost.

The arrival of the first wine of the harvest is a great excuse for a wine-tasting party, but, hey, any reason will do. Joe and Diane S. Hudachek of Newtown, Pennsylvania, for instance, wanted to celebrate the first weekend of summer. They contacted us a couple of years ago to ask how to give a Champagne-tasting party, "just because it sounds like fun." You bet! We offered some advice and later asked how it went. Here's their response:

Sometimes things just come together, and this party was one of those times. It was a perfect summer evening. We held it on our screened porch with its paddle fans and candles. We were able to arrange the seating so that everyone could see and hear everyone else. Champagne has a way of raising expectations, and everyone came prepared for fun.

We spent a good deal of time researching Champagne. Ultimately, we decided to divide the Champagne by "style," or depth of body for want of a better description. There were six couples at the party, and each couple brought two bottles of Champagne (or sparkling wine) in their assigned category: aperitif style, blanc de blanc, medium-bodied, full-bodied, rosé, and "foreign" *(not French and not American). One bottle was to cost under $30 and the other over $50. Also, we asked guests to avoid Champagnes with which we were all familiar. We had hors d'oeuvres and desserts so that we could see the difference in taste that various foods produced.*

Everyone was at ease and so not at all shy about sharing his or her opinion. We had gotten the names of the bottles everyone was bringing beforehand, so that we were able to provide a sheet with the names and spaces for ratings and comments to each guest. The party lasted for five hours. We were drinking Champagne with good friends and learning about each other as well as about the various styles of Champagne. It was one of those evenings that you hate to see end.

Thanksgiving

How to Hail a Good Cab

"My daughter, who is temporarily living in Los Angeles, decided to have this first Thanksgiving away from home at her house. She did the turkey and stuffing with all the trimmings. I thought I would pick up a bottle of Champagne for the special occasion of her first turkey. My wife and I went to the store with the intention of picking up some bubbly. Then I saw an odd-looking bottle. It was sparkling Chardonnay from Australia. It was perfect. We had it with the turkey as well as the dessert. It was the exact thing to make the occasion more special. There is nothing like the soft pop of a cork and a nice wine to put an 'l' on a dinner." —**JERRY McILVAIN, CHICAGO**

We were scheduled to talk about Thanksgiving wines on National Public Radio. Before the appearance, the producer, Karen Grigsby Bates, sent us this note:

Let's figure out some scenarios:

Plain ol', plain ol' June Cleaver Would Have Done It This Way roast turkey.

Cajun-style fried turkey.

Turkey rubbed with southwestern spices and roasted.

Tuscan-style turkey—rubbed with garlic, rosemary, olive oil, and spun on a spit.

Then we should probably talk traditional side dishes:

What wine does one drink with greens? With brussels sprouts?

If you're serving savory and *sweet things (creamed onions, sweet potato casserole) is there one wine for both?*

And does it make sense to serve dessert wine, or should we just serve coffee and pass the Port?

If any single note ever summed up the problems of pairing your Thanksgiving dinner with wine, this was it. And that's not all. This is the premier dinner of the whole year. It's likely that you'll have friends or family over for dinner, so the stakes are really high here. There are two important things to keep in mind:

1. Relax. It's the thought that counts. We wouldn't have suggested a sparkling Australian Chardonnay to Mr. McIlvain, but, as he said, "It was perfect." Was that because the tastes melded perfectly, or was it because the family was together for a very special Thanksgiving? This is all going to work out fine.

2. You shouldn't make the wine an afterthought. Think about how much effort you put into planning your Thanksgiving meal. You don't buy just any turkey or any dinner rolls. More than just about any other meal of the year, this is the one where you'll spend the extra money on the fresh turkey and maybe the fancy bakery's finest. You should put as much thought into the wine and be willing to spend a little more on it than usual, too.

We cook a very traditional Thanksgiving dinner: roast turkey with bread stuffing, sweet potatoes with marshmallows on top, some sort of green vegetable, canned cranberry sauce, and corn soufflé. John likes white meat, and Dottie likes dark meat. Even with such a relatively straightforward dinner—it's not like we have mincemeat pie or Jell-O mold—pairing the meal with wine is a challenge.

The first step is easy: go American. Thanksgiving is a special American holiday, and it's appropriate to serve American wines. Start with an American sparkling wine, either while cooking or when guests arrive, to get the day off on a festive note. Bubbly is also quite good with light appetizers, so you can take it to the table, too. Not too long ago, there were few good American sparklers. That sure has changed. Now American sparkling wines are excellent, widely available, and often great buys. They are usually made from the same grapes as Champagne—mostly Chardonnay and Pinot

Noir—and are crafted the same way. Here are some very good, widely available, and reasonably priced American bubblies (only Champagne from the Champagne district of France can really be called Champagne, though we think life's way too short to spend much time worrying about that). Most of these are nonvintage, and all cost under $20. At the holidays, if you shop around, you can sometimes find them for $10 to $14.

Oh, one more thing: since some people don't drink red wine, they can stick with the bubbly throughout the meal. Most of us rarely drink sparklers with food, but they're often an excellent match, and some hit their heights with food. Also, remember that the traditional rule of thumb is that there are six glasses of wine in a bottle, so keep that in mind when you're shopping.

Some American Bubblies

Roederer Estate Brut (Anderson Valley). Our top choice. Clean, fresh, nicely acidic, and vibrant. This is much livelier than most and not at all heavy.

Chandon Brut Classic (California). A bit heavy, with lots of taste, but pleasant and hunger inducing. Because we often saw this on sale, this was our "house bubbly" for many years.

Chandon Blanc de Noirs (Carneros). Full, bold, and lemony, with some tastes of yeast and toast. Big enough to have with dinner. (Blanc de Noirs means the bubbly was made primarily with Pinot Noir and Pinot Meunier, while Blanc de Blancs means it was made primarily with Chardonnay.)

Mumm Cuvée Napa Blanc de Noirs (Napa Valley). Pink-tinged, with very aggressive bubbles. Fruity and pleasant, with some hints of raspberry. Very romantic.

Pacific Echo Brut (Anderson Valley). Honeyed and flowery, with honeysuckle notes. Consistently easy to drink, but not a subtle wine.

Piper Sonoma Brut (Sonoma County). So very drinkable. Clean and nicely lemony, with a lovely integration of taste and bubbles. A truly festive wine and good for just sipping.

Now, on to the main wine. What's best? That's tough. Think about the riot of flavors on the table—the light meat, the dark meat, the sweet potatoes, the green beans. Here's our solution: an American Cabernet Sauvignon with some age on it. Cabernet Sauvignon is the great red grape of Bordeaux and of America's most storied red wines. At its best, it has class and elegance made for a great Thanksgiving dinner. A Cabernet Sauvignon with some age is "red" enough for the heavier parts of the meal, but—because its tannins have broken down a bit—soft enough for the white meat and the lighter parts of the meal. Not only that, but a fine Cabernet Sauvignon with some age is an appropriate example of the bounty of America, and, like the meal itself, it will be interesting as it changes through the courses. Think we're kidding? Consider some of our own Thanksgiving wines, each from the 1974 vintage, which we used to collect, presented here with our contemporaneous notes.

Thanksgiving 1992. ***Heitz Martha's Vineyard 1974.*** Looks its age, vibrant but yellow at edges. Nose is awesome—concentrated fruit. Taste: Wow. Sweet with fruit yet dry. After it's open for fifteen minutes, the fruit is going, leaving alcohol and . . . what? After thirty minutes, a balance. Almost a heavy sweetness, not at all light. Heavy. Lots of alcohol but also lots of fruit. Fascinating.

Thanksgiving 1993. ***Louis Martini 1974.*** It looks a bit tired, but nose is terrific—rich and woody and fruity, with tobacco. Taste at first is terrific, big, rich, classy, and old; just great. But it's short-lived; after it's open for fifteen minutes, it starts getting simple, losing some of the depth. Still lots of fruit, but old.

Thanksgiving 1994. ***Freemark Abbey 1974.*** Wow. What a powerhouse. Taste is massive, fruity, with lots of black currants, cherries, and cloves. Huge, explosive finish. Cassis. Portlike. Perfect to drink now. Huge yet balanced, with lots of ripe fruit.

Thanksgiving 1995. ***Beaulieu Vineyard Georges de Latour 1974.*** Huge Cabernet nose. First taste is pretty well perfect, classy and elegant, with a long-lasting, cinnamon finish. Mouth-filling, but more with memory than with taste. Ephemeral, haunting.

Unfortunately, most people don't store old Cabernets, and most corner wine stores don't carry any. But they're out there. You have to spend some time finding one and be prepared to spend more money than usual. Here are some tips for buying an old Cabernet:

1. Start shopping early.

2. Go to a good wine store. Sometimes you can find an old treasure at a second-rate store, but that's chancy, especially because you don't know how the wine has been stored over the years.

3. Ask what kind of California Cabernet Sauvignon the store has that's at least five years old. If they look at you blankly, you're probably in the wrong store. Even though most wine is sold young and meant to be drunk right away, five years isn't very old at all for a fine red wine. You're not looking for something from the nineteenth century, after all, just something from, say, 1999. (You can do some of this shopping on the Internet, especially if you live in a state where wine can be delivered from other states.)

4. Look at the bottle. How does it look? How is the "fill"—that is, how far up the neck of the bottle does the wine come? If the fill is low, beware. Too much air in the bottle harms the wine. Is the bottle covered with dust? Has wine dripped down the label? Use common sense. A five-year-old wine isn't ancient. It shouldn't look like it is.

5. Check the price. Don't be embarrassed to put it back down if it's too expensive, though you should be prepared to spend at least $50. Hey, it's Thanksgiving.

6. Remember that older wines require some special handling. For some tips, see "Open That Bottle Night."

It's impossible to give you a specific list of wineries to look for because some of the best older Cabernets are made by lesser-known, smaller wineries, and there's no telling which—if any—old Cab you might find in your store. To be sure, the most famous wines of California, such as Screaming Eagle and Harlan Estate, would be excellent at any age. But these are hard to get and cost a fortune. For this chapter we spent a glorious week opening several of our own old Cabernets (and some good red blends) to get a sense of how they're doing. We didn't open ancient bottles or wines from cult wineries (well, maybe one) because we're just trying to give you an idea how good a decade-old Cabernet can taste, even from a small winery you might never have heard of. How were they?

Diamond Creek "Volcanic Hill" (Napa Valley) 1991. One of California's famed wineries for a reason. Black as night, with a blackberry nose filled with fruit, spice, and pepper. Nicely tart, but then it dissolves in the mouth into clouds of sweet fruit. "Every mouthful is an experience," Dottie said. It's earthy, and as it opens, the earth gets more and more pronounced, until it's like standing in the middle of a field of sweet, black earth after a spring rain. Big and gutsy yet structured and classy. The only problem: it's still very young, with a long, long life ahead of it, and it was our last bottle of this.

Durney Vineyards (Carmel Valley) 1993. Absolutely gorgeous to look at—garnet and vibrant, without a hint of age. Nose is filled with fruit, oak, cedar, spice, and tobacco. Taste is elegant, crisp with fruit, and simply lovely. Not intense or powerful, but classy. Some real undertones of tar give it backbone. Maybe a hint of age, but just a hint.

Ferrari-Carano Vineyards and Winery "Reserve" (Sonoma County) 1992. This red blend was made from the five classic grapes of Bordeaux: Cabernet Sauvignon, Cabernet Franc, Merlot, Malbec, and Petit Verdot. But, interestingly, it tastes mostly like a big California

Zinfandel—massive, filled with blackberries, spice, and pepper. It looks, smells, and even tastes dark. It's a powerhouse wine, with many years ahead of it.

Jarvis "Lake William" (Napa Valley) 1993. A blend of Cabernet Sauvignon and Cabernet Franc. Massive, rich wine, filled with awesome dark black cherries. Chewy. "Tastes like you're getting the whole grape," Dottie said. Nice lemony acids, so it's good with food. Many years ahead of it. This is a real American wine—big, bold, and proud of it.

Bernard Pradel Vineyard "Signature Selection, Howell Mountain Ranch" (Napa Valley) 1992. This is clearly showing age—it's earthy and dusty—and has the round, comforting taste of an old Pinot Noir rather than a Cabernet. Dottie calls it "a classy old dowager." It has sweet, old fruit but retains real class.

Peju Province "H.B. Vineyard" (Napa Valley) 1991. Nose is filled with vibrant fruit. The wine is classy, crisp, and structured, not rich but almost intentionally austere. Still plenty of tannins. It has age on it in a good way, with tobacco and cedar—a kind of humidor smell and some eucalyptus.

During our tasting, we talked a great deal about why we think these wines are so perfect with Thanksgiving dinner. Dottie finally nailed it while we were drinking the Peju Province, and what she says goes for all of these wines: "This is a special-occasion wine. You celebrate with it. It's not just that it goes well with the food. It goes well with the occasion. Old Cabernets have a kind of graciousness that's very Americana, that takes you back someplace very special and puts you in touch with other times and places. This wine says to your guests, 'This is a taste you'll remember forever.'"

One other thing: a central element of your Thanksgiving tradition should be an appreciation of the bounty around you, whether it's locally grown pumpkins, fresh brussels sprouts, or wine from a local vineyard. As part of our tasting of old wines, we opened a bottle of Millbrook Vineyards & Winery Cabernet Sauvignon 1991, from the Hudson River region of

New York State (we'd bought it at the winery; see "Visiting American Wineries"). It was the biggest surprise of the tasting, with the kind of structure, elegance, and class we associate with fine Bordeaux but the guts we expect from an American wine. It was also still vibrant and very much at the top of its game. Many local vineyards offer "library wines" going back many years. Visit a local winery and purchase one of its older red wines. Because these have been kept in pristine conditions for all these years, there's a good chance it will be especially good—and, of course, the fact that you bought it directly from the local winery will make it taste better, too.

The second-best choice after a Cabernet with some age is simply a good Cabernet, from even a recent year, from a classy producer. Here are half a dozen names that would be great to look for as an accompaniment to Thanksgiving dinner—and if you happen to see an older one, so much the better.

The vintage we tasted is in parentheses with its price, but these are excellent wines year after year. Note that all of them are from the Napa Valley. While excellent Cabernet Sauvignon is produced all over California and throughout the United States, you do increase your chances of success with a high-end Cabernet if you look for *Napa Valley* on the label.

Some Thanksgiving Cabernets

Caymus Vineyards (Napa Valley). Filled with sweet fruit. It actually tastes a bit like cranberries and herbs, and what could be more perfect with the dinner? Long, lovely finish. A real winner. (2000; $72.95)

Heitz Cellar (Napa Valley). A classy name for many years. Inky and roasted. Rich and lovely. Its dense chewiness would pair well with some of the "flatter" tastes of the turkey and the herbal stuffing. Could age well. (1999; $39.95)

Joseph Phelps Vineyards (Napa Valley). A great name in California wine, always reliable. This is so young it tastes like it came right from a barrel. Still hard and tough but tasty. John thought this would be too young and aggressive to serve with Thanksgiving dinner, but Dottie had another thought: "It's perfect. Thanksgiving is a long dinner. You want to have small sips of this wine. You can't gulp it. It makes you linger at the table and talk." (2000; $36.95)

Staglin Family Vineyard (Rutherford, Napa Valley). One of our favorites for years, though it was certainly more affordable when we first started drinking it. This exudes class and elegance and is filled with sweet fruit. But it's challenging, too: quite young, with a nose of lilacs and roasted wood and an aggressively herbal background. Most remarkably, it has a finish that's dry as dust and almost bitter in its dry intensity. Its combination of richness and austerity should do your white and dark meats proud. This could live forever. (1999; $84.95)

Steltzner Vineyards (Napa Valley, Stags Leap District). This is harder to find than many but is one of our all-time favorites, both young and older. It's dark and rich-looking and smells like a meal. Rich cherry-blackberry fruit. Sensuous and lusty. Classy and approachable, with everything well integrated. It really sparkles and then has a nice, acidic kick that would add a whole extra dimension to dinner. Could age for a long time. It's a real bargain, too. (1999; $29.95)

Sullivan Vineyards "Coeur de Vigne" (Rutherford, Napa Valley). The phone number for this winery is 877-Big-Reds, so you can guess what this wine is like. It's big, heady, and young, with a purity of fruit that's simply awesome. It's massive yet elegant, with nice, lemony acids for food. Thanksgiving is an event, and this is an event wine. It would be great for Thanksgiving 2020, too. (1999; $85)

Now you've heard our point of view. Many people passionately disagree with us. They believe the most appropriate wine to have with Thanksgiving dinner is Zinfandel, because it is America's own great grape. Its origins were mysterious for decades. DNA sleuths now have proven that Zinfandel actually hails from Croatia, but that doesn't change anything. Because Zinfandel was an enigma for so long, there has been no "standard" to which it could be compared. American Chardonnay could be tasted against white Burgundy, Cabernet Sauvignon against Bordeaux, Riesling against great German whites. But Zinfandel? American winemakers were on their own, and they had a great time playing with the grape. They made massive, alcoholic, late-harvest wines; they made elegant ones, with fine structure but still that special Zinfandel zest; and, for better or worse, they even made a simple, slightly sweet pink wine out of it. At its best, Zinfandel is a wine with the class and structure of a fine Cabernet or Bordeaux but with far more power and almost peppery tastes.

Unfortunately, we rarely see Zinfandel at its best anymore. To begin with, we would most certainly warn you away from Zinfandel under $20 for your Thanksgiving dinner. We have found most of them far too simple, far too alcoholic, and sometimes far too sweet to pair with any meal, much less a special one. There are some outstanding higher-end Zinfandels. Our very favorite Zinfandel for years has been Rafanelli, but there are other great ones, too, such as Turley. These are hard to find and expensive, but they can be very exciting experiences. How exciting? Consider these.

A. Rafanelli Winery (Dry Creek Valley, Sonoma County). High art. The nose is massive and peppery, and so is the taste. It tastes like tiny, concentrated berries, like pellets of fruit. Peppery and spicy, but it's not overwhelming or too powerful to simply enjoy. Aggressive, intense herbs and spices, with a real earthiness. Real complexity for a wine of such power. This is Zin. (2000; $60)

Turley Wine Cellars "Duarte" (Contra Costa County). It's as though the wine has been boiled down to the essence of great Zinfandel. It even smells black, filled with black currants, spices, and pepper. The fruit is so massive and the winemaking so confident that the wine has a certain majesty, with a long, Portlike finish. It almost tastes like distilled raspberry-blackberry-blueberry wine with a bit of fermented black pepper. As it opens and warms in the glass, it gets a little creamy, reminding us of blackberry cream pie. The only downside: at this young age, it might overwhelm a Thanksgiving meal, not just in its tastes but in its power. It might be better after the meal, served as Port would be, paired with good conversation and perhaps an after-dinner walk. (2000; $85)

Indeed, that's just the problem with most young, high-end Zinfandels: they will likely overpower your Thanksgiving meal. It's not just that the tastes are too big for the lighter parts of the meal but that their high alcoholic content seems overwhelming during a meal that is already over the gustatory top. But, if you are going to get a Zinfandel to have with Thanksgiving dinner, here are some good names to look for and some tasting notes from recent vintages. All of these will cost $20 to $40. If you can't remember anything else, remember *R*: Ravenswood, Ridge, Rosenblum, and Renwood.

Some Classy Zinfandels

Franciscan Oakville Estate (Napa Valley). Elegant and restrained, but with really good Bing cherry fruit. Intense, spicy fruit but not overwhelming. This is a very classy wine, with a fine blueberrylike finish. (1999)

Kenwood Vineyards "Jack London Vineyard" (Sonoma Valley). Plenty of pepper and spice, with bright cherry fruit, but just a bit thin for our taste. Easy to drink, which may make it more approachable for your choice of dishes, but lacking power. (1999)

Niebaum-Coppola Estate Winery "Edizione Pennino" (Napa Valley). Huge wine. It's dark and even looks rich in the glass. The taste is deep and roasted, with hints of lilacs, chocolate, and cream. The finish is woody and filled with pepper and spice. (2000)

Ravenswood "Dickerson" (Napa Valley). Lovely, with lots of plump fruit. Easy to drink. It's not intense or very "Zinny," but it's relaxed and good with food. It has a certain softness that Merlot lovers would really like. (2000)

Rosenblum Cellars "Annette's Reserve, Rhodes Vineyard" (Redwood Valley). Rosenblum makes a wide variety of Zinfandels; remember the name because it's a very reliable label. This one was a total winner, easy to drink, yet with real Zinfandel character. With food, it gets spicier, with more intensity. There's tobacco on the nose and the kind of structure we'd expect from a good Bordeaux. (1999)

Renwood Winery "Jack Rabbit Flat" (Amador County). A huge, awesome Zinfandel, massive and very American. Filled with fruit, but it's awfully young and still tastes quite alcoholic (it's 15.3 percent!). (2000)

Ridge Vineyards "Lytton Springs" (California). One of the great names in Zinfandel. This one is tough but very "Zinny," a bit like fermented black pepper. Challenging, rich, and dark. This would clearly overwhelm some parts of the meal, though it would be great with a heavy, savory stuffing. (2001)

If you stick with Zinfandel and you find a bottle with some age on it, this would be a special treat. Good Zinfandel ages well. It still has that Zinfandel character but is a bit softer and easier to drink, pairing better with dinner. For instance, we opened several old Zinfandels from our own cellar, including an older version of one of the wines listed above. Here's what we found, which we pass along just as examples of what older Zinfandels can taste like, if you're lucky enough to find one.

Dickerson Vineyard (Napa Valley) Limited Reserve 1992. It smells like sweet fruit and, indeed, is absolutely bursting with awesome, ripe, sweet fruit. It has the layers of a good Bordeaux and even some tobacco on the nose, but it's clearly a powerful American wine, with many years ahead of it.

King Estate (Oregon) 1994. Zinfandel from Oregon? Just goes to show again that interesting wines are being made all over the map these days. This is a real Zinfandel—big, rich, and peppery. Its age has softened it a bit, so it has some smoothness to contrast with its spice. Beautiful wine. (Sadly, King Estate stopped making Zinfandel.)

Niebaum-Coppola Estate Winery "Edizione Pennino" (Napa Valley) 1994. Roasted fruit, but an older, more relaxed taste, filled with sweet fruit. Still many years ahead of it, but quite lovely already.

Nalle Winery (Sonoma County, Dry Creek Valley) 1993. Absolutely charming. Fairly light, filled with creamy fruit tastes. Not intense, but loaded with character and absolutely bursting with fruit. This really would be great with Thanksgiving dinner.

For our own Thanksgiving dinner in 2003, we opened a special treat: a bottle of 1978 Amador County Zinfandel from Sutter Home that we received as a wedding present some years after our wedding. It looked, smelled, and even tasted like a fine old Burgundy to us, with brown-tinged edges, a nose of chocolate and soft fruit that reminded us of prunes and earth. The finish was all Zinfandel, though, filled with pepper and spices. It was clearly quite old, but its elegance and stature made our special meal that much more memorable. This twenty-five-year-old wine matched the meal perfectly—not necessarily because its tastes were the best complement to the food but because this was an "occasion" wine and Thanksgiving is a great occasion.

Finally, two more notes about Zinfandel for Thanksgiving:

1. We aren't big fans of decanting. We like to taste a wine from beginning to end as it unfolds in our glass. However, if you are serving a young Zinfandel with Thanksgiving dinner, we'd urge you to decant it an hour ahead of time to soften a bit and perhaps let some of its alcoholic headiness blow off.

2. Be careful about the temperature of Zinfandel, especially young ones. If you serve it at room temperature, it will be too warm and will almost surely taste alcoholic and sharp. Put the wine in the refrigerator for a couple of hours before you take it out to decant it. That should allow you to serve it closer to "cellar temperature"—about fifty-five degrees—which will make the wine taste much better.

· · ·

Now, how about Karen Grigsby Bates's question about dessert? To begin with, don't even ask your guests if they want dessert wine. They will surely say no—maybe because they're already stuffed or, more likely, because they think they don't like dessert wines. Here's your chance to make a lasting impression. After a big, blowout dinner like Thanksgiving, you certainly don't want a dessert wine that's heavy or high in alcohol. So remember this name: Muscat. The Muscat grape is made into honeyed, delightful wines all over the world. The wines are sometimes light and airy and sometimes pretty syrupy. Moscato d'Asti from Italy is one of the sunniest, most delightful wines on the planet, slightly sweet and a bit spritzy. We usually prefer it as an aperitif, but after a huge meal it can be quite good as a kind of digestivo. Dessert wines are also a great excuse for you to use those pretty little wineglasses. Sticking to American wineries, there are quite a few lovely Muscat wines that would end your meal just on the right note. Take these right out of the refrigerator and pour. They are great with simple fresh fruit, but they're also good with pumpkin or apple pie. Most of those we've listed here come in half-bottle sizes. These are generally pretty light and low in alcohol—11 percent or less—and are better young.

Some Muscats for Dessert

Eberle Winery Muscat Canelli (Paso Robles). Our favorite. It's like nectar, filled with honeysuckle and flowers, but it's light as a feather. This would be absolutely perfect immediately after the plates are cleared away. (2001; $14)

Robert Pecota Winery Moscato d'Andrea Muscat Canelli (Napa Valley). Lovely, year after year, with flowery honeysuckle flavors. It's so ephemeral that the wine just seems to float into you. Dottie describes it as "sweet sunshine." (2001; $12.99 for a half-bottle)

St. Supéry Vineyards & Winery Moscato (California). Pleasant, with plenty of sweet-fruit tastes. Not as interesting as some others but still quite lovely. (2001; $18)

La Famiglia di Robert Mondavi Moscato Bianco (California). Absolutely charming. Very light and happy, with a little spritz. It's also low in alcohol (7.5 percent), which might make it perfect after a big dinner. It's impossible to drink this wine and not smile. (2000; $13.99 for 500 ml)

Bonny Doon Vineyard Muscat "Vin de Glacière" (California). Bigger taste than others, filled with flavors of stewed peaches and prunes, apricots, and a bit of sweet earth. It has some weight, but its 18 percent residual sugar is nicely balanced. Serve this with nuts and fruit—especially peaches. (Nonvintage; $21 for a half-bottle)

Beaulieu Vineyard Muscat de Beaulieu (California). A bit heavy and alcoholic (18 percent alcohol), almost Portlike. Would be better at the very end of the evening. Tastes like roasted nuts, peaches and apricots drenched in honey, with a velvety, thick finish. (Nonvintage; $9 for a half-bottle)

The Day After

So you had a special wine for Thanksgiving. What are you going to drink with the leftovers? Leftovers? You bet. By pairing last night's dinner with a new wine, you'll have a new meal tonight instead of just remnants. A fun wine—something far more informal than the wine served the night before—will add new interest and zest to what might otherwise be just sandwiches.

Just as we have a traditional Thanksgiving dinner, we have a traditional leftover dinner the next night (and the night after that and the night after that . . .): turkey sandwiches on rye with Russian dressing, warmed stuffing, leftover cranberry sauce. To be sure, one of the very best wines for this meal is the just-released Beaujolais Nouveau (see the previous chapter). It's seasonal, like Thanksgiving itself, and it's so fresh and lively that it gives new verve to the leftovers. Think about why cranberry sauce goes so well with roast turkey and you'll have an idea why the exuberant red-berry freshness of Nouveau is so good with the sandwiches. But what else would be good with leftovers? We once conducted an experiment to find out. We picked up dozens of different wines and tried them all against our leftovers. We spent around $15 or less a bottle because these *are* leftovers after all. We didn't get any whites—we suspected that leftover turkey, stuffing, cranberry sauce, and such would be too heavy and complex for most whites, and, in any case, the crisp air outside calls for red. We did pick up a few rosés, just to see what would happen, but they weren't big enough to stand up to the food. Not only that, but a chilled wine paired with cold turkey sandwiches didn't add anything at all. Ditto for even a nicely acidic sparkler. It was clear that our original thought, that red would be best, was right, especially with the Russian dressing on the sandwiches. But which red?

We tried all kinds. We tried some heavier wines: a Rhône from France, an Australian Shiraz, an inexpensive Bordeaux, and others. We found each one too big for the food. They overwhelmed the sandwiches and didn't taste good at all with the leftover cranberry sauce. Finally, we found the perfect match, and it surprised us: Rioja, from Spain. Rioja is one of those wines we're all kind of familiar with but don't buy that often, which is a shame, especially since it's often so inexpensive. It's made in the Rioja region primarily from the Tempranillo grape. It's rich and flavorful but, at the same time, understated and a little woody tasting—something like the various tastes of turkey itself. Rioja also tends to have a certain relaxed, easy taste, which is pretty well perfect with leftovers. You don't want to take a turkey sandwich too seriously, but there's no reason not to improve it with a good wine. Here are some names to look for. A few are often available for under $10, while others cost closer to $20.

Some Riojas for Leftovers

Marqués de Cáceres.   Our top choice because it's usually available and always reliable. Looks young and vibrant, with rich, sweet fruit on the nose. Quite tasty and a touch creamy. Light and easy to drink. So very pleasant. (1998)

Marqués de Riscal. Our "house Rioja" for years. Delightful, a little earthy, with nice, lemony acids and a hint of age to give it character. (1998)

Castillo Rioja (Bodegas Palacio). Austere, dusty, and interesting. Good dark-cherry flavors, but very lean. Filled with fruit, but not even a little sweet-tasting. Real wine. (2000)

Loriñon "Crianza" (Bodegas Bretón y Cía). Year after year, one of our favorites. Fruity, extremely pleasant, and easy to drink. Simple but very nice. (1999)

Viña Alberdi "Reserva" (La Rioja Alta). Cranberry nose. Deep, rich fruit. Beautifully balanced and quite complete. Light-bodied and easy, yet with some layers of taste. (1998)

Viñas de Gain (Artadi). Rich, with real body, nice acids, and abundant, bricklike, almost dusty fruit. (1999)

Viña Real (Cune). Woody, soft, and comforting. Light body and good acids, with sweet, rustic fruit. Utterly easy and pleasant, with relaxed tannins. (1999)

And finally, since we brought it up, a word about Jell-O mold. Among the most charming things about Thanksgiving are those traditional dishes that families serve every year whether anyone really likes them or not. No wine is perfect with Jell-O mold or with challenging, sometimes bitter vegetables such as turnips and brussels sprouts or that decidedly odd dish, creamed onions. In the frenzy of the season, though, this is the most important thing to keep in mind: every wine goes well with family and tradition, and that's what really matters.

We called Kraft Foods, the maker of Jell-O, to ask if they had any advice for pairing wine and Jell-O molds. They didn't, but they did tell us, for our own wine-pairing purposes, that the two most classic Thanksgiving Jell-O molds are Spiced Cranberry Orange Mold, with cranberry gelatin, cranberry sauce, cinnamon, oranges, and walnuts, and Jell-O & Juice Mold, with straw-berry gelatin, orange or cranberry juice, pineapple chunks, and orange seg-ments. So we suppose that if we had to come up with separate wines with side dishes, we'd suggest maybe a flowery American Riesling with the Jell-O molds and maybe even the creamed onions, though actually sparkling wine might be good with both of them. With turnips and brussels sprouts, we'd stay green, with a grassy Sauvignon Blanc.

After we wrote about this in the newspaper, you'd be amazed at how many people wrote to us about Jello-O molds. This was our favorite note:

My husband's favorite "wine" pairing with a Jell-O mold of any flavor is, in an annoying high-pitched singsong: "Do I have to eat this?"
                                        —*Karen Winterkamp Picciano, Miami*

Christmas
The Greatest Gifts

"Since my family is of Italian origin, it is always nice to give an Italian wine as a gift to others. Sort of stirs the soul a bit. Over Christmas, I offered to bring the wine to my mother's lovely dinner of pollo rollatino, sautéed peppers, pasta with bread crumbs, and a beautiful salad. At the time they were going through a phase of serving white Zinfandel with everything unless you brought the wine. I brought a bottle of Pio Cesare Barbera d'Alba from Italy. My wife and I usually drink a glass of wine apiece with dinner, but we finish the entire bottle anytime we open this one up. It runs about $20 a bottle around here in Texas, but I have to have it brought in special order as no one really buys it enough to keep it in stock. My parents loved it." **—ANTHONY V. COLELLO, DALLAS, TEXAS**

The United States ranks thirty-fifth in the world in per-capita wine consumption, just ahead of Finland. There is just one brief, shining moment during the year when we look like a nation of wine drinkers: Thanksgiving through New Year's. Some wine stores tell us that the last six weeks of the year account for 40 percent of their entire annual sales volume of fine wine. And why not? The holidays are prime time for family, for celebration, for memories, for good times, for optimism—all of those things that wine is really about. Unfortunately, that also means it's prime time for wine angst. What wine do I take to a friend's house for the holiday dinner? What do I serve at the big party? And the really big one: What do I give my wine-loving friend for Christmas that he'll really like— and won't make me look dumb?

Take a deep breath. Don't forget that it really is the thought that counts—and that the circumstances themselves favor success. Think about Mr. Colello's experience. He was visiting his parents; his mother was making a delicious dinner; he cared enough to take along a bottle of wine he really liked himself and that he had to make an extra effort to get. Is it any wonder the choice was a big success? We're going to offer you a cornucopia of advice about how to make wine a great part of Christmas, starting with something we heard about from a reader.

The Wine Swap Party

Rod Brooks of North Stonington, Connecticut, is in sales, but for his office's Christmas parties his wife, Paige, sold him on one of her ideas. Instead of the cookie swap party that her office holds, his office now has a wine swap party. Because it has been such a success at their workplace, they have adapted it for their annual open house at Christmastime. Here's how it works: each guest is asked to bring two bottles of wine—one to open and share with other partygoers and one, concealed in a bag, for someone to take home. The Brookses recommend attaching a note to the take-home bottle that gives some background about the wine, including why it was purchased. "It's nice when it's something that matters to you, something that you've had before," Mr. Brooks told us. Other tips in the note might include how long the wine should be kept before it's opened and foods that might make it sing. As guests arrive, have them deposit all of the take-home bottles in a pretty decorated box near the door. When guests leave, they reach in and select a bottle to take home. Since the bottles are all bagged, what people select is a delicious mystery. This also eliminates the possibility that people will fish around in the box looking for something specific. One can hope that what they select is safely out of their comfort zone. What fun! The Brookses sometimes set a price range for the wine; sometimes not. It can be anything—red or white, rosé, sparkling, or dessert.

The wine swap party is an excellent way to discover new wines. Mr. Brooks told us, "At the first swap, someone brought a Viognier," a unique white wine mostly associated with the Rhône Valley of France. "It was really good, and that led us to try others that were new to us. Someone else brought a Shiraz from Australia, which I hadn't had before." The entertainment is built in, just friends sitting around sharing wines and getting caught up on each other's lives. With all of the wine, don't forget to have plenty of food and water, still or fizzy. The Brookses plan their menu weeks in advance and usually feature two major dishes and several appetizers, a selection of cheeses, and, for folks who don't want wine, beer and liquor. "Instead of having a sit-down dinner, we run it like an open house," Mr. Brooks explained. "There's always something coming out of the oven. What you eat depends on when you arrive."

The Perfect Present

John's younger brother, Kris, loves golf, so every year for a long time we searched high and low for the perfect golf-related Christmas present. We bought balls with his name stamped on them, fancy doodads that measured distance, and some lovely golf-club covers. Here's the problem: we don't know anything about golf. It was years before we realized that a serious golfer would scoff at our presents, although Kris accepted them with great grace. In other words, we know how hard it is to buy a useful, sure-to-be-appreciated gift for the wine enthusiast in your life. But not as hard as you think. Ask Karen MacNeil, the head of the wine department at the Napa branch of the Culinary Institute of America and the author of *The Wine Bible*. She still remembers the greatest wine-related Christmas present she ever received. She was twenty-two at the time. "It was Hugh Johnson's *World Atlas of Wine,* and I treasured it because, for the first time, I realized how significant, historic, and extensive the world of wine was. It seemed daunting and thrilling at the same time." Andrea Immer, author of *Great Wine Made Simple,* told us: "My favorite-ever wine-related gifts have been food. The all-time topper was a duo of utterly decadent oils. It's not an exaggeration to say they changed my wine and food life. They were truffle oil and pumpkin-seed oil, and I swear to God that eating them on toasted bread or a plain baked potato or scrambled eggs makes the most extraordinary wine-loving fare."

See? It's not so hard after all to give gifts to your wine-loving friends this holiday season. Here are simple ideas for presents at all price ranges that any wine lover, whether neophyte or veteran, would enjoy. Two places to look for wine-related presents are wineenthusiast.com and iwawine.com. We don't recommend those sites over any other websites or stores, but they have a large selection, so they're a good place to start for some ideas and a general sense of prices.

> *Everyday Glasses.* Glasses for a wine lover who surely has dozens? You bet. Too many people give fancy, expensive glasses as gifts. Those usually get put away somewhere and aren't used for fear of breakage. In fact, no wine lover has enough everyday glasses. They should be clear, the glass fairly thin, with a bowl that curves in slightly near the top and a nice, long stem. Most important, a glass should hold at least twenty ounces. No, you don't fill it up; you just pour a little. We prefer glasses that hold at least twenty ounces because that gives the wine plenty of room to breathe and also feels generous and comforting in our hands. We usually spend about $6 a glass and rarely more than $10, so we don't have to worry about breaking them. You might even enclose a note that says: "These are meant to be used every day until you break them." Our favorite wineglasses for the money are Spiegelau Vino Grande Pinot Noir Burgundy glasses, which hold twenty-five ounces and cost about $10 each or less. Crate & Barrel also has good glasses at you-can-afford-to-break-them prices. Riedel is a very important name in glasses, well known to all wine lovers. These will be more expensive than our favorite everyday glasses, but a set of them—they come in all sorts of styles and prices—is a special gift. Another idea along the same lines: *everyday Champagne glasses*. Everyday Champagne glasses might sound like an oxymoron, but it shouldn't be. Remember that the best glasses for bubbly are flutes. If you pack them up with a bottle of Champagne and a note that explains that every day should be an occasion for Champagne, it becomes a very special present.

> *A Glass Drainer.* Speaking of glasses, isn't washing stemware a pain? We once ran across something called a Stem Mat for around $12. It's

a very simple little perforated plastic mat on which you can put your glasses upside down so they dry well. It seemed like a good idea, so we bought it. Now we don't know how we ever did without it. We have suggested this to many people over the years, and they always thank us.

Corkscrews. Yes, of course, all wine lovers have corkscrews, but they can always use another. Here are three ideas:

A Screwpull. Yes, we use one of those fancy, expensive lever systems to open our wine, but we open six to ten bottles every night and we're old and our wrists hurt. For most people—and for us before we were wine writers—the plain old Screwpull can't be beat. We know your friend already has a Screwpull, but it's a funny thing: as Screwpulls wear out and break over time, people can't stand to throw them out because they do work, with some effort. A new one would always be a treat.

A Sterling-Silver Tiffany Corkscrew. Talk about a present wine lovers would never buy for themselves. It's pure retro luxe, like a martini glass—classic. It's an old-fashioned, use-your-muscles corkscrew with none of the state-of-the-art usefulness of the prong or even the easy-to-use Screwpull. But who can improve on that elegant design? Some friends gave us this as a present and—and, well, it's really fun to use because it's just so incredibly extravagant. This is expensive: around $150.

A Personalized Corkscrew. This is the ultimate in thoughtfulness. Kevin Zraly, the former wine director of Windows on the World and author of *Windows on the World Complete Wine Course,* told us: "For Christmas 1977, I gave personalized corkscrews to all of the captains, who made me look good by selling wine. They were small waiter's corkscrews, hard black plastic, and each came in a case. I got them engraved with Windows on the World and their names. It will always be theirs."

Cheese. Wine and cheese are a natural combination. The cheese culture in the U.S. is booming, with new and better cheeses available all the time. Ms. Immer's second-favorite present of all time? "A giant wheel of Vella Bear Flag Dry Jack from Sonoma." The present we give most often to wine lovers on our own list is a big wedge of Parmigiano-Reggiano from Williams-Sonoma. It's such a luxury that few people would buy it for themselves, but breaking off a little piece every night to pop into your mouth with a nice red wine during winter— well, that's the kind of present that really keeps on giving. Our personal favorite—especially during the winter, since it goes so well with Port and other heavy red wines—is blue cheese from Maytag Dairy Farms. More generally, wine-friendly foods make a great, unexpected gift. As Ms. Immer said about her oils: "It doesn't matter the wine, but all your big guns are worthy with this food, so it's an easy excuse to open the good stuff."

A Way to Save Notes and Labels. For Christmas 1979, John's parents gave us a loose-leaf binder with a soft cover that read *The Cellar Key Wine Diary and Catalog.* Inside were simple 8 1/2- by 11-inch lined pages, like a legal pad, with headings for the date, number of bottles, name of the wine, and our comments. The first bottle we cataloged: Christian Brothers Cabernet Sauvignon 1974 ($7.59). We never would have guessed we'd be the type to keep notes on wine, but we have, because of that book. This turned out to be the best and most important wine-related Christmas present we ever received. If you can't find a simple book like that, it's easy to make one from any kind of loose-leaf notebook. Add a photo album with those sticky transparent pages, which is perfect for saving wine labels. Just write a little note for the spine that says "Wine Labels" and maybe take off one wine label and place it on the first sticky page before you gift-wrap the album, to sort of prime the pump. Then add some label savers, those adhesive strips you see in some wine shops and on-line that rip the label right off the bottle.

A Good Book. Like Karen MacNeil, we found Hugh Johnson's book very important as we began to learn about wine, so we're big fans of giving books as presents. But what about wine enthusiasts, who, you fear, already have all the best-known books? Think about an old book. Because there's a new vintage every year—not to mention new wineries—wine books often have short shelf lives. That means people get rid of them, which is why it's easy to find old books at used-book stores. We're lucky: Years ago, a friend of John's family named Mel Kutzer, who was in the spirits business, had a load of old books to throw out, so he brought them over. We treasure our 1928 edition of *The Wines of France,* which talks about the vintage of 1858 like it was only yesterday, and our 1960 *Guide to California Wines* that writes warmly of wineries that long ago ceased to exist. One of the many great things about wine is the way it connects with history, and these weathered books offer a unique sense of time and place. Go to a used-book store or a used-book website such as alibris.com and you'll find plenty.

An Insulated Bag for Wine. Whenever we want to travel with a chilled bottle of wine, we put it into a bag meant for a six-pack of beer, because we got it free at a New York Mets baseball game. Everyone needs something like this sometime, and there are more elegant alternatives than a New York Mets beer carrier.

Wine-of-the-Month Club. A few years ago John's brother Kris, who is better at giving us wine presents than we are at giving him golf presents, sent us a year's worth of wine from Lynfred Winery in Illinois. Once a month a bottle would appear on our doorstep directly from the winery. What a treat! Since then we've always been huge fans of wine-of-the-month clubs, but because of state shipping laws, some clubs can ship to certain states and not others. We're shut out of many because we live in New York, which has restrictive shipping laws. Every state has different laws, so it's impossible to know which club or winery can deliver to a particular place. Still, this really is an excellent present if you can find an outfit that delivers to the state where your recipient lives. The fact that you went to the trouble will mean something, too. One bit of advice: think about asking a winery—maybe even a local winery near you or in the recipient's state—if it has a club and if it can deliver to your friend. Wines that come directly from the winery are great fun (and, after all, completely fresh and well cared for) and often are available only to people on the mailing list.

A Bottle Coaster. After you pour wine, drops sometimes travel down the bottle and stain tablecloths. This isn't something we thought about much until someone gave us a bottle coaster, which is basically just a little dish to put a bottle on. We've seen them for hundreds of dollars, but ours, with John's initials on it, didn't cost anywhere near that. Because Dottie collects vintage linens, we use it every day. Which brings us to . . .

Nice Tea Towels. This might sound like an odd present for a wine lover, but it's perfect. Dottie collects antique linens from thrift shops and flea markets. We use them to help open Champagne (we hold one over the cork), to dry glasses, and to wrap around a bottle that has just emerged from an ice bucket or the refrigerator. You can find elegant little towels not only at thrift shops and flea markets but sometimes at antique shops too, and lovely new ones can be purchased at department stores and through catalogs that specialize in linens.

A T-Shirt from a Local Winery. There are commercial wineries in every state now. Go visit one near you and send your friend something special. We mean, geez, anyone can wear a T-shirt from Robert Mondavi, but only John runs around Central Park wearing his T-shirt from Habersham Winery of Helen, Georgia.

A Wine Saver. These simple devices pump out air from unfinished bottles so that the wine will keep for a few days. In a test we found that these manual pumps actually work. There are all sorts of other systems for saving wine, but this one is easy, inexpensive, and lasts forever. About $14.

"The Worldwide Sampler." This is a case of mostly inexpensive wines from all over the world. Novices will enjoy this because it will show them what a wide world wine is; wine lovers will enjoy it because most of these are wines they don't buy every day. See the list that follows.

One Great Bottle. Especially for people who already love wine, one expensive and very special bottle of wine, perhaps with something nice written on the back label, is always appreciated. We know what you're thinking: Well, what if they already have this wine by the case? But there are unusual wines out there that even wine lovers don't buy for themselves often enough. See the list following "The Worldwide Sampler."

The Worldwide Sampler

Here is a case of wines from all over the world—most of them for less than $15 and many of them for less than $10—that would give a budding wine lover a delicious global taste of wine. Talk to any good wine shop about putting together a case along these lines. It's impossible to know what's in stock at any store, and some of these might be hard to find, so be open to substitutions. Also, more wine is entering the U.S. from unexpected places, so any wine from, say, Moldova would be an unexpected treat. One of our all-time favorite wines is Chateau Musar from Lebanon, but we don't see it very often and it can be expensive. If you're lucky enough to live in an area where Canadian wines are available, one of those would be a good choice, too.

Keep your eyes open. We were once at a little suburban wine shop that rarely has anything very unusual and spotted a Cabernet Franc from Uruguay. We asked the merchant why he was selling that, and he explained that the bicycle repairmen down the street were from Uruguay and told him that they'd fix his bike for free if he could get them some wine from their country. So there it was, a wine called Catamayor from the 2001 vintage. The back label had a map showing where Uruguay is in South America and included this note signed by the winemaker: "The name of Catamayor means 'Good Tasting.' Each wine comes from the best tasted lot. The wines were made with our own grapes harvested by hand. The vineyard, in the San José region in the south of Uruguay, is with a clayey soil. The climate is temperate and maritime influenced by the Rio de la Plata, which allows favorable temperature fluctuations for grape maturation." We bought it, of course (for $10.99). It had Cabernet Franc's classic "pencil shavings" smell. It lacked any of the intensity or sharpness we might expect from Cabernet

Franc, but it was soft, very mellow, and delightful. If we served this to a party full of Merlot lovers, without telling them it was from Uruguay, they'd all demand to know where to buy it. This is just the kind of experience that would change someone's whole view of the world of wine—and how can you give a better Christmas present than that? Here are some ideas:

Prosecco from Italy. Light, bubbly, and delightful. This is perfect as an aperitif—not complex, but simply drinkable and fun.

Gewürztraminer from Alsace. A peppery and dry white wine and one of the best values in the world. Great with pork and apples or veal with a cream sauce.

Pinot Noir from New Zealand. This is the hot new thing among those in the know—juicy, somewhat grapey, and delicious. It might be hard to find. If so, fall back on Sauvignon Blanc from New Zealand— vibrant, fresh, alive, and totally mouthwatering.

Vinho Verde from Portugal. Get it young and fresh. This light, refreshing white pops in your mouth. This is great alone or with any type of seafood.

Albariño from Spain. Albariño is the same grape used to make Vinho Verde, though the grape is called *Alvarinho* in Portugal. If it's possible to find both of these—and they are both sometimes hard to find—it's a real eye-opener about how the same grape can make such very different wines. While Vinho Verde is light, Albariño is a wine of real weight and mouthfeel, with vibrant tastes of peaches, melon, and soil. It's great with food.

Chardonnay from Israel. Yarden is our favorite, but Dalton is a good name as well. Both are rich and filled with fruit. They're kosher, too, which might help change the recipient's mind about today's kosher wines.

German Riesling. It's important for many people to get over their perception of German wines as sweet and simple. So many are beautifully made and inexpensive because they're not popular. Look for Kabinett and Riesling on the label and you'll be fine (Riesling is the grape, and Kabinett means it's light and fairly dry).

Pinotage from South Africa. Kind of the national grape of South Africa. Quite peppery and herbal. Dottie always says this red "tastes blue."

Malbec from Argentina. Meaty, distinctive, and inexpensive. Great with grilled meats and vegetables. Sublime with a juicy hamburger and lively Cajun dishes.

Merlot from Chile. Everybody knows Merlot, but tasting a Merlot from Chile will make it clear how different wines from various places can be. Chilean Merlot often has slightly peppery, herbaceous tastes that give it great character and is often a great buy.

Vacqueyras or Crozes-Hermitage from France. The Rhône Valley is home to robust, wintery reds that are too often overlooked. There's a whole world of reasonably priced Rhône wines on shelves, and these are excellent examples.

Anything from Australia except Chardonnay or Shiraz. At this point everyone is familiar with Australian Chardonnay and Shiraz. But all sorts of wines are coming from Australia that most people haven't had. Look for anything unusual. Two possibilities: Grenache, an earthy, herbal, and rustic red, or Sémillon, a white with tastes that are so weighty it sometimes seems chewy to us.

That One Great, Expensive Bottle

Here are some very special bottles—most of them expensive—that wine lovers would love to receive as gifts. In terms of price, the sky's the limit for just about all of these, depending on the year, the producer, and other factors.

Condrieu from France. This is a distinctive, somewhat weighty white wine made from the Viognier grape in the Rhône Valley of France. Only those in the know have heard of it.

Grand Cru Chablis from France. Chablis—the real thing—is one of the world's great white wines, but wine lovers don't often treat themselves to the very best.

High-End Shiraz from Australia. It's amazing what spending a little more can get you here. These are often huge, black-pepper red wines that linger in your memory for a long time. In the case of Australia's most famous Shiraz, Grange, it's pure elegance. Isn't that the type of present you want to give a special friend?

Barbaresco from Italy. This great red wine from Piedmont is often overshadowed by its neighbor, Barolo, and is somewhat harder to find, too, making it an excellent gift.

Côte Rôtie from France. This black, "roasted" red wine from the Rhône Valley can be downright exciting.

High-End Meritage Red from the U.S. These special red blends are all the rage among American winemakers as consumers begin to look for something beyond varietals.

Top-Notch Oregon Pinot Noir. We disagree about Oregon Pinot—Dottie likes many of them, while John finds many too fruity—but this is an exciting region producing unique wine. The better ones tend to be expensive, which is why one would be a great gift.

Petite Sirah from California. Intense and special, the best versions of this very American red wine are a treat.

Vendange Tardive from Alsace. A rare and very special sweet wine. Perfect at the end of a special evening.

Spätburgunder from Germany. From a country known for its great white wines, these ephemeral reds made from the Pinot Noir grape are rare and a treat. They're not usually very expensive, but they are hard to find, making them a special gift.

Austrian Dessert Wine, such as a Beerenauslese. Some outstanding wines are coming from Austria these days. They're not widely available, but if you see one—any one—grab it (especially the reds, which are particularly hard to find). This is an intense dessert wine that will truly excite the recipient.

Icewine from Canada. Icewine (Eiswein in Germany) is made from frozen grapes, which concentrates the juice into pure nectar. The combination of sweetness, acidity, and intensity is explosive and exciting. Incredibly, there are even some sparkling Icewines—an utterly over-the-top experience.

Château d'Yquem from France. In our minds the most majestic wine in the world, a Sauternes that's sweet and earthy at the same time. It is very expensive—depending on the vintage, it can cost from $150 up—but it's the kind of present that even the most committed wine lovers don't buy for themselves very often. (For more about Yquem, see "Newborns.")

The Perfect Wine to Take to a Friend's House

You've been invited over to someone's house and asked to bring the wine. The pressure is on—and, to be sure, we have heard some pretty horrifying stories over the years, like this one, from Todd Owen of New York City:

I am usually tickled whenever I get invited anywhere, but it is especially nice when I get invited over for dinner. A few months ago a friend invited Kati and me over for dinner. I really enjoy going to the wine store and selecting the wine to bring for dinner, looking for something unique and tasty, but this time we were very busy during the day and I didn't get a chance to go wine shopping. No problem, I thought; I've got lots of wine at home, and there is apt to be a bottle on my shelf that is worthy of bringing to dinner. We finally get home from a day about town, late, and there is the big rush through the apartment to get cleaned up and dressed up for dinner. Just before we leave, I sift through my red wines and find a bottle from California that looks very interesting. I don't remember seeing it before. It must be one of the "dynamite" selections that Joe at the wine shop talked me into. This should do nicely for dinner.

We arrive for dinner, and I proudly present the wine. The hostess takes the wine and says, "So Todd, we're regifting, are we?" She had brought that bottle to my place for a dinner some months earlier, but it had been unconsumed that night. We know it was the same bottle because that wine is unavailable in New York—she gets a case annually direct from the winery. That bottle, and several others just like it, went very nicely with dinner.

Based on our experiences and recommendations from readers, here are tips for taking a wine to a friend's house. Number one, of course, is to remember Mr. Owen and not take the same bottle of wine the friend brought you last time. In addition:

    If you've been asked to bring wine for dinner, ask whether it should be red or white. You want to make sure your wine is appropriate. (If you haven't been asked to bring wine and arrive with a bottle anyway, consider it a gift. If the host opens it with dinner, great; if not, don't be offended. It's just that the host already planned the food-and-wine matches and will save your wine to enjoy another day.)

    Go to a good wine shop or a supermarket with a strong selection of wine. Maybe you usually shop at the dank little store on the corner. Stretch a bit.

    It's impossible to say how much you should spend. That depends on the occasion, the friends, the dinner, and much more. You want to make sure your wine is equal to the meal, so be prepared to spend more than you usually do when you're having something simple at home.

℃ Stick with dry, still wines unless you've been asked to bring a dessert wine or a sparkling wine. Most people prefer dry, still wines with dinner.

℃ If you bring a white, chill it before you arrive. Don't buy it already chilled. It might have been sitting in the store's cooler for years. If you're in a hurry, just put it into water and ice for fifteen minutes.

℃ Don't take big risks. We love trying new things—Malbec from Argentina, Pinotage from South Africa—but unless your friends and their guests are into wine and like experimenting, it's better to go with more familiar tastes.

℃ At the same time, do try to bring a wine that's a bit unusual. In other words, even if you get a Chardonnay, buy one that you don't see every day.

℃ Try to know something about the wine you bring. If you can say to your host as you present it, "I read that New Zealand is making some fine wine these days," that will show care and concern.

℃ If you're asked to bring wine for the whole gathering, the rule of thumb is that there are six glasses to a bottle. We figure a half-bottle per person. It's better to have too much than too little.

℃ Don't talk about the wine as it's being served. Let others discuss it if they like. Your job is to sit back and enjoy it, without making people feel self-conscious about it.

Now, here are six specific suggestions, three white and three red:

Special Chardonnay. Chardonnay is always a safe choice because almost everybody loves it, but it can be boring. Here are three Chardonnays that are not boring, but all will cost $20 or more: Rombauer, Robert Mondavi Reserve, and Beringer Private Reserve.

Special Merlot. Ditto, ditto, ditto. In the $25-and-up category: Whitehall Lane, Joseph Phelps, Dry Creek Reserve.

Pinot Gris from Oregon. Pinot Gris is a white wine of some weight and considerable charm, especially from Oregon, where it hits a high note. Good Pinot Gris has a marvelous combination of citrus flavors and nice acids that make it great with food, plus a hard-to-describe dimension that reminds us of crème brûlée and flan. Some good names to look for: Firesteed, Adelsheim, Eyrie, King Estate, WillaKenzie, and Sokol Blosser. Expect to pay less than $20 in most cases.

An Expensive Zinfandel. Especially if it's cold and you've been asked to bring a red wine, look for a Zinfandel that's more expensive than what you're used to buying. Many inexpensive, well-known Zins today lack character, but, at the higher end, some small-production Zins offer great tastes. Remember the *R*s—Ridge, Rosenblum, Renwood, and Ravenswood—and be prepared to spend at least $25.

A Really Fine Red Bordeaux. All of these will cost somewhere over $30, but wait till you see your friend's eyes light up: Châteaux Beychevelle, de Fieuzal, Gloria, Lafon-Rochet, and Phélan-Ségur.

A White Bordeaux. This would certainly be a surprise. Bordeaux is known for its reds, of course, but there are some outstanding whites, too, made primarily from Sauvignon Blanc and Sémillon grapes. Look for whites from the Pessac-Léognan area, which is a choice part of the Graves region of Bordeaux. Because these are unusual, they tend to be good buys, but your host doesn't need to know that.

One last thing: Even if you open your presents on Christmas morning, you should give your loved one a single present on Christmas Eve: a really nice bottle of Champagne that you've put, already wrapped, into the refrigerator. December is pretty crazy in our house, and there's nothing quite like that quiet time on Christmas Eve, after the kids have finally gone to sleep and all of the work is done. Every year one of us gives the other a special bottle of bubbly on Christmas Eve. We take out the good glasses, pop the cork, and sit in front of the Christmas tree, enjoying each other's company. A cold glass of Champagne rarely tastes better than that.

New Year's Eve

The Perfect Champagne, at Any Price

"Then other questions began to surface. Are the bubbles all the same size from bottle to bottle? Does temperature affect the bubble size?" —BILL LEMBECK, *WINE & SPIRITS* MAGAZINE, **1988**

There's really just one important question people ask about New Year's Eve: which Champagne should I pop open? About 60 percent of Champagne and sparkling wine consumed in America is sold in the last two months of the year; in fact, almost 25 percent is sold between Christmas and New Year's alone, according to Korbel, the big producer of sparkling wine in California. When we were growing up, our parents rarely bought wine, but we'd always have a bottle of bubbly—usually Korbel, as it happens—to open with great ceremony at midnight, as we watched Guy Lombardo on television. So we'll get back to the big question, but let's answer three other, far less important questions first.

How Many Bubbles Are in a Bottle of Champagne? Okay, we know you've never really wondered, and neither had we, until we heard about Bill Lembeck. He wrote an article on the subject for *Wine & Spirits* magazine in 1988, citing the figure forty-four million. We tracked him down and asked how he'd come to calculate such a figure. "At the time there were a few people lecturing about Champagne, and they would be asked this question. They would always answer none. There aren't any bubbles in a bottle of Champagne until you open it. It was a fake answer. One day a PR guy in the field who had heard that answer asked me to see if I could figure it out." Mr. Lembeck is a retired senior research scientist and a professional engineer, and he helps his wife, Harriet, run the New School's wine program in New York City. "So, I thought I could figure it out. After two weeks, I wrote an article that has since been republished all over the place." After consulting with an expert on Champagne, Mr. Lembeck said he changed his calculation to reflect greater pressure in the bottle and came up with the figure forty-nine million bubbles. He admits that it's not of earth-shattering importance, just a fun calculation, and even he's amazed at its shelf life. He recently saw the figure quoted in a magazine about Austrian wines.

How Do I Make a Good New Year's Eve Toast? Several years ago, right before New Year's, we received a call from a reporter for the *Los Angeles Daily News*. She said she was doing a story about how to make a good New Year's toast and wanted our advice. Truth is, we pretty much always celebrate New Year's Eve alone, so our toast is really simple:

DOTTIE: *To your face.*
JOHN: *To your bottom.*

Somehow, that didn't seem like the right thing to tell the reporter, so we simply said, "Saying something heartfelt is always appropriate, and the briefer the better." Well, we were amazed at the play that article got. It was run on the wire services and must have been picked up by half the papers in the country. We wish we had said something more profound. The experience made clear to us that the rituals of New Year's, including the toast, really are important. So, in terms of the toast, here is our advice: be sincere. Say what's on your mind, as long as it's really sweet. Avoid irony unless you're really good at it. Keep it short. Try something like this: "May the next year be the greatest vintage of your life."

Will There Be a Champagne Shortage This Year? Before the millennium celebration, some brilliant marketer came up with the idea of predicting a "Champagne shortage." This caused prices to rise and many trusting people to rush out and get their Champagne early. We predicted early on that there would be plenty to go around, and, of course, there was. But the success of this hype—at least for wine stores—has meant that just about every year we hear about the possibility of a "Champagne shortage." It won't happen. The Champagne district of France alone produces 250 million to 300 million bottles of Champagne a year and often has a big surplus. Even a bad vintage isn't devastating to supply because most Champagne is a blend of several different vintages. Regions all over the world produce good sparklers, too. Prices for all kinds of bubbly have been fairly flat for years, which tells you all you really need to know about supply and demand being in a nice balance. So relax and buy your Champagne at your leisure.

Now, let's get down to real business. What Champagne should you have for New Year's Eve? One of the great things about bubbly these days is that there is such a great selection at a wide variety of prices. The fact that you're not a millionaire doesn't mean you can't enjoy popping a cork at midnight. Real Champagne is made only in the Champagne region of France, and it is indeed special. It is made from Chardonnay, Pinot Noir, and Pinot Meunier grapes and tends to have a special, intertwined relationship between the bubbles and the taste that is unique in the world. But outstanding sparkling wines are being made all over the world now, often from those same grapes. Here are some of them in a variety of prices:

Under $10

For under $10, it's hard to beat Cava, which is the formal name of sparkling wines from Spain made in the traditional Champagne method—that is, with the second fermentation, which causes the bubbles, taking place in each bottle under great care. The wines generally come from the Penedès region in northeastern Spain and are made from white grapes with unfamiliar names, mostly Macabeo, Parellada, and Xarel-lo, and sometimes red grape varieties like Garnacha Tinta and Monastrell. Since the late

1980s, some of the sparklers have included Pinot Noir and Chardonnay, the traditional grapes for Champagne. Cava ranges from dry to sweet and sometimes is made pink. Two giant producers of Cava, Freixenet and Codorniu, are ubiquitous around the United States. Here are three of our favorites.

Cristalino Brut. Our top choice when we can find it. It has a great Champagne nose — toasty, floral, and filled with fruit and minerals — and a very special vibrancy. Even the bubbles are especially lovely. This is a great deal.

Freixenet "Cordon Negro Brut." Yeah, yeah, we know that this wine in a black bottle reminds you of your college days, but it really is still a great party wine. It's happy, easy and bubbly, and straw-colored just like Champagne.

Marqués de Gelida Brut. Nutty, refreshing, and very pleasant. Crisp and easy to drink. A little bit of honey. Nice weight and good acids make this better than most with those little finger foods that you might pass around while you wait for the clock to strike twelve.

$10 to $20

For this price, California bubblies are the best choice. For a look at some our favorites, see "Thanksgiving."

$20 to $40

Now we're getting into "real" Champagne territory. Keep this in mind: the best Champagne for New Year's is probably the one that's most special to you. For instance, while other Champagnes have done better in our blind tastings through the years, Taittinger will always be our Champagne of choice for special occasions. Why? Because it was the first Champagne we opened on our first cross-country train trip together and the Champagne we served at our wedding. Others may taste better in blind tastings, but when we know we're drinking Taittinger, well, it always tastes great to us.

Most of the Champagne at this price will be nonvintage — that is, blends of various vintages to create a consistent taste. Because so many of these are made in large quantities, stores often compete on price, so be on the lookout for bargains. Speaking of bargains, here's an important point: sometimes it's better to skip the well-known names. Any sparkling wine from France that says *Champagne* on the label has to be the real thing. There are hundreds of little Champagne makers you've never heard of who send a bit of wine to the United States. These are often excellent wines at good prices. Here's a little secret: on each bottle of Champagne, look on the label for the Champagne's registration number, which will be in very small type. Most will begin with *NM,* meaning it's made by a négociant that blends and ships the wine. But you might see one marked *RM.* This is a grower's own wine, and drinking it can be a very special experience. These are often full of personality, and they tend to be good buys because nobody has heard of them. We have listed some below, but only as examples of the small-production wines on shelves. Don't look for these, but look for Champagne labels you've never seen before and squint hard for those little identifying letters and numbers.

At this price, Champagne isn't the only option. Some American bubbly producers make a small amount of high-end stuff. These are definitely worth a try. They are often from specific vintages. We've listed some of our favorites, but there will probably be more recent vintages on shelves now. *Brut* means that wine is dry, while *Extra Dry* means it's a bit sweet. Go figure.

WELL-KNOWN CHAMPAGNES

Heidsieck & Co. Monopole "Blue Top" Brut. Consistently impressive. Yeasty and chewy, bursting with fruit. Classy.

Charles Heidsieck Brut Reserve. Lots of lemony fruit, lots of yeasty taste. A more approachable style than Heidsieck & Co., but just as classy.

Jacquart "Brut" Tradition. A big nose of yeast, lemons, flowers, honeysuckle, and even some molasses. Very pleasant. It tastes familiar and comfortable.

Lanson "Black Label" Brut. A very complex wine, with all sorts of things going on in the glass: nuts, yeast, and flowers. We always think of this wine more as a meal than as just a glass of wine.

Laurent-Perrier Brut "L.P". The nose alone is delicious, with chalk, lemon, fruit, and yeast. It tastes like ripe fruit, and the bubbles and the taste are so inextricably bound that it's almost a primer on what Champagne should taste like.

Piper-Heidsieck Brut. Deep, rich, nutty, and honeyed. Elegant and seamless, with real finesse. Many people take Piper for granted because it's such an old standby, but it's an old standby for a reason: it's consistently good.

Pommery Brut "Royal." Real Champagne nose, with yeast and straw. Elegant, a beautiful wine. Romantic, smooth, and seductive. Easy and effortlessly classy.

Taittinger "La Française" Brut. Our favorite bubbly for many years. Elegant, with yeast, toast, and even a hint of rich soil. It has more mouthfeel and weight than many. It's heady and simply yummy.

SOME LITTLE GUYS OF CHAMPAGNE

Albert Le Brun Brut "Carte Blanche." Big, with plenty of taste. Plenty of yeast and even a little caramel. A flavorful, heavier style, with toast and almonds.

Camille Saves Brut "Carte d'Or Grand Cru" (Bouzy). Fabulous Champagne nose and cascades of perfect bubbles. Austere and very dry, with an endless, sparkling finish.

Delamotte Brut (Le Meslin-sur-Oger). Elegant bubbles, with some nice chalk on the nose. Nutty, classy, with nice citrus flavors and good depth. A big Champagne with a great deal of character. It really tastes hand-crafted.

Jean Vesselle Brut "Prestige" (Bouzy Grand Cru). Real-thing nose, with chalk, nuts, and fruit. Beautiful straw color and plenty of bubbles. When we tasted it, we said, "Somebody's wine," because it was so highly personal. It has such good acids that it would be terrific with food—maybe seafood with a rich cream sauce.

J. de Telmont Brut "Grande Réserve" (Damery). Nutty and flavorful. Bigger and so not as elegant as some others, with some interesting crème brûlée tastes. Big enough to be good with food.

Leclerc Briant Brut "Extra." A bit rustic and yeasty, with plenty of substance. It seems a touch sweeter than the others. For those who like full-flavored bubblies.

René Geoffroy Brut "á Cumières Premier Cru." Flowery, elegant, and soft, great as an aperitif. Very ephemeral, utterly charming, and elegant tastes. It reminds us of Audrey Hepburn.

HIGH-END AMERICAN BUBBLIES

DVX by Mumm Cuvée Napa. Our top choice. Real Champagne nose, with toast and yeast. Just a few languid bubbles, but, interestingly, the taste is filled with sparkles. Like an outstanding Champagne, the bubbles themselves seem to hold the taste, with little explosions of flavor bursting in your mouth. A bit of cream on the finish. Really fine. This may cost more than $50. (1995)

Roederer Estate L'Ermitage Brut (Anderson Valley). Terrific nose, filled with toast and honey. Classy, with a nice yeastiness and good lemon tastes that suffuse the wine. Big enough to have with dinner. One of our perennial favorites. (1997)

Iron Horse "Classic Vintage" Brut (Sonoma County, Green Valley). A wine of real gravitas, with hints of chalk, yeast, and even mushrooms. It's almost like a woody Champagne, if you can imagine that. This would be great with heavier food. (1997)

Gloria Ferrer "Royal Cuvée" Brut (Freixenet Sonoma Caves). We don't often see this, but if you do, grab it. In 1999, we found a bottle of the 1988 for just $17.99 that was utterly charming, with crisp, lemony, honeyed, vibrant tastes. In Tallahassee, Florida, in 2003, we ran across a bottle of the 1993 for just $16.95, which is almost criminally cheap. It was a stunning, impressive wine, nicely acidic and fruity, and the age gave it a round, deep taste that was incredibly impressive. We felt it could easily compete with midrange versions of the real deal from Champagne.

Domaine Carneros Brut by Taittinger. Not as complex as some others, but interesting cream and caramel tastes and very easy to drink. (1997)

Over $100

Maybe rappers and movie stars routinely spend more than $100 on a bottle of Champagne, but few of us real people do. So when we do, we want it to be the right choice. That's why so many people fall back on the best-known high-end sparklers, especially Dom Pérignon and Louis Roederer Cristal. John proposed over a bottle of Cristal, and it will always have a special place in our hearts. "Prestige" Champagnes are expensive for a reason. They are made only in the best years, with great care, and are often coddled and aged at the winery for many years before release. They frequently have a very special, otherworldly combination of ephemeral tastes and seriousness that simply must be experienced. Here are some of our favorites. The tasting notes are based on the vintages noted—because older vintages are often on shelves, we have listed more than one vintage of some of the wines—but these are good year after year.

Billecart-Salmon "Grand Cuvée" 1989. It looks so elegant, with pinpoint bubbles that say "Champagne." So shy that you need to give it time to open up and to grow on you.

Billecart-Salmon "Grand Cuvée" 1990. All the right tastes—toast, chalk, fruit—but in such a relaxed, laid-back, and elegant package that John said it was "very after-midnight."

Bollinger "Grande Année" 1996. Languid bubbles in a roasted, almost thick bubbly, with all sorts of yeast, nuts, and toast on the nose. Lots of taste, yet with a very clean finish. Bold and full-flavored.

Bollinger R.D. 1988. "R.D." stand for "recently disgorged," which means this wine sits on its yeast and other sediment for an exceptionally long time, giving it a special weight. In some years it can be downright somber, not really appropriate to a lively celebration. But it's always a wine of gravitas that tastes expensive. This one has especially nice acids that give it a little underlying liveliness. It would be great with a fine meal.

Charles Heidsieck "Blanc de Millénaires" 1990. Languid golden color, with a rich nose like a hot-buttered croissant—maybe that's why the smell itself seems chewy. A real powerhouse Champagne, with rich tastes and an exceptionally long finish.

Jacquart "La Cuvée Nominée" 1988. Wow. This is the one to serve to your wine-loving friend who thinks he's tasted everything. This is a bubbly of real stature, with great fruit flavors—even some tropical fruits—and fine acids. This is a very serious Champagne.

Louis Roederer Cristal 1994. An exceptionally lovely, bubbly "nose" and an edgy, fascinating taste, almost a bit bitter at the front, nicely yeasty in the middle, and a little sweet at the end, with an ephemeral finish. Real body. This is a winemaker's wine.

Louis Roederer Cristal 1996. Quietly rich, with a long, almost creamy finish. Very classy and very clean. It's more elegant and has less obvious tastes than some others, but you're rewarded for stopping just a minute and thinking about the great tastes that are coating your mouth and throat.

Moët et Chandon Cuveé Dom Perignon 1990. This was the hottest wine for the millennium celebration, said to be so popular that it would soon be gone. In fact, more than a decade later, it was still available and may be even better for the extra age. It's simply beautiful and so very elegant. There's so much going on in the glass. This has *classy* written all over it.

Moët et Chandon Cuveé Dom Perignon 1995. Perfect pinpoint bubbles, a golden appearance, and a vibrant nose that says "Champagne." It's pretty well perfect: Exceptionally clean and easy to drink because of its bright acidity, yet all sorts of layers of taste underneath. It sparkles, and not just because of the bubbles. Even without the famous name and label, this is a wine anyone would like.

Pol Roger Cuvée Sir Winston Churchill 1988. A perennial favorite. All of those classic Champagne tastes—yeast, chalk, nuts, buttered toast, fruit—in perfect proportion and a taste that lingers in your mouth forever. Beautiful wine—not showy, just delicious.

Pommery Louise 1989. Interesting, complex layers of taste, but very shy and restrained, as though there's a little bit of flavor inside every bubble. It has a "you come to me" quality that's very fetching and a little mysterious.

Salon "Le Mesnil" Blanc de Blancs 1990. Yowee. It even looks expensive, like liquid gold, simply gorgeous. Real Champagne nose, with yeast, smoke, molasses, and brown sugar. The wine is elegantly large, like a meal—rich, nutty, and bold. Utterly satisfying.

Veuve Clicquot Ponsardin La Grande Dame 1995. We like this every year. The nose bursts with flowers, honeysuckle, and almonds and immediately transports us to a field in bloom. Some chalk-earth underpinning gives it a sense of place, and the long, lemon-cream-toast finish lets you linger there. Classy.

What Glasses Do I Use?

New Year's Eve is all about celebration, memories, tradition, friends, and family. For all of those reasons, don't be shy about using old-fashioned bowl glasses, the ones whose shape is supposedly based on Marie Antoinette's breasts. To be sure, those might not be the best for the Champagne itself since they allow the bubbles to dissipate quickly and make it harder to smell the wine. Flute glasses are best—they concentrate the bubbles and the "nose" of the wine, and we love watching the bubbles rise up, up, and away. But "best" is subjective. If those wide glasses add to the celebratory sense of the moment, use them. Ultimately, this night isn't really about the Champagne.

How Do I Open the Bottle?

Right after Christmas 2002, our country cabin was covered in twenty-three inches of snow. The scene was really quite beautiful. As soon as the snow stopped, we bundled up and ventured outside. Media and Zoë carried their sleds. We carried a bottle of Champagne. Because we were outside on more than an acre of land, John, feeling particularly celebratory in the beautiful moment, tore the foil off the bottle, pointed it down toward the frozen stream, and popped the cork. Wow! We had no idea a cork could fly quite so far. We found it in spring, after the snow had melted. We mention this for a reason: even on New Year's Eve, don't let the cork go flying. It's bad for the wine—it allows the bubbles to escape—but, far more important, this really can be dangerous, especially in a crowded place like at a party. Champagne is under tremendous pressure—that's why it's in such a heavy bottle—and flying corks can do serious damage. Instead, open the bottle this way:

1. Take off the foil.

2. Put a towel over the top of the bottle.

3. Put your hand under the towel and take off the metal jacket. Sometimes the Champagne will pop as soon as you do this, so be careful.

4. Take your hand out of the towel and then grasp the cork firmly through the towel. Twist.

5. When the cork starts to come out, exert some pressure to make sure it comes out slowly. It should pfffft, not pop.

The advantage of this method is that, even if the cork does pop out, it will be kept inside the towel. No, it's not quite as festive as letting the cork fly across the lawn or the room, but starting the year with an injury is really a bad omen.

Why Does Champagne Give Me a Headache?

We've read that there are real physiological reasons that sparkling wines are more headache inducing, something about the bubbles carrying alcohol to the bloodstream more quickly. Personally, we think the reason is simpler: People drink too much of it because (1) they don't usually have it and it tastes really good, (2) the mood is festive when they are drinking it, so they're not aware of how much they're drinking, and (3) they're usually drinking it without food. Bottom line: be careful.

I Didn't Finish the Bottle; Can I Keep It?

There's a tragic rumor out there that, once you open a bottle of Champagne, you might as well dump it down the sink if you don't finish it. Hogwash. Put a cork in it and put the bottle in the refrigerator. When you pour yourself a glass over the next couple of days, you'll remember the celebration, enjoy the idea of having a glass of Champagne for no reason at all, and find that the bubbly still tastes mighty good, even if it has lost some of its bubbles.

I Didn't Open Them All. What Now?

W e're asked this question quite frequently. People buy a couple of bottles for the holidays, open only one (or perhaps buy twelve and open only eleven), and become convinced that if the bottle stays in the refrigerator it will go bad; if it's taken out, it will be like one of the characters in Shangri-la who leaves and immediately turns to dust. Relax! The bottle will be fine in there until Valentine's Day. Or take it out if you like and leave it in a dark place with a fairly constant temperature. It will be fine there, too. In fact, it might be even better next year. Readers ask us all the time if Champagne can age. There is much debate about this. The British like their Champagne with some age on it; the French think this is nonsense. In our experience, Champagne and good California sparklers do indeed improve with age, getting rounder and a bit richer and losing some of that overaggressiveness. We've even had some really old Champagnes that were still quite delicious, with their youthful exuberance replaced by a kind of less-bubbly seriousness, much like many people we've known.

Newborns

Baby's First Bottle

"My daughter Katie was born two years ago (what joy!). My wife and I would like to purchase a few cases of 'birth wine' from 2001 for her. As a bit of background, we had the wonderful experience a couple of years ago, when visiting some dear friends at their home in Burgundy, to share a bottle of their eldest son's birth wine. I would appreciate your thoughts on the best way for a relative novice like myself to go about this." —**TOM HONAN, SANTA ANA, CALIFORNIA**

This is one of the questions we're asked most often. What a lovely sentiment. But first things first, and we do mean first: let's talk about the baby's birth.

It took us five long years, lots of money, and some really great doctors before we conceived our first child, Media. When Dottie was pregnant, someone told us that it's a French tradition to touch Champagne to babies' lips as they enter the world. That sounded like a great idea to us. So John got a very special, rare bottle of Champagne—Salon "Le Mesnil" 1979—and, with the Miami doctors' hearty approval, touched a bit to Media's lips before they rushed her off to the ward for premature babies. When Zoë was born less than two years later, the doctors in New York disapproved, so John smuggled a small bottle of Taittinger into the delivery room so Zoë could also enjoy Champagne as her first taste in the world. It's not clear that this really is a French tradition—some say yes, some say no, and some say it's actually a tradition in countries all over the world—but it's a tradition for us (not that we expect to be continuing it, personally). If it's okay with your doctors, we would urge you to consider doing this. It is a lovely way to celebrate such a proud occasion. Daddy can always enjoy the rest.

In terms of bottles to lay down, this definitely is a tradition. In the classic 1965 episode of the television show *The Avengers* called "Dial a Deadly Number" (see "The Oscars (and Emmys)"), Steed is talking to an old gentleman in a wine cellar. When they taste a 1928 wine, the man exclaims: "Twenty-eight? Now that was a great year. Put a hogshead down for Jeremy when he was born for his twenty-first."

"A most civilized gift," Steed replies. "Did he enjoy it?"

"Enjoy it? The brigade turned him down. Young fellow went straight into the church. Had to drink it all myself. Oh, well."

As with that old gentleman, the British often lay down fine Bordeaux, especially the "first growths"—Châteaux Lafite Rothschild, Latour, Mouton Rothschild, Haut-Brion, and Margaux—and that's great if you're a multimillionaire. Sometimes people expect the children to open the bottles on their twenty-first birthday or for their college graduation or their wedding day. The idea is the same: a case of wine that will mature gracefully and gain some wisdom, symbolically mirroring the child. Of course, each bottle will also be a memory of the givers of the wine and a reflection of their hopes and dreams for the child when he or she was born. So, what would we recommend? It's a very difficult question to answer because we're being asked to suggest something that will be good twenty years or more down the road. We can tell you that this will require more thought and more money than you probably usually spend on wine because you want to avoid the kind of modest wines most of us usually drink as our everyday wines. We once received this note from a woman in Illinois:

> *"I have a bottle of Liebfraumilch from a brother-in-law that was bottled in 1979. My daughter noticed that it was her birth year and asked me to keep it until she turned twenty-one. I have, and I would like to share it with her, but can't find info about it, or food recommendations. I was thinking a meal or even cheeses. Do you have any suggestions, and any reason why I'm having trouble finding info from all sources?"*

She was probably having trouble because no one wanted to tell her the truth: that Liebfraumilch from 1979 should have been drunk no later than, well, 1980. While you can never know for sure what wines will and won't age well, you can increase your chances with some well-considered selections. Twenty years isn't nearly as long as it seems when it comes to good wine. Many Bordeaux from 1982 are still great; in fact, twenty years after the vintage, many experts were talking about them "just coming around." In California, 1984 was a great year for Cabernet Sauvignon, so anyone turning twenty-one in 2005 would be in for a treat if some generous relative had laid down a case. Here's an important point, though: in this situation, storage matters. In general, we always say you shouldn't get obsessive about storage, since most wines are drunk right away, but these will be around for many years. A gift of a few bottles shouldn't require you to buy an expensive storage system, but keep these gifts someplace dark and dry, with a fairly constant, moderate temperature, where they won't be disturbed. And here's another important point: take your time. Any wine worth keeping all those years won't be released to the market for at least a couple of years after the child is born anyway, so you have plenty of time to research this. If your child is born in early 2005, for instance, the grapes in most places won't even be picked for several months. It will be quite a while after that before anyone knows how good the wines are—this is for upper-tier fine wines, after all—and years more before they are released to the public.

Do some research. Look around for good prices. While usually we don't dwell on vintages very much, because there are so many variables and most wines are made to be consumed immediately, this is one instance where you want to consult a vintage chart (they're often next to the cash registers at wine stores, and there are plenty on-line, too). There are some so-so years in Bordeaux, for instance, in which the wines aren't likely to be long-lasting, while the same year might be a great one in, say, California. If your child was born in 1968, for instance, you would have been quite disappointed in any Bordeaux twenty-one years later, since it was a particularly awful year there. However, it was a classic year in California, and any child with a case of fine 1968 California Cabernet in 1989 would have had a case of very good—and now very expensive—wine.

Assuming it's not a year when weather wrecked havoc on the vineyards, a midrange Bordeaux is a good idea. Our favorite, Château Gruaud-Larose, would be a treat in twenty years, for instance, if it's from a good year. If the child happens to be born in a year that was great in Bordeaux, even a lesser-known, lower-priced Bordeaux would be fine. We were lucky: Media was born in 1989, and Zoë was born in 1990, both excellent years in France, so we had many choices. Here are six midrange Bordeaux wines that are good year after year and generally available:

Château Beychevelle (Saint-Julien). Filled with verve. Plenty of pepper and big fruit, with marvelous hints of soil. Bright and lively, with a bone-dry finish.

Château de Fieuzal (Pessac-Léognan). Always a good buy because it's our secret. Lively fruit with plenty of "stuff " underneath and nice structure.

Château Gloria (Saint-Julien). Lovely nose. Somewhat rich, with real backbone. Just about anybody would like this.

Château Gruaud-Larose (Saint-Julien). Rich and classy. Year after year we find it soulful and earthy, with deep, almost chewy fruit. We have had more vintages of this than any other Bordeaux, some quite old, and always enjoy it.

Château Lafon-Rochet (Saint-Estèphe). Classy and elegant, with good fruit and excellent structure. Very pleasant.

Château Phélan-Ségur (Saint-Estèphe). Nicely made, with lovely, fruity fruit. Not profound and deep, but very friendly.

Here are a few more ideas for wines to lay down for your child:

A Big California Cabernet Sauvignon. Truth is, most California Cabernet under $20 is meant to be drunk this minute and won't age well, though there are clearly exceptions: We, and many of our readers, are constantly amazed at how well the inexpensive red wines of Louis M. Martini Winery age. As it happens, Louis P. Martini, son of Louis M. Martini, kept a cellar for each of his children beginning with wines from the year they were born. His daughter Carolyn, who grew up to head the company, brought a 1947 Barbera, from the year of her birth, to the *Weekend Journal*'s Open That Bottle Night party that we threw in Napa in 2000. It was still delicious. A better bet these days are more-expensive Cabernets that are clearly built to last. Some wineries have reputations for making "big" wines. The Cabernets we listed in "Thanksgiving" are all pretty good suggestions. Don't be shy about calling the winery itself, explaining what you're planning, and asking for a recommendation. Winery people are generally very nice and helpful. You can also find your own Cabernet or other red wine to save—and have fun doing it. Ask a wine merchant for a recommendation and take it home. Open and drink. If you find it difficult to drink because it's so full of tannins that it makes your mouth pucker—if it tastes "hard," which you'll know when you taste it—then it's probably a good candidate to lay down, assuming, of course, that you like the general taste of it. If it's soft and approachable, it probably isn't a good candidate for a long life.

Barolo, the Great Wine from the Piedmont Region of Italy. These wines, made from the Nebbiolo grape, are great ones to lay down because many of them seem to last forever and just get better and better. The problem with Barolo, we think, is that it's so big and so powerful that it might overwhelm a twenty-one-year-old who is just beginning to learn about wine.

Vintage Port. Port—the real thing, from Portugal—is pretty complicated. There are all sorts of levels, such as tawny and late-bottled vintage. Stick with the top of the line, vintage Port, which is made only in the best years. It lasts forever and gets better with age, and it's not even released for years, giving you plenty of time to think about it. Port is such an elegant, grown-up drink that it has a special resonance in marking a coming-of-age. The problem is that not every year is good enough to be called a vintage year, so you can't be sure you will be able to save a case from the child's birth year.

Sauternes. Here it is, our top recommendation and, in fact, what we laid down ourselves. This great wine from France is sweet, like the child, and it gets better with age. Not only that, but the wine gets more beautiful in its clear bottle as the years go on, changing from yellow to gold to orange, like a sunset that lasts many years. This means the child can appreciate the wine for years before he or she can drink it, just by looking at it. In fact, this was the "birth wine" Tom Honan enjoyed in Burgundy, which he talked about at the opening of this chapter. "It was our first exposure to Sauternes, and having it along with some foie gras was not only a gastronomic experience but also a very emotional one," he told us. There are all sorts of fine Sauternes on shelves. Classic names include Châteaux Bastor-Lamontagne, Coutet, Doisy-Daëne, Guiraud, Rayne-Vigneau, Rieussec, Suduiraut, and the wine some people, including us, consider the greatest wine in the world, Château d'Yquem. Thomas Jefferson and the grand duke of Russia were big fans. When Napoleon III commissioned France's famous Classification of 1855, in which the great wines of Bordeaux were ranked, Château d'Yquem (dee-*kem*) was the only wine rated "grand premier cru," even above the great "first growths" such as Château Lafite Rothschild. Sauternes, sometimes even corrupted to *Sauterne,* was long appropriated by winemakers around the world to mean "cheap sweet wine," but the real thing, from the Sauternes region of Bordeaux, is a wonder. It is made primarily from Sémillon and Sauvignon Blanc grapes that are attacked by a mold called *Botrytis cinerea,* or "noble rot." This concentrates the juice in the grapes, leaving a tiny amount of nectar.

The highest expression of Sauternes is Yquem. First, the grapes have to get just right—ripe and moldy. Then they have to be picked by hand, one by one, when they're perfect. So little is made that each vine makes a single glass of wine. The creation of the wine itself is intensive, too, with great care including years of aging in expensive new oak barrels. There are only two problems with laying down Sauternes: (1) There are some years when top estates make no wine at all because conditions aren't right for the natural creation of noble rot, or the crop is lost because it needs to stay on the vine such a long time into the fall and weather and critters have their way with it. (2) Some of these, especially Yquem, tend to be expensive, at

$150 and up a bottle . We would still urge you to consider this, however, because these wines get better and better and better with age (and, after all, you certainly don't have to buy an entire case; even a single bottle laid down for your child's twenty-first is very special). We recently bought some older vintages of Yquem at stores—incredibly, they're usually available, since these wines aren't in as much demand as they should be—and here are some notes that will give you an idea of how delicious these will be when your child graduates from Harvard:

1986. $325. Young, vibrant, and lemony. Zesty. Lovely, with real stature, but really young and a bit hard. It's not yet as well integrated as it will be in a few years. Plenty of acids and lively. Tasted blind, no one would guess that this is seventeen years old. This will just get better and better.

1988. $325. The nose is so rich that it's like fertile, damp soil and so big it's almost like a red wine. Tastes of toasted almonds, honey, and orange blossoms. It's still a bit thick, but its tastes are so earthy and real that it somehow seems to touch our souls in a very special way. In another ten years or so, watch out.

1990. $250. Luscious but still filled with acids and tastes of young wood. Honeylike, with a long, mouth-coating finish. Peaches and cream yet still somewhat austere and quite young. Awesomely classy. Truly liquid gold and not just because of the price.

1991. $150. Blonde-wood color. Earth and nuts on the nose. Smells thick with a surprising amount of alcohol on the nose. Honeylike and rich. Stewed peaches, prunes, and apricots. Mouth coating and luscious, but not as intense as the 1986 or the 1988 and more drinkable now.

Finally, the most important point: In the long run, the very best wine to lay down is one with some special significance to you, and that significance could be merely that it's your favorite wine. Listen to Nick May, from Portland, Oregon:

My wife Janyce and I are the proud parents of a cute six-month-old, Chloe. Since Chloe's birth, I have been putting together a time capsule of her first year. Along with the typical copies of newspapers and her first blanket, I thought it would be fun to put aside something that was a little more unique: a bottle of wine. I wanted to add something that most time capsules lacked: the taste and smell of an earlier time.

The wine we chose was a Cabernet Sauvignon by Beaulieu Vineyard. Janyce and I grew up in central California, so the Napa and Sonoma area was always just a short drive away. On one of our trips, we toured Beaulieu Vineyard and just loved the whole experience. There is something about the way things etch into your memory. I remember the cool air of the winery compared to the heat of the July day. The aroma of wine slowly aging. The friendly staff of the winery. Of course, being there with Janyce and the feel of her hand in mine. All of these memories helped us to choose the wine that we wanted our Chloe to experience. Perhaps the word experience sums it up. I could have chosen one of dozens of different bottles to lay down, perhaps some better than the choice we did make. But there would not have been that connection to our experience that is really at the heart of it all. Perhaps, one day, Chloe will visit the BV grounds. When she does, she might imagine Janyce and me walking around, holding hands, and thinking about the future.

Valentine's Day

Bring in da Funk

"Huge, chocolate, rich, sensuous nose. Gorgeous color, red and lots of gold, like a sunset on the Pacific aboard the *Coast Starlight.* Taste is big, rich, gorgeous. Sweet with fruit, plump, tongue-coating. Increasingly big and sweet with fruit." —OUR NOTES ON A **1961** CLOS DE VOUGEOT RED BURGUNDY FROM J. THORIN

Lovers everywhere want to get lucky on Valentine's Day, and we don't mean that in the modern, lurid sense—well, maybe a little. What we mean is that we want the day and night to be perfect. We want the roses to smell just right, the restaurant to have an available table, and the wine to fit the mood. Wouldn't the wine from the tasting notes above, from Valentine's Day in 1996, make anyone feel lucky?

Wine is a romantic beverage, so it's perfect for Valentine's Day, and Valentine's Day is perfect for wine. Because so many people go to restaurants on Valentine's Day—and often fancy, expensive places with good wine lists—we thought we'd first offer some advice on how to make the most of that experience. You should also be sure to read "Restaurants," about wine lists, but here is some Valentine-specific advice.

Before You Go, Check the Internet. It's a whole new world. We're hardly high-tech experts, but we plugged in "wine list" on the popular search engines, and dozens of wine lists, from all over the world, popped up. Spend some time browsing through them, getting a feel for what various wine lists look like. Restaurants rarely give you enough time to get comfortable with their wine lists. Now you can do it at home, on your computer. The restaurant you've chosen might well have its list on-line. Besides, at the table, you want to be looking into your loved one's eyes, not down at the wine list.

Preorder Your Wine. Yes, we know this seems scary, but at least think about it. Drop by the restaurant sometime before Valentine's Day; tell them you have a reservation and ask if you can look at the wine list now. Have a seat and choose a bottle (truth is, the restaurant will likely be so charmed by this that someone might come over to give you some advice). Ask them if the bottle can be on your table when you arrive. Trust us on this: when you're led to your table and there's already a bottle of wine sitting there that you chose ahead of time, your date will be impressed and touched. Dottie sure was when John surprised her this way on her first birthday as a resident of New York City.

Order Bubbly First. If you haven't ordered the wine ahead of time, when the waiter comes over and asks, right after you've been seated, "May I offer you a cocktail or a glass of wine?" say, "We'd like to see the wine list, please. But could we start with two glasses of Champagne?" You're going to pay real money for those two glasses of Champagne, but, hey, it's Valentine's Day. This will both impress your date and give you enough time to decode the wine list.

Be Somewhat Conservative. We believe you should usually be very adventurous at restaurants, but Valentine's Day is an exception. While you don't want to go with the same old boring stuff—do you want to seem boring on Valentine's Day?—you can stay within your comfort zone and still try something new. If you like Chardonnay, stick with Chardonnay, but try a new one. Remember that this is a day for tenderness and sensuality. Highly acidic, sharp wines, such as Sauvignon Blanc, don't taste very romantic to us. We'd also avoid particularly massive wines that might overpower the moment, such as some huge and powerful Zinfandels. This might be a good time for a particularly rich, buttery Chardonnay or an American Pinot Noir.

Say Something. When the wine is served, clink glasses and say something romantic—something simple like "Happy Valentine's Day, Sweetie." You'd be surprised how many people become mute at this critical moment. Just say something!

Don't Rush. Even if you're planning to do something, shall we say, more exciting later on, try to linger over dinner. Let the wine slow you down so that you can really talk and look at each other and even hold hands. Let the anticipation of later pleasures build. The evening is young, and you're with the most wonderful date on the planet.

Save a Little Bit of Wine in Your Glass. When you get to the last sip, lift your glass, clink again, and say something else romantic.

You Can Take It with You. Don't be embarrassed about this: Tell your waiter you want to take the empty bottle, or at least the label, with you. Tell your date (even if your date is your spouse) that you want to save the label to remind you of such a perfect evening. The restaurant will be flattered and pleased to do it.

Now, the truth is that we'd urge you to consider avoiding restaurants on Valentine's Day. They're so crowded and rushed that day that they seem quite unromantic to us. Besides, in our minds, this should be one of the top wine days of the year, and the kind of wines we'd recommend for this special day are either unavailable or ridiculously expensive at most restaurants. Our best advice: prepare a special meal at home and spend some of the money you save on a really special bottle of wine instead. Light some candles, buy an extra dozen roses, and cuddle. What wine? We have some suggestions, but first some ideas from people we consider experts at romance. Among the thousands of notes we have received over the years are quite a few from couples who clearly know something about love, romance, and making the most of time together. We got back in touch with several of them and asked, "What is the perfect wine for Valentine's Day?"

Lois Pannone Shaughnessy and Dan Shaughnessy, Brooklyn: "I think of white satin or red velvet, berries, luxurious foods, shrimp, caviar, and thus wines to match these things," Ms. Shaughnessy told us. "Nothing too heavy with red, and rich buttery whites to accompany that rich, luscious euphoria of being in love. I recall taking my husband to Aureole in New York City for his engagement gift and ordering a Sonoma-Cutrer Chardonnay. It was so perfect and smooth and seductive but in a sexy little demure way, not in a big, obvious way."

Jennifer and Adam Thackery, Morristown, New Jersey. "A smooth, full-bodied red, such as a Cabernet," Ms. Thackery told us. "It is perfect for sipping in front of the fire on a snowy evening with your honey. I have also found that we tend not to rush through dinner and leave the table when we are appreciating the wine."

Marcia and Martin Freed, McMinville, Oregon: "A late-harvest Riesling or Gewürztraminer. Why this choice? First, they are served at the end of the meal, so you can settle back, relax, and sip and savor the evening and the wine slowly, and this is nice especially if you have had to (frantically) prepare the Valentine's dinner for an hour or two beforehand. Second, the wine can stand alone as a dessert or with some nice fruit, and after some heavy entrees these wines can be a lovely contrast. The third reason is that they are unusual and special and make for a memorable end to the meal."

Joe Norton and Trip Weil, San Francisco. "Well, honestly, what would we say? Anything with a cork on it just has a certain sensuous *je ne sais quoi* about it," Mr. Norton told us. Mr. Weil added: "For me the most romantic is Cabernet Sauvignon. You've often pointed out that wines change during the course of an evening, and in my experience that evolution is most apparent with a Cabernet. The constant evolution, the way a Cabernet can be treasured for so many different qualities over time, is what I like about our relationship. What I appreciate now is so different from what I appreciated five years ago, and that from what I appreciated ten years ago. Cabernet is the same, only the years are minutes."

Trish and Tim McDonald, Torrance, California: "We love Chardonnay as our 'first love/teenage crush' wine, with its powerful fruit and smooth, creamy, buttery complexion," Ms. McDonald told us. "Now that we are more mature—as Tim notes, both oenologically and chronologically—Pinot Noir is our second love: rich, smooth, and velvety, with lively fruit memorable of youth, but also hints of depth and mystery."

Lisa D. McNary & T. J. Green, Columbus, Georgia: "We spent our first three Valentine's Days as a married couple apart (Lisa was finishing her PhD across the country from T.J., who was on an engineering project). So we vividly recall our first Valentine's Day together, which was in the restaurant of a winery of a local vintner in Ohio, where we were living at the time. After moving to Georgia, we tried the same thing—doing something around a local winery where we were living and on occasion visiting (Missouri, southern California, New Mexico are a few). In keeping with the spirit of the holiday, the wines are mostly red."

Cindi Cohen and Jeff Bloom, Vienna, Virginia. "Cindi thinks Burgundy because there's the French romance aspect to it," Mr. Bloom told us, "but I think any Pinot Noir would do. It has a seductive feel that works with so many things. I would start with a glass of Champagne and have Pinot the rest of the meal."

Tamra and Tony Rollins, Sonoma, California. "Valentine's Day is definitely a red wine day. Even a noncook can go to the store, pick up some great already prepared dishes and a great wine, and enjoy a very special Valentine's Day celebration."

Our advice? Here are four ideas.

Saint-Amour

As we wrote in "Wine-Tasting Parties," Beaujolais is one of the world's most delightful wines and generally a bargain to boot. Nouveau is the simplest, made to drink right away. "Real" Beaujolais arrives about a

year after the harvest. A step up in quality from plain Beaujolais is
Beaujolais-Villages, which has to come from specific areas. Then there are
ten areas within Beaujolais that are the best, and they are allowed their
own appellations. One of them is Saint-Amour and, really, what wine could
be better named for Valentine's Day? It's not just the name. The wine is
excellent for romance, too. Here are Dottie's verbatim comments on
the 2002 Saint-Amour from Georges Duboeuf, which costs less than $10:
"It's fruity, earthy, lusty, and sweet in a romantic way, like raspberries and
chocolate. It's exuberant, charming, and romantic. The earthiness means
your feet are on the ground, but the sweet fruit puts your head in the
clouds. You know, like Cupid." Geez, no matter how much you spend, it's
hard to beat that. Buy the youngest vintage you see and chill it for an hour.
Duboeuf is the name you're most likely to run across and that's fine because it's consistently excellent. Just don't tell your date that the name actually has nothing to do with love. We asked the official Beaujolais group
Union Interprofessionnelle des Vins du Beaujolais about the name, and it
responded: "In 286 in Saint-Maurice-en-Valais, a Roman légionary by the
name of Amor escaped a massacre of which a good number of his comrades
in arms fell foul. They had refused to march against the Christians. The
soldier sought refuge in Gaul and became a missionary there. He is said to
have given his name to the village of Saint-Amour. Today there is a stat-
uette to his honour near the church in a niche carved into the corner of a
house." Oh, well. This will just be our secret.

Red Burgundy

We believe that red Burgundy, made from the Pinot Noir grape, is
the most romantic wine in the world. Our notes at the beginning
of this chapter should give you some idea how we feel, and we're certainly
not alone. A famous chef once told us, "With Burgundy, there's often a little funk that I find *very* sexy in the right amount at the right time." It's
hard to explain why Burgundy is so romantic, but partly it's the red-velvet
consistency, partly it's the rich earthiness—a lusty, musky quality. Here,

unfortunately, is the problem: red Burgundy is notoriously inconsistent. Pinot Noir is a finicky grape to begin with, and there are so many growers and so many different Burgundies that it's very hard to be sure you've picked up a winner. The good news is that, if you do choose a good one, you simply can't beat it. Pair a fine Burgundy with a simple meal, even just roast chicken, and you will have the most romantic Valentine's Day ever. To narrow your search, we'd suggest you look for wines from these three areas: Gevrey-Chambertin, Chambolle-Musigny, and Savigny-lès-Beaune. Here are some good ones we've had recently that will give you an idea why we're so crazy about these wines. These will cost somewhere between $30 and $50.

Domaine Bachelet Gevrey-Chambertin. Earthy, cherry-fruit nose. Deep and complex, with vibrant fruit. John found it a bit too plump, but Dottie thought it was lovely. (1999)

Dominique Laurent Gevrey-Chambertin Premier Cru Lavaux Saint-Jacques. Rich, with good fruit and some depth. Nice earthiness and soul. Fuller tastes than most. (2000)

Labouré-Roi Chambolle-Musigny Premier Cru. Grapey and round, with sweet raspberry fruit and nice hints of earth. Notably dry, almost dusty finish. (1999)

Bruno Desaunay-Bissey Chambolle-Musigny "Combe d'Orveaux." Charming, with all sorts of up-front cherry fruit. (1999)

Domaine Heresztyn Chambolle-Musigny. Deep color, serious nose, and surprisingly chewy mouthfeel. Beautifully made, though we wish there were more fruit. (1999)

Domaine Jean-Jacques Girard Savigny-les-Beaune Premier Cru Les Lavières. Nice acidity and quite charming, with some layers of flavor. Improves with some air. (1999)

American Pinot Noir

We never thought we'd say this, but a Pinot Noir from the United States would be a safer bet for Valentine's Day. Just twenty years ago, there weren't many fine Pinots in America, and some experts said there never would be. Gosh, were they wrong. As the years have gone on, winemakers have discovered where to plant Pinot Noir, in both California and Oregon, and how best to tame it. Not only that, but in the past few years they've begun to get that great taste of the earth, the underpinning that gives Burgundy its grounding and, yes, its funk that helps make it so soulful and sexy. We have found over the past couple of years that Pinot Noir under $20 is the most consistently good buy among American wines and that Pinot Noir over $20 is very often worth every penny. The sky is the limit on some, but for $20 to $50 you should be able to get a Pinot that will knock your socks off. Under or over $20, it will be hard to go wrong with any one of them, but here are some of our favorites. Personally, we'd urge you to go upscale on this one since Valentine's Day is so important, but you have many choices at all price ranges.

UNDER $20

Clos du Bois (Sonoma County). Beautiful wine. Elegant, with layers of flavor. Bright acids, good soil, and interesting pomegranate fruit tastes. (2001)

David Bruce Winery (Central Coast). Quite drinkable and pleasant, with interesting depth. Simple at the front of the mouth, more complex on the finish. Very classy. (2001)

Echelon Vineyards (Central Coast). Rich and chewy, with real depth and a bit of attractive toughness. A wine to talk about. (2001)

Firesteed Cellars (Oregon). Delightful, easy, and fruity, a bit like Beaujolais. More of a gulping wine than others, fun and exuberant, with very nice fruit. (2001)

Kendall-Jackson Vineyards & Winery "Vintner's Reserve" (California). Classy, with some real "stuff," yet quite easy to drink. Good with duck. (2001)

Meridian Vineyards (Santa Barbara County). Really good fruit that simply tastes good. John thought it lacked depth; Dottie agreed but didn't care. (2000)

Napa Ridge Winery "Coastal Vines" (North Coast). Very clean cherry-berry fruit that leaps off your tongue, but also some firm structure, nice earth, and good acids. (2001)

$20 TO ABOUT $50

Acacia Winery (Napa Valley, Carneros District). Reliable name. *Very* dry, with hints of "sweet tar" and blackberries. Black, intense, and classy. Almost rustic in the sense that it tastes like concentrated blackberries and blueberries pressed and left for a while in oak barrels, their fruity berriness intact. (2001)

Archery Summit "Premier Cuvée" (Oregon). Black as night, with a rich, sensuous nose. Chewy, rich, and velvety. Deep, rich, and very serious. Massive fruit, with a dusty, dry finish. (2000)

Au Bon Climat (Santa Maria Valley). Very good. Interesting, lovely nose. Interestingly, it's chewy yet dry at first, then velvety and smooth as the night wears on. Hmmm—that might be just right for Valentine's Day. (2001)

Beringer Vineyards "Stanly Ranch" (Los Carneros, Napa Valley). Challenging. Fruity and tight. Plenty of structure, like a Cabernet Sauvignon, with a long, lemon-fruit finish. Filled with personality. Great acids and real purity of taste. (1999)

Cambria "Julia's Pinot Noir" (Santa Maria Valley). Filled with charming fruit, with all sorts of layers of taste, good acids, and a bracing, coffee-ground finish. Reliable name. (2000)

Cristom Vineyards "Jessie Vineyard" (Willamette Valley). Elegant and beautiful, with intense fruit, clarity of taste, an underpinning of rich soil and great acids that give it a surprising jazziness as part of the endless cherry, pepper finish. (2001)

Gary Farrell (Sonoma County). Good name to look for in elegant Pinot. Pleasant and a bit creamy, with an interesting, nicely acidic finish. Really fine with salmon. (2001)

Miner Family Vineyards "Garys' Vineyard" (Santa Lucia Highlands). Massive, cherry-berry, roasted lilac nose that you can smell across the room. Nose bursting with fruit. Classy and tight, with Bing cherries and blackberries. Serious wine, clearly expensive. Layered with tobacco and cedar, vanilla, and spices. It's like a meal, with a *long* finish. Truly classy, with a touch of cream. "I could wear this behind my ears," Dottie said. (2001)

Morgan Winery (Monterey, Santa Lucia Highlands). Filled with rich fruit, depth, and really ripe blackberries. Mouth coating, with an endless finish and an interesting, attractive hint of bitterness at the end. Warming, with great balance. (2000)

J. Rochioli Vineyards (Russian River Valley). One of the most sought-after Pinots in California. Vibrant and light on its feet, with a squirt of citrus and a heavenly scent of blue flowers. Ephemeral and lovely. (2000)

Sterling Vineyards "Winery Lake Vineyard" (Carneros, Napa Valley). Sterling has had its ups and downs over the years, but this is a winner. Quite rich, with some nice funk, especially in the very dry finish. Quite earthy and soul satisfying. It tastes *real.* (2000)

Ken Wright Cellars "McCrone Vineyard" (Willamette Valley). A real heavyweight. Rich, roasted fruit and almost thick with tastes of plums, dark cherries, and blackberries. Lots of stuffing, almost dense-packed with flavor. (2002)

Rosé Champagne

Sigh. What could possibly be more romantic than a glass of beautiful pink Champagne bubbling next to a dozen roses? Pink bubbly is one of the world's greatest treats, but it tends to be so expensive that only an event like Valentine's Day could be worth it. Here's something interesting about rosé Champagne: the juice from fine-wine grapes is colorless. What makes a wine red is contact with the dark skins. Leave the clear juice in contact with the skins for just a short time and, voilà, a rosé wine. A few rosé Champagnes are made that way, too, but most are made by blending a little red wine, often Pinot Noir from the appropriately named Bouzy region of Champagne, into the white wine. Not much rosé Champagne is made, and it's an expensive process, so these do tend to be pricey. Here are some of our favorites, with very approximate prices.

De Venoge Brut Rosé. Pretty light color, pale and elegant, and quite pink. Pleasant, with a bit of lemon cream. Easy to drink and charming. The light color is romantic, and the taste is fetching—"subtle and teasing," Dottie said. (Nonvintage; $32)

Pommery Brut Rosé. Our very favorite year after year for its combination of taste and value (we sometimes see it for as little as $35). Golden, with salmon highlights. Very clean and fresh, with hints of nuts and toast. This is a very classy Champagne, especially for the price. (Nonvintage; $45)

Louis Roederer Cristal Brut Rosé. Delicate, elegant, and very dry, with lovely acids. It simply tastes beautiful. Only downside: it isn't very pink—and it is really, really expensive. (1995; $299.99)

Perrier-Jouët Brut Rosé "Blason de France." Orange-gold color. Nicely lemony and floral, with good yeast and toast, but with really large bubbles. Dottie called it "a garden wedding Champagne," which seems pretty good for Valentine's Day. Its nice acids made us think of food, so this might be good if you're making a special dinner. (Nonvintage; $74)

Pol Roger Brut Rosé. Lovely, with great balance and a perfect color. Nutty. More giving than some and quite romantic. (1995; $65.99)

Veuve Clicquot Ponsardin Brut Rosé Réserve. Full-bodied, but surprisingly light on its feet. Really good fruit flavors and balancing acids. A bit bold, but not too blustery or overaggressive for Valentine's Day. (1996; $59.95)

Oh, one last thing. Remember Lois Pannone Shaughnessy, who told us about "the rich, luscious euphoria of being in love" earlier in this chapter? A few months later, when we were doing our last-minute fact checking for this book, we dropped her a note and received this in response:

"Good afternoon, John and Dottie. I am covering for Lois as she is out on maternity leave. She had a beautiful baby girl, Mia."

Open That Bottle Night

Loss, Renewal, and "the Gift of the Grape"

"Last night we consumed a 1982 Château Cantemerle to celebrate Open That Bottle Night. This bottle has survived our fortieth and forty-fifth wedding anniversaries and both of our seventieth birthdays plus numerous other events. We just didn't have the guts to open it—a classic reason for OTBN. Words cannot describe how wonderful this wine was. Dinner was peppercorn beef tenderloin, garlic mashed Yukon Gold potatoes, plus veggies and salad. Just a super evening! We are looking forward to next year, when we will celebrate our fiftieth and OTBN—with Château Gruaud-Larose, our last 1982."

—ROBERT AND JOAN WICKLAN, BELLEVUE, NEBRASKA

Okay, it's an occasion we invented ourselves, but, still, the *Wall Street Journal*'s Open That Bottle Night has become an international celebration of family, friends, and memories. If you're not familiar with OTBN, here's the very simple explanation: Many of us have that one very special bottle of wine that we can't bear to open. Maybe it's from a wedding or a vacation or a departed loved one. Whether we have one bottle in the house or a cellar full of wine, there's always that precious bottle. We save it for a special occasion, but no occasion seems special enough. With each passing momentous event, the next one has to be bigger and bigger. So the bottle sits forever, unopened. When we began our column in 1998, we heard from so many readers about that special bottle that we decided we should open it together, on the same night, and celebrate the memories that come with it. Thousands of people took part all over the world, and OTBN became an annual event, celebrated every year on the last Saturday of February. In short, a glorious, life-affirming ritual.

> *"We opened a bottle of wine we brought back from Italy. The wine was just a simple vino da tavola from the Antico Ristorante Sibilla in Tivoli. Was the wine or the memories wonderful? Judging from our hugs and giggles, both. Thanks for permission to open. We would have saved that wine forever."*
> *Belinda and Bill Nygren, Denver, Colorado*

As the years have gone by, Open That Bottle Night has become an excuse for families and friends to get together to have fun, remember the good times, celebrate surviving the bad times, and maybe get carried away a little.

> *"Once again Margie and I participated in what is rapidly becoming a most anticipated annual event; this time, however, we were with our best and dearest friends. After surviving unfortunate first marriages, they met for the very first time at our house approximately fifteen years ago. One thing led to another, as so often happens, and they have blissfully been wedded for the last fourteen years! Thinking to celebrate their marriage and OTBN, Margie and I uncorked a bottle of 1989 Château l'Evangile Bordeaux, paired with the menu of standing rib roast and Cabernet au jus; caramelized onion horseradish mashed potatoes; spring asparagus with lemon; mixed greens with vinaigrette dressing; and topped off with fresh Florida strawberries in brandy, followed by coffee, Cognac, and Girl Scout cookies. The wine was about the best we have ever had; I seem to remember one of our friends with her tongue in the very empty bottle!"*
> *Dave and Margie Osborn, Longboat Key, Florida*

OTBN has also been a time for intimacy and romance. Some of it is suitable for children's ears.

> *"We've been saving a bottle of 1993 Cristal Champagne for several years now. I mentioned it was Open That Bottle Night to my boyfriend, and he suggested we open the Cristal. However, I had confused the dates and thought it was Saturday, Feb. 15, not Feb. 22. We already had dinner plans*

for Valentine's (we deliberately planned for dinner on Saturday instead of Friday), and I suggested we do this at the next OTBN, when we could plan a menu around the bottle. We went to the restaurant and had a fantastic dinner. After the entree plates were cleared, the waiter placed Champagne glasses on our table. I whispered to Casey that the waiter was really screwing things up tonight because we hadn't ordered any Champagne. The Cristal was then placed on the table, and the waiter prepared to open the bottle. It finally dawned on me that Casey had surprised me by bringing the bottle into the restaurant earlier that day. Panic-stricken, I said we had to stop the waiter; it was the wrong night! My boyfriend just smiled, and then he proposed."

Grace Huang and Casey Fleck, Pasadena, California

And some of it is not suitable for children's ears.

In 1978, on our first trip to Paris, my wife and I went shopping one cold, misty weekday morning at Fauchon's. We purchased two things: a 1975 Château Léoville-Barton and a large bunch of Muscat grapes, which we had never seen in the United States. We decided to take a walk, and when we got to the Tuileries we sat on a wooden bench to eat our grapes. We huddled together on the bench for warmth while we ate. Soon after we sat down, another couple joined us on the adjacent bench. Both were wearing full-length rain coats. They huddled also, then kissed, the raincoats ended up unbuttoned, they wore nothing underneath, and, well, you can guess the rest. It was certainly unlike any lunchtime encounter we had ever witnessed in Tulsa, Oklahoma. Even today, whenever we see a bunch of large green grapes, my wife and I will look at each other and smile. So it was with some trepidation that we decided to open that 1975 Léoville-Barton on OTBN. I mean, we weren't young when we took that first trip, and here we were, twenty-five years older. We were not at all sure we were up to what opening that bottle should fully entail.

Since it was very cold on OTBN, we couldn't picnic outside, as we had planned. Instead, we fixed a more conventional candlelight dinner for two. Because of 1975 Bordeaux's reputation for hardness, we let the bottle breathe for two hours. It was still closed when we tasted it, but as dinner progressed, and we laughed our way through the Tuileries story and reminisced about twenty-five years of traveling together, the wine, and we, softened. I will end the story there, except to say that we acquitted ourselves very well, thank you. Vive la France!

Michael D. Graves and Kathleen Page, Tulsa, Oklahoma

Actually, while most people don't have vacation memories like that, it is amazing to us how many people have a bottle socked away from a vacation to Tuscany or California's wine country.

"Our 1997–1998 Christmas and New Year's holiday consisted of three days in San Francisco, leading to three more days at a bed-and-breakfast in wine country. We brought home a bottle of Benziger 1995 Cabernet Sauvignon and their 1995 Merlot as souvenirs of that lovely vacation. Those souvenirs have sat in our basement ever since then—until last night. We opened up the Benziger 1995 Cabernet Sauvignon. Tasting the wine brought back memories of that trip. There was a moment driving up to Sonoma where we just had to stop the car to enjoy one of the most beautiful sunsets we have ever seen—vibrant orange and red and violet filling the whole sky. Or morning walks, just experiencing the quiet splendor of the open fields with the morning mist still rising from the ground."

Paul Hilger and Isabel Czech, Park Ridge, New Jersey

Open That Bottle Night is about remembering good times. It's about remembering good people, too.

On February 14, a good friend of mine lost his battle against brain cancer. Two days later, the Baltimore-Washington area (and all points north) had a snowstorm for the record books. Because of the storm, the family had to make multiple changes to the services and other arrangements. People couldn't get in for the funeral, or they couldn't get out after the services were delayed several times. This was not a low-stress occasion for his wife, family, or friends. We were finally able to say our good-byes and hold the service on the 20th.

On OTBN, my wife and I went over to the eastern shore where they lived so that I could do some maintenance on the house that hadn't been done for the last eight months. My wife Dottie reminded me that it was OTBN and that we should take something nice with us. We took a bottle of Io (1996) and a bottle of Chateau Potelle Mount Veeder VGS Zinfandel (2000). While I worked through the maintenance list, Dottie and Anne sat by the fire, talking and sipping the wine. I waited until all the electrical work was done before I was able to enjoy any of the wine. We started with the Zin as we knew it was still young, and besides, we wanted to finish with the larger taste of the Io. To tell the truth, while the wines were good, we won't remember them. But we will remember the night where good friends talked, laughed, cried, and sat in silence together as we shared our times with Jim. That is what it is all about.

Larry Elletson, Ellicott City, Maryland

Here are twelve tips for enjoying Open That Bottle Night.

1. Choose the bottle. Remember that what's important here isn't the pedigree of the wine but the quality of the memories it invokes. Consider this note we received from Richard Streit of Dubuque, Iowa:

"Last Saturday night we hosted Open That Bottle Night in Dubuque, Iowa. I had a 1972 bottle of Blue Nun, which I knew would be vinegar, but this gave me a good excuse to open it. It was not vinegar but was no longer a white wine. The taste was not good at all. Anne Mulgrew brought a 1993 Clos Du Chateau Chardonnay, which she had sent home from France in 1994. It was rather good. The find of the night, however, was a gallon bottle of homemade Concord wine which Gary Hancock brought. It had been stomped by four nuns from the Presentation Convent in Dubuque in 1965. The taste was that of a fairly good Port wine. Gary was sorry he had thrown out the rest of the jugs in previous years."

2. Consider spending the evening with friends or family. Wine has a special way of bringing people together.

"We are members and spouses of the Kansas City, Missouri, Rotary Club Bowling League, and we gather after bowling at some restaurant to enjoy friendly fellowship over a nice dinner and a glass or two of wine. With the exception of a couple in the group who claim to be collector/experts (they

visited Napa Valley once upon a time), most of us don't have a special-occasion bottle saved since they seem to dissipate once available for un-corking. One member said he qualified to celebrate OTBN because he 'saved it all the way from the liquor store to my house.' So be it. We used your OTBN as an excuse for a variation on our weekly routine, and it was a delightful evening. I had each guest list and comment on the wine they brought. I'm afraid they would not meet your standard of comments, but what do you expect when the thought of the moment is 'get me a glass and let me sample the hors d'oeuvres'? Al and Mary brought a Columbia Crest Merlot 1993 received as a prize in 1995 at the Rotary Bowling Banquet. Al's contribution for discussion was that 'you twirl your glass clockwise in the northern hemisphere and counterclockwise in the southern hemisphere.' There's one in every crowd."—BOB WEIR AND ANN O'DELL, OVERLAND PARK, KANSAS

3. Consider making a special dinner. Over the years, most OTBN celebrants have opened their bottle with some very special meals. Sometimes that just means a pizza from their favorite local joint. Sometimes readers tell us about truly jaw-dropping, extraordinary meals. After one OTBN, Deborah and David Lazear of San Diego sent us their wine and food menu:

༅

STOLT SEA FARMS "STERLING CAVIAR,"
BUCKWHEAT BLINI

Piper Sonoma Select Cuvée Brut NV

TUNA TARTARE IN A CUCUMBER ROLL, ASIAN INFLUENCE

Billecart-Salmon Champagne, Mareuil-sur-Ay NV

DUCK CONFIT & MOREL TORTELLINI IN A DUCK CONSOMMÉ

Vincent Girardin Pommard Les Grands Epenots 1er Cru

MEDALLIONS OF EMU AND SHITAKE MUSHROOM CAPS

VEAL DEMIGLACE

CREAMY POLENTA

Beringer "Private Reserve" Cabernet Sauvignon

BABY GREENS & BELGIAN ENDIVE SALAD WITH CREAMY
GOAT'S MILK CHEESE

RASPBERRY VINAIGRETTE

CHOCOLATE GÂTEAU WITH
CHOCOLATE GANACHE ICING

FRESH RASPBERRIES

FRENCH CHOCOLATE TRUFFLES

COFFEE

2000 Alsheimer Rheinblick, Auslese, Rheinhessen

෨෧

4. Stand the wine up (away from light and heat, of course) for a few
days before you plan to open it. This will allow any sediment to sink to
the bottom.

5. Note the temperature. Don't drink your white wine too cold or your
red wine too warm. Both reds and whites—and especially older whites—
are often better around "cellar temperature" of fifty-five degrees. Your
wine might be old and delicate. If your white is too cold, the chill might
hide what's left of it; if your red is too warm, the flavors might be too
diffuse. Put the bottle in the refrigerator for two or three hours—maybe
a little longer for a white, a little shorter for a red, but it depends a
great deal on the temperature at which you've kept the wine.

6. With an old bottle, the cork may break easily. The best opener for a
cork like that is the one with two prongs, but it requires some skill. If
you're planning ahead, use the days that you have before OTBN to
practice using one of these on less precious bottles. Otherwise, be
prepared for the possibility that the cork will fall apart with a regular

corkscrew. If that happens, have a carafe and a coffee filter handy. Pour just enough of the wine through the coffee filter to remove the pieces of cork.

7. Otherwise, do not decant. We're assuming these are old and fragile wines. Air could quickly dispel what's left of them.

8. Have a backup wine ready for your special meal, in case your old wine really has gone bad.

9. Serve dinner. Then open the wine and immediately take a sip. If it's truly bad—we mean vinegar—you will know it right away. Even if the wine doesn't taste good to you right away, don't rush to the sink to pour it out. Give it a chance. We've heard from many people over the years who find that the wine gets better and better as the night goes on—and sometimes even longer.

Here at the McDonalds', Open That Bottle Night arrived concurrently with the kids' Open That Baseball Season Day 5 (OTBSD), and, in order to feed the resultant team of junior sluggers who drifted to our home that evening, Barbecue That Wahoo Night. Our family calendar looks like a scratch pad with so many erasures and cross-outs. The day originally was set as GBCNO (Girls' Book Club Night Out). But when "We're moving so we're emptying our freezer" Gramma and Grandpa showed up loaded (to the gills?) with a catch of wahoo, we changed plans. The book club dropped by anyway and joined the bottle sampling. One guest hit a real home run by bringing a bottle of 1975 Chateau St. Jean Alexander Valley Belle Terre Vineyard Cabernet Sauvignon. We carefully tried to open the bottle, but the cork just crumbled out. On tasting, it seemed that after twenty-eight years and an apparently bad cork, the stuff pretty much struck out. We resealed the bottle and put it aside to use for cooking. Following your advice, we had backup plans and so enjoyed a not-so-old but still very special pair of Babcock vintages: the 2001 Grand Cuvée Chardonnay and the 2000 Mt. Carmel Pinot Noir. And that, we thought, was that.

The next morning I spied the bottle of Cab there next to our range. I don't really know what possessed me at that early hour (well, to tell the truth, I guess I do know), but I just had to try the wine again. What came out of that bottle didn't look, feel, or smell anything like the sample from the night before. It was clear and soooo smooth, with an understated complexity still very much Cabernet in character.

In hindsight, we should have given much longer for the bottle to breathe and for the sediment of cork and whatever else to settle. But come next year we plan to add yet another event to our family calendar: OTBAM, for Open That Bottle Again Morning!

Tim and Trish McDonald, Torrance, California

10. Reminisce. We've found that talking about the person who gave you the wine, or the circumstances under which you received it, makes the wine resonate in a very sweet and personal way. Most people find their wine tastes surprisingly good under these circumstances. This is what happened to John and Mary Jo Runnion of Acworth, Georgia:

I was really intrigued by the concept of OTBN when I first read about it, but I wasn't sure we were going to participate because I didn't think we had a bottle of wine on hand that qualified as a special bottle that we had been saving forever. We began drinking wine regularly a little over a year ago when I first started reading your column, so prior to that time we almost never bought wine for ourselves and rarely had a bottle on hand. Then, several weeks ago, I mentioned OTBN to Mary Jo, and she said "Well, there is that bottle of sparkling wine we were given when Colleen was born." Colleen, our daughter, turned four years old last November. After a brief search, we found the bottle. It certainly wasn't a special wine, Martini & Rossi Asti, but the circumstances under which we received it were very special. We hadn't opened the bottle when we received it, because quite frankly, we didn't think we would like it very much. A sweet sparkler like this one isn't something we would have chosen for ourselves, even back in those days. Eventually, the bottle got pushed to the back of the cabinet, and we forgot about it.

So, we had our wine and we thought we could enjoy it if we planned the right menu. We made grilled pork tenderloin with a cranberry and brown sugar glaze, baked apples with sugar and cinnamon, Moroccan carrot salad, and herbed green beans. We thought we needed foods that would stand up to the sweetness of the wine, and we were right! The wine went well with our food choices, and we enjoyed it! I don't know if it was the food, the special circumstances under which we received the wine, or the bit of extra time the wine had in the bottle, but it tasted much better than we expected as we reminisced about our lives in 1998 (and in 1993 when our son, Andy, was born).

11. Enjoy the wine for what it is, not what it might be or might once have been.

12. Save one last glass of wine in the bottle. At the end of the evening, after the dishes are done, pour the remainder of the wine into your glasses (pour it through a coffee filter if there's a great deal of sediment and you're squeamish). Then drink up and enjoy those very last moments of a lovely night.

If you do this, you will find that wine has a way of conjuring memories the way few things do.

"I write to you from Cancun, Mexico, where my husband and I are celebrating our fifty-fifth wedding anniversary. Last night we enjoyed our OTBN at the hotel's French restaurant with a bottle of Château Margaux 1970. We hold a special fondness for this wine as we first drank it at the Eiffel Tower during our second honeymoon celebration in Paris many years ago. Last night the sommelier decanted our wine and gave us a small sample. The initial impression was a lovely aroma and a pleasant taste. We let it breathe more. The wine had improved, and we both found it delightful. As I stared out onto the Caribbean Sea, I couldn't help thinking about Paris, an ocean and a lifetime away, and the man I loved seated next to me with whom I shared it."
        Iris N. Spencer (Mrs. Robert W. Spencer), Bloomfield, Michigan

Ultimately, Open That Bottle Night is about things way more important than wine. In a sermon just after Christmas, the Rev. Ronald D. Campbell of Elmwood Park Presbyterian Church in Illinois used Open That Bottle Night to make some significant points. This is what he told his congregation:

The Wall Street Journal *made a suggestion last year that I thought had some important lessons. It was in their weekly column about wine. If you stay away from all alcoholic beverages, don't be offended. You will see how this can still apply to you.*

They chose a specific date when they said everyone should open and drink that special bottle of wine set aside someplace in the house with some people who are important to them. The message is very simple: that while it is important to have hopes and dreams, and to set things aside for the future, it is equally important to celebrate with our families and loved ones now. Gather some people together who are indeed special to you, and important to you, and literally make that the special occasion where you can share the wine together. Now, again, wine is not the important part. What is important is recognizing those people in our lives—typically the people on our Christmas card lists—who are truly and genuinely an important part of our lives. Find a way to share with them in this coming year—not just with an annual Christmas card. At some point during the year, make, create a special occasion when you can celebrate those friendships, because life is short and we never know what the future holds. Celebrate the gift of life that God has given us every day, for that gift is indeed special.

Nobody understands that better than John Watson of Maple Glen, Pennsylvania. Of all the many thousands of people we have heard from in our years of celebrating OTBN, no one has touched us more deeply than Mr. Watson. The first year of OTBN, he wrote lovingly of two bottles of wine he and his wife had brought back from London many years before—a 1961 Burgundy and a 1983 Châteauneuf-du-Pape from the Rhône Valley of France. On the first Open That Bottle Night, he opened the '61 and wrote us: "I can only express one regret. Had we found an occasion last year to open this great 'gift of the grape,' my bride of over fifty years could have been present to enjoy this event in person rather than in spirit only."

The second year, Mr. Watson opened the Rhône wine. "I decided the wine this year should again be shared with family (daughters, sons-in-law, four guests in all) and paired with an appropriate regional cuisine. The meal was enjoyed by everyone present, but the Châteauneuf did not live up to our expectations. Perhaps wines are like life itself: They each have their moment in time. Or maybe wines, like memories, fade with the passing years."

Then came the third Open That Bottle Night, and we received this letter from Mr. Watson:

> *When I wrote my OTBN letter in 1999, I was in a period of sad reflection on the death of the true love of my life. I assumed those wonderful days of shared companionship, discovery, and romance with a very special person were all behind me. But as I drifted down the Dordogne River during a wine tour in France in 2001, I met Mary. As we sampled wines at châteaux from Bergerac to Bordeaux and slurped oysters in the seaside village of Arcachon, we discovered the similarities of our feelings for our lost loves and the thoughts we each had about the future. We realized that with more of our lives behind us than ahead of us, it was time to create some new memories. So, in spite of being separated by a continent (she lives in Portland and I live near Philadelphia), we agreed to share new experiences whenever we could. One of these experiences, we decided, would be OTBN. Thus, on Saturday, Feb. 23, we sat at a candlelit table, looking out a picture window at the twinkling lights of Portland reflected on the river below us. Our wine for the evening was a 1994 Château Pichon-Lalande we had purchased at the château. As we finished our romantic repast, we raised our glasses in a toast of thanks.*
>
> *Life is wonderful, and miraculous, too. If Mary and I didn't have a love of wine, neither of us would have been in the same place at the same time in France. So, here's to the "gift of the grape."*

By the fourth Open That Bottle Night, Mr. Watson's note was signed "Mary and John":

> *In our continuing quest to create some new memories, it seems Mary and I are destined to revisit the familiar. When Mary and I met in France, during a wine tour in 2001, we purchased our first bottle of Château Pichon-Lalande, and this was the wine we opened and wrote about for the last OTBN. Then, this spring, as we toured the coast of Oregon, we discovered an intimate little restaurant, which had a very extensive wine list. There*

among the prizes was a bottle of 1997 Château Pichon-Lalande, which we just had to have as we enjoyed a delightful and exceedingly well-prepared meal in the quiet ambience of that great little restaurant. What a treat to enjoy this wine again. It made us feel as though we were back in Bordeaux.

Finally, this winter we attended an estate auction, which included a well-cellared collection of some great wines. Among all those cases and bottles of some of the top producers in the wine industry was a case of Château Pichon-Lalande 1987. The bidding was fast and furious, and the price escalated beyond what we had hoped to pay, but we persevered and ended the evening with our treasured case of wine. We had thought that we would open a bottle each year on the anniversary of our first meeting (in May) but could not wait that long and decided OTBN would be an appropriate occasion.

So, for OTBN we once again sat at our table by the picture window overlooking Portland and the Willamette River below us and enjoyed our meal accompanied by this now familiar wine. Even though this wine was sixteen years old, it had stature and refinement that we have not witnessed in any other wine, full of subtle flavors and essences of berries and a great smooth finish.

*As we raised our glasses in a toast, we mused at how, if we were to celebrate each future OTBN with a bottle from our cache, we would be enjoying the last bottle of the case in 2014, when the wine will be twenty-seven years old and John will be **ninety years old.***

What an incentive for longevity.

What a raison d'être.

Here's to the "gift of the grape."

The Oscars
(and Emmys) Take Our Quiz:
"Blood and Wine"?

Bad guy: "Do you like wine, Mrs. Peel?"

Mrs. Peel: "In moderation."

Bad guy: "I was referring to your interest, not your capacity."

Mrs. Peel: "So was I."

—*THE AVENGERS,* "DIAL A DEADLY NUMBER," 1965

Why should the stars have all the fun celebrating the Oscars and the Emmys? You can have a good time, too—and you don't have to suffer fashion know-it-alls making fun of your clothes, either. Who does Joan Rivers think she is, anyway? One fun and easy way to celebrate the stars of the Big Screen and the Little Screen is to throw a party and ask guests to bring a wine that they think represents the nominees. A muscular, unrestrained Rhône would fit Russell Crowe, for instance, while Denzel Washington might be a velvety-smooth red Burgundy, Matthew Broderick a puppy-dog-friendly, eager-to-please Rioja, and Tim Roth a kinky, inky Zinfandel. Group the bagged wines according to awards categories— Best Actor, for instance—and taste them blind, trying to guess the wines' celluloid personas. Perhaps you could test whether Richard Gere knew what he was talking about when he told Julia Roberts in *Pretty Woman* that strawberries "bring out the flavor in the Champagne." (It's probably a tip-off that he then reveals he doesn't drink.) Another possibility would be a quiz. Have everybody come up with wine questions from movies and television and see who can answer them.

Wine has played a role in television and movies from each medium's early days. Sometimes its screentime bolsters a major theme, such as the healing power of food and wine in *Babette's Feast*. Sometimes it's used for celebration ("The Night They Invented Champagne" in *Gigi*) or for suspense (what really is in that bottle of 1940 Pommard in *Notorious?*). However, and sadly, we have found in general that wine is rarely treated with real affection in movies or television, with the exception of the otherwise forgettable *French Kiss*. More often, wine is used to showcase snobbery or as a joke:

Count Dracula: "This is very old wine. I hope you will like it."
Guest: "Aren't you drinking?"
Count Dracula: "I never drink . . . wine."

Here are twenty questions and answers to start the fun with, most from movies but some from television, since it would be a crime to leave out a classic *I Love Lucy* episode, for instance. Got your thinking cap on? Let's go.

1. In *Year of the Comet*, what is the famous bottle of wine to which the title refers?

Château Lafite from the 1811 vintage—the year of "The Great Comet"—is considered by some the greatest Bordeaux ever made. In the movie, a giant bottle of the wine is the object of a bizarre chase. By the way, Lafite became Lafite Rothschild almost sixty years later.

2. What did Hannibal Lecter consider the perfect wine with liver? (Careful: trick question.)

We all remember that, in the movie *The Silence of the Lambs*, Dr. Lecter said he'd once eaten a census taker's liver with "some fava beans and a nice Chianti." But in the book he says, "I ate his liver with some fava beans and a big Amarone." Amarone is the intense, dried-grape wine from northeastern Italy (look for Cesari, Santa Sofia, or Masi), but, personally, we'd prefer the somewhat fruitier, livelier tastes of Chianti with liver.

3. In the movie *Joshua Then and Now*, how does James Woods get back at the man who makes a pass at his wife?

The man is a wine collector with a massive wine cellar. Joshua, played by Woods, steams all the labels off (we wish they really came off so easily; see "Saving the Memories"). That leads to a scene where the two meet on a street. "I've been burglarized," says the man. "What did they take?" asks Joshua. Man: "Nothing. Worse." The scene shifts to the cellar, where the wine lover says: "Some snake, some pervert, he steamed all of the labels off my bottles, and he's moved them around so I can't tell which is which. Why would anyone do such a thing to me?" Joshua replies: "Fortunately, a man of your educated palate, he could pop open any one of these babies and be able to tell not only the vineyard but the vintage as well." The man brightens.

4. In the 2000 movie *Keeping the Faith,* Ben Stiller plays a rabbi named Jacob Schram. Why did we find this amusing?

Jacob Schram was a pioneering winemaker in California, founder of Schramsberg, which produces excellent sparkling wine. Its top-of-the-line bubbly is called J. Schram. We figured this couldn't be a coincidence, so we called the movie's writer, Stuart Blumberg. He never heard of Jacob Schram the winemaker. Oh, well.

5. In the movie *Blood and Wine,* what wine does Jack Nicholson drink after suffocating Michael Caine?

Despite the title, this movie has very little to do with wine. Look closely in this scene, however, and you'll see that Nicholson enjoys a glass of Opus One, the expensive, collectible red from California.

6. In the movie *Disclosure,* why is a bottle of wine important, and what is the wine?

In Seattle, Michael Douglas's new boss, played by Demi Moore, invites him to her office after work and tries to seduce him with dirty talk and a bottle of Pahlmeyer Chardonnay 1991, which had been a special wine to them when they were dating years before. Pahlmeyer is an excellent wine that was a cult favorite in the nineties. When Douglas sues for sexual harassment, Moore claims that the meeting was spur-of-the-moment. Then Douglas's lawyer points out that Pahlmeyer Chardonnay isn't available in Seattle wine stores, proving that Moore must have been planning this seduction for some time. No, it doesn't sound very convincing, and it didn't seem like the mediator hearing the case thought much of it, either.

7. In the movie *A New Leaf,* what is Elaine May's "wine" of choice, to the horror of Walter Matthau?

Matthau plays a broke playboy who is wooing geeky May for her money. At a fancy restaurant, as the waiter pours red wine, Matthau says: "Fifty-five was a glorious year for Mouton Rothschild, better than '53, I think. Don't you?" To which May replies: "Have you tasted Mogen David's Extra-Heavy Malaga Wine with soda and lime juice? It tastes a little like grape juice, and every year is good." Matthau says, "Why don't you just drink grape juice?" and she answers: "It's not as sweet." She calls this "a Malaga cooler."

8. In *Funny Face,* arriving at a meeting with Audrey Hepburn, before she's introduced to the fashion press, Fred Astaire proudly shows her a bottle of bubbly imported from where?

We're always amused by the scene in which Astaire, in Paris, proudly announces that the wine is "imported all the way from Napa Valley, California." Finding California bubbly in Paris in 1957? Only in the movies.

9. In the Keanu Reeves howler *A Walk in the Clouds,* where does the "mother vine," the one from which a huge vineyard sprung, come from?

The mother vine came from Mexico, the source of some early wine grape-growing vines in California. What's truly odd in this very odd movie is that, after a fire levels the vineyard, Reeves pulls the ancient vine up with his bare hands and gives it to the patriarch of the family—and odder still that the patriarch is pleased about this.

10. At which winery was the old prime-time soap opera *Falcon Crest* filmed?

The series, which ran from 1981 to 1990, was filmed at Spring Mountain in Napa Valley. We remember the first Spring Mountain wine we ever had, a 1976 Chardonnay. Our notes: "Delicious! Huge yet crisp, but also soft and very creamy. Very complex, with contradictory tastes." During the TV show's heyday, the winery had a second label called Falcon Crest.

11. In *From Russia with Love,* how does Sean Connery know that Robert Shaw is a bad guy?

Aboard a train, James Bond is having dinner with Shaw, who is pretending to be a fellow agent, and they both order grilled sole. Bond tells the waiter: "I'll have a bottle of the Blanc de Blancs." Shaw says: "Make mine Chianti—the red kind." Minutes later, he knocks Bond unconscious. When 007 wakes up, with a gun in his face, the first thing he says is: "Red wine with fish. Well, that should have told me something." Shaw fires back: "You may know the right wines, but you're the one on your knees."

12. In *French Kiss,* what two items does Kevin Kline smuggle into France?

A stolen bracelet and a tiny vine, so he can use some American rootstock to revitalize an old vineyard. The way he discusses his love of wine with Meg Ryan is quite touching.

13. In the *Avengers* episode "Dial a Deadly Number," how does Steed impress the wine-loving villains?

In a wine cellar, they each take a glass and walk twenty paces in a blind taste-off. Steed sniffs the wine and says: "It's either a '65 Algerian red or a premier cru—Château Lafite Rothschild. It's old, very old. Definitely pre-1914, but no earlier than 1880." Then he says "1908," and the bad guys smile, but Steed quickly adds: "would not be the year. 1909—from the northern end of the vineyard." The bad guy is so shocked that the monocle falls right out of his eye.

14. In the television show *Frasier,* Niles and Frasier face off over what position in their wine club? Extra credit: How does Niles win?

In an episode called "Whine Club," the brothers compete to become "corkmaster." Amid a grotesque amount of swishing and swirling, Niles wins by correctly guessing that a wine is made primarily from Merlot; Frasier guesses Cabernet Sauvignon. After Niles's victory, he is serenaded by the club:

Hail, Corkmaster, the master of the cork.
He knows which wine goes with fish or pork.

15. Why was Lucy chosen to stomp grapes at a winery in Italy?

In the classic TV episode, Lucy decides to visit a winery to research her hoped-for part in a movie called *Bitter Grapes.* The vineyard manager decides she should help stomp the grapes because "Look at those feet—like large pizzas." She gets into a fight in the vat and loses the role because she's stained purple when the director visits later in the day. Even after all these years, that fight makes us laugh out loud.

16. In *Casablanca,* what Champagne does Captain Renault order for Major Strasser?

Veuve Clicquot 1926, "a good French wine."

17. But later in *Casablanca,* as Dooley Wilson sings "As Time Goes By," what Champagne do Rick and Ilse share?

We all remember Humphrey Bogart saying, "Henri says he'll water the garden with Champagne before he'll let the Germans drink it." What's the bubbly? Mumm Cordon Rouge.

18. In the 1998 remake of *The Parent Trap,* Dennis Quaid plays a California winemaker, but what kind of wine does he share with his bride? Extra credit: At which winery was it filmed?

Look closely. He pours Where the Dreams Have No End, an Italian Chardonnay—or at least he pours from a bottle with that label, because the wine that comes out is red. The movie was filmed at Staglin in Napa Valley, which makes an outstanding Cabernet Sauvignon. Shari Staglin says she and her husband, Garen, found the filming at their home "exhilarating and invasive, but all in all, we just loved doing it." Some of the people involved in making the movie have dropped by since to visit, but she's still waiting to see Quaid again. "He's a real cutie," she says. As a fund-raiser for a charity several years ago, Staglin auctioned off an item called "A Walk in the Clouds" that included some of its wine and the privilege of dressing up like Lucy and stomping Staglin grapes. It sold for $56,000.

19. In the 1973 *Columbo* episode titled "Any Old Port in a Storm," Peter Falk's detective is trying to solve the mysterious death of a

womanizing winery owner. The chief suspect: the man's wine-snob brother. How does Columbo solve the case?

Adrian Carsini is a California winemaker played by Donald Pleasence. When his brother, who owns the winery, tells him that he is selling it to "the Marino brothers," Adrian sputters: "The sixty-nine-cents-a-gallon Marino brothers? They don't make wine. They don't even make good mouthwash." The brother responds: "Don't worry . . . I'm sure the Marino brothers will let you lick the labels of their new carbonated rosé." This is too much for Adrian, who knocks his brother out and drags him to the wine cellar. Then Adrian turns off the air-conditioning and flies to New York for a week, leaving his brother to suffocate in an unexpected heat wave. Later, he dumps the body in the ocean, to make it look like a drowning. During the investigation, Columbo secretly serves Carsini a bottle of Carsini's own wine from the cellar, and Carsini declares it has been ruined by heat—proving to Columbo that the victim actually suffocated in the wine cellar and that Carsini did it. Okay, so the stone cellar probably wouldn't be airtight and wouldn't get that hot—over 150 degrees, they say—even without air-conditioning, but it's a great episode. And it includes this classic exchange:

Lt. Columbo: "How can you tell a good wine from an average wine?"

Snooty wine merchant: "By the price."

20. In *Notorious,* what was in that 1940 bottle of Pommard?

Fine Burgundy wine. Tricked you! It's the 1934 Pommard that has the uranium ore in it. This Hitchcock movie is the granddaddy of wine movies to us. After all, one of the central points of tension is whether there will be enough bottles of Champagne for guests at a party. That's because if they run out, bad guy Sebastian (Claude Rains) will have to go to the cellar, where he will find good guys Devlin (Cary Grant) and Alicia (Ingrid Bergman), who have discovered the bottles of ore. How central is wine to this movie? Consider that, in Hitchcock's traditional cameo, he's seen drinking a glass of Champagne.

Wine-Tasting Groups Your Neighbors Are Doing It

"Our health care retirement facility has a wine-tasting club. We meet in one of our fellow inmates' rooms. Our most senior member, ninety, married a babe of sixty and promptly moved out to get away from all those old people." —JOSEPH SCHMIDT, BUCKINGHAM'S CHOICE CONTINUING HEALTH CARE RETIREMENT COMMUNITY, FREDERICK, MARYLAND

When you think of a "wine-tasting group," you probably think of something like the insufferable wine snobs on the television show *Frasier* who got together to impress each other with ridiculous descriptions and pompous pronouncements. But even Jon Sherman, a wine lover and an executive producer of *Frasier,* who co-wrote the show's classic "Whine Club" episode mentioned in the preceding chapter, knows that's not really true. "The wine club seen on *Frasier* isn't really about wine; it's about exclusivity," he once told us. "While wine snobbery is plenty good for jokes on TV, it's terrible for you, your wine, and your tastings. Wine clubs should bring people together, not set them apart. So if you belong to a wine club like the one on *Frasier,* I'd encourage you to quit and start a new one."

There are thousands of wine-tasting groups all over the country, most of them informal get-togethers among friends whom you'd never consider wine snobs. We'll let you in on a secret: somewhere in your neighborhood, there is a wine-tasting group. They're everywhere, all around you. If you have some good friends who are like-minded, you might think about doing this, too. Not only can you experience a wider variety of wines with people you enjoy, but if you're lucky, the members will grow and change, improve as time goes by, like a fine wine. Your group will develop its own rituals that can become a very important part of your life year after year.

When we were just starting our affair with wine, we joined a nationwide group, Les Amis du Vin, which held several tastings and wine dinners throughout the year. The local chapter in Miami brought in winemakers like Cecil De Loach and wine legends like the late Harry Waugh, a director of Château Latour. Mr. Waugh presided over an amazing vertical tasting—tasting the same wine in a progression of vintages—that included a heavenly scented brown wine that he said had been made almost entirely by women because the men had been called up to fight in the Great War. In the mid-1980s, the club also introduced us to wines from Australia, our first glimpse of the juggernaut that would overcome France in 2002 as the second-largest source of wine by volume imported into the United States. A handful of colleagues from the *Miami Herald* were members of the Miami chapter, but mostly our passion threw us in with complete strangers who weren't strangers after a glass or two.

Because the Les Amis tastings didn't come fast enough, the newspaper contingent also formed a separate group. We'd meet at each other's homes, and everyone would bring a bottle of wine from an agreed-upon type and an appropriate dish. When we did high-end Chardonnays, Pat brought Far Niente and Bob brought Kistler. On another occasion, the two Freds treated us to Vega Sicilia that they'd brought back from Spain. We remember introducing our friends in the steamy tropics to what we'd decided was the world's best white Zinfandel, from De Loach. The meals were whatever we felt would go well with the wine of the night. For a tasting of bubblies, we brought chilled lobsters. One time, instead of ordering twenty-four squares of quiche from a fine French bakery in the neighborhood, Dottie ended up with twenty-four pies that we desperately foisted on our guests as they left. One of the Freds, Fred Tasker, who is now the *Miami Herald*'s wine writer, and his wife, Catherine, once served a whole roasted baby pig.

The tastings were blind, and everyone arrived with bottles in bags. There was always spirited discussion about each wine, what we tasted in it, how it tasted with the food. We didn't do anything formal—no tasting sheets or votes. (Though John and others jotted down some notes for themselves. That's how we know, for instance, that we tasted Zinfandels on February 16, 1980, and the best of tasting was a 1976 from David Bruce Winery with "beautiful balance.") We'd eat and drink late into the night, usually a Saturday, and make sure everyone got home safely. Our group consisted of eight hard-core members (four married couples) and sometimes swelled to twelve, including a couple of single men. Once a year, on the night before Joe's Stone Crab opened for the season, our group and a few others would join Dr. Robert Hosmon, associate dean of the University of Miami School of Communications and wine columnist for the South Florida *Sun-Sentinel* newspaper. Alone at Joe's, except for a small number of waiters, we sat for hours and sampled white wine after white wine, trying to select the one that went best with stone crabs. When we moved from Miami to New York more than a decade ago, these were the people we missed most.

We have heard from hundreds of wine groups, and, really, they're everywhere. Think we're kidding? Let's take a quick tour.

Valencia, California: The Earthquake Group

At 4:31 A.M. on January 17, 1994, an earthquake brought Patti and Gene Mellevoid of Valencia, California, together with wine-loving neighbors. Married for only a year, they and their neighbors were jostled awake at that hour by the powerful quake that killed fifty-seven people and caused more than $40 billion in damage. Mr. Mellevoid was tossed about, dislocating his shoulder and breaking several ribs. On their return from a harried trip to the hospital, the Mellevoids were stunned to find their neighbors, many of whom they'd never met, sitting in their driveways drinking wine. It is interesting how some people react to calamity. After they'd assessed the physical damage they and their homes had suffered, the wine helped them reflect on what they'd just survived and to celebrate being alive. Mrs. Mellevoid told us she remembers thinking: "These are people I need to get to know."

"It was then we discovered what some of them were drinking was really great stuff," she told us. "Heaven forbid an aftershock would take out the remaining great reserves and vintage wines some of us had. And hence, we became a group of wine tasters and gourmet cooks and shared some amazing wines and great dinners."

Boston, Massachusetts: Sisters Who Sip

About seven years ago Stephanie Browne, senior manager for Blue-Cross BlueShield in Boston, realized that when she and several friends got together, their conversations invariably touched on wine. So she pulled them together—some knew each other from serving in the local Boston chapter of the Coalition of Black Women, Inc., a national organization that focuses on social and political issues—and asked each to invite a friend to form a wine-tasting group. That group became Divas Uncorked, whose website, divasuncorked.com, calls them "Sisters Who Sip." Although the ten members come from different professions—they're entrepreneurs, an artist, and a lawyer, figures in the media, in health care, and in sports, and homemakers—they had in common, even before wine, a love of volunteering. "It's a lot of work, doing fund-raising, doing committee work, so we were looking for something that was pure fun," said Callie Crossley, an award-winning television producer and commentator who also works for the Nieman Foundation at Harvard. The Divas meet monthly at members' homes, with the hosting diva deciding a theme, buying all the wine, and providing all the food. Each member contributes $20 for each gathering, whether she's present or not, although Ms. Crossley said "that doesn't begin to cover" the cost of the evening because some members do rather elaborate dinners. Added Karen Holmes Ward of the local ABC affiliate, WCVB-TV, "There are many B. Smiths and Martha Stewarts in our group." The wines are tasted—sometimes blind, sometimes not, tried with and without food—and then graded.

Some of their themes have been "The Art of the Wine Label," in which wine was selected by the artistry of the label; "In the Pink," with blush wines and spicy foods; "New England Clambake Whites (And Some Reds)" to pair with lobster and seafood; and "Oregon to the Mediterranean," with Oregon Pinot Noirs matched with Mediterranean food. Each member receives printed information about the evening's wines to take with her. "It's absolutely key," Ms. Crossley said. "The hostess has to have an information packet, general information about the wine she's featuring, either it specifically or the genre it's from. Also in the packet are comments from critics, the cost of the wines, and the stores where they were bought." One tradition that they enjoy is giving each member a wine-related party favor to take home after each meeting—a corkscrew, wine tags, once even inexpensive clocks set in a face of Bacchus.

The group has grown so popular that now it even holds wine dinners open to the public. During Boston's big Wine Expo, they host a wine dinner at a fancy restaurant, featuring wine professionals, from African-American vintner Mac McDonald and his Vision Cellars Pinot Noirs to Joshua Wesson, founder of the chic Best Cellars wine stores. The Divas also organize an annual French wine dinner to which spouses and other significant others are invited. They've traveled to California wine country twice, and they're planning an overseas trip. They also conducted a one-day seminar, "Wine, Women and . . .", which was open to the public and geared to women "because they're intimidated about going into a wine store," Ms. Crossley said. Part of the day was a discussion on how to start a wine club. The day culminated with a banquet, of course.

In the beginning, Divas Uncorked could be divided into those who liked only white wine and those who liked only red, Ms. Crossley told us. Now, everyone enjoys sipping all sorts of wines. "I feel very comfortable going to a restaurant, even though there's a list of something that I don't know about. I feel comfortable asking questions of a wine person or discussing with the table what they might like. I'm particularly attuned now to what it's like to have a wine that works well with food. It's great to find a fun thing and to share it with people." In fact, the only problem is that the divas constantly have to fend off requests from people who want to join the group. Said Ms. Crossley: "It would feel weird to expand this intensely bonded group."

Yakima, Washington: The Five Fs

Thomas Gates, a stockbroker in Yakima, Washington, has been part of a male wine group for eleven years. The group has eight members. "We were interested in increasing our knowledge of fine wine," he said simply. Initially they met five or six times a year, but as their enjoyment grew, they met more frequently. Now it's once a month, and, because their wives felt left out, they hold an annual blowout dinner to which the wives are invited. Sometimes, he said, they go on road trips with their wives to places like Sun Mountain Lodge, a posh resort with an impressive wine list, just outside of Winthrop, in the Northern Cascades.

Mr. Gates's group calls itself the Five Fs, which stands for the Forty-Five-Minute Finer Ferment Fraternity, according to member Dr. Palmer P. Wright, who lent his wit to its name. He told us that the forty-five-minute designation was supposed to put pressure on the host to get the tasting done between forty-five minutes and an hour because many of the members have family and professional obligations that require their time. Among the members are a dentist; an ear, nose, and throat specialist; a teacher; a farmer; the owner of a fertilizer company; and Mr. Gates, a stockbroker who starts his day at 4:30 A.M. Still, most gatherings last a couple hours, and that's a good thing considering what they're tasting. The Five Fs is different from many groups in that its members drink almost entirely from their own wine cellars. These cellars—all except one member has one—contain from five hundred to four thousand bottles. The depth and breadth of their eclectic collections, Mr. Gates said, means that they can taste "old wines, verticals, and horizontals," but apparently it all needs to be red. "One guy springs whites on us, but we prefer reds," Mr. Gates said. One tasting that was popular was wines made from Syrah grapes in the Rhône Valley of France, Washington state, California, and Australia. One member likes to taste the wines blind, but Mr. Gates said, "If it's really good, I want to know what it is." The host provides all of the wines and the appetizers, and the cost is not shared. "It's nothing fancy," Mr. Gates explained.

Hartford, Connecticut: The Women's Group

A female group in Hartford has been meeting since 1995. An aerobics instructor and some of her friends form the nucleus. One key to its longevity, said Colette Nakhoul, a private-equity portfolio manager, and Jane Booker, a union legal aide, is that the members have different professional interests but share a love of wine, much like the male group in Yakima. Just like the Five Fs, the women invite spouses and boyfriends to a special gathering once a year. Why just females? "Women and men are different in the way they experience things and enjoy things," said Ms. Booker. "Men might be more focused on swirling and sniffing and writing down the score because men are really into measuring things. Women are more, 'What do you see and what do you like?'" When the female group in Hartford started, members simply chose a country to focus on. "Narrowing it down to a country gave us an entire year's worth of tasting subjects," Ms. Nakhoul said. The first two years they kept themes simple. "One of Jane's tastings was a varietal taste-off between a couple Pinot Noirs from Washington and Burgundies from France." The group of seven meets every two to three months. The hostess pays for everything. The group is talking about going to Tuscany together.

Frankfort, Illinois: The Teachers

More typical of the groups we talked to were coed ones such as the one Joyce Cekander started together with single and married friends in 1968 in Frankfort, a southern suburb of Chicago. At the time most of them were high school teachers and college professors. "Being very young and very poor and wanting to know more about wine, we decided that we'd get together. We started out bringing a bottle of wine and having cheese at somebody's house. Then we'd pool money and buy more expensive wines, so it evolved." In June 2001, the last of them retired. "After thirty-four years from the onset of the group, we have grieved together, celebrated together, grown together, and become an important part of each other's lives," Ms. Cekander told us. "Friendships have flourished, we

have all matured, and we enjoy each other's company when we are together."
There are ten people. The group has regular wine-tasting parties, and its
members host many "tweeners," more or less impromptu gatherings. "Being
all educators, we were never at a loss for topics of discussions," Ms. Cekander
said, "and we're never all in agreement." Some members meet in Florida
every February. Three of them went to France together in September 2002.
A few years ago six female members and one male member rented a boat
in Burgundy and sailed it themselves. "It was catastrophic; we almost cap-
sized. It was just awful, and I loved every minute of it," Ms. Cekander said.

Al Sowa, at seventy the group's elder statesman, built a boat, *Ishmael,*
with his wife, Grace, over more than two decades. Its various stages of
completion gave the group numerous occasions to celebrate. Mr. Sowa rel-
ishes the freedom that the hosts have. "The person who hosts the party
buys all the wine and makes the program, and they can do as much research
as they care to," he told us. "I've enjoyed making maps. Once I did Italian
wines from various parts of Italy, so I made a big map of Italy that covered
the whole table, and we put the bottles in Piedmont and Friuli."

Not all well-researched efforts turn out as planned. Ms. Cekander told us
she once tried to pull off a tasting of wines from the Baltic States. There are
large pockets of people in the Chicago area who can trace their origins to
these places, so the more she thought about her plan, the more excited
she became. "I went out and researched it and eventually changed my
mind," she said, explaining that she found few wines from those regions.
So she instead "made a half side of lamb and moussaka, and it became a
Mediterranean-Greek tasting."

Mr. Sowa also enjoys being a guest. "The host is responsible for all of
the food. Nobody brings anything to the party except a check to pay for
the wine. So you're not obligated to fix an appetizer or a dessert. You come
completely unfettered." His best piece of advice? "I would not limit the
creativity of the host." He and Grace have been creative. She once did supermarket wines recommended by *Consumer Reports.* Mr. Sowa once
poured the same wine from a half-bottle, a regular bottle, a magnum, and a
double magnum. "Invariably, the one from the largest bottle tasted the
best," he said. Another time, the group tasted the same wine in different
glasses: a little one, a medium-size one, and a big one. "I told them they

were different wines," he recalled. "The larger glass produced the best wine experience." Still, he added: "Sometimes people get lazy and run out and buy some stuff the day of the party, and that's okay, too. It doesn't have to be very involved all the time."

Columbia, Missouri: The Taste Travelers

Other groups do things differently. Margo and Richard Pettway's group in Columbia has eleven members who meet six or seven times a year, with summers off, said Mr. Pettway, a finance professor in the business school of the University of Missouri, Dottie's alma mater. The host decides what type of wine they'll taste, buys it, and provides cheese, crackers, and dessert. Everyone brings glasses and a hearty hors d'oeuvre. At first the wines were under $10. Now they're around $15. Once they had four reds, and the challenge was to see if they could pick out the Zinfandel, Cabernet, Merlot, and Shiraz. Sometimes they'll taste bottles of the same type of wine but from different countries. "It's a wonderful coming-together experience," said Mrs. Pettway, who taught Spanish at Missouri until retiring in 2000. "You begin to get more interested in geography and people and languages and the food from a certain region," she added. From northwestern Spain, they tried white wines that go with seafood, for instance. "It makes us think: maybe I'd like to travel there and experience it."

Houston, Texas: The Twenty-Year Group

In Houston, Henry and Betty Jane Bernstein started a wine group more than twenty years ago when a couple across the street, who had belonged to one in Atlanta, suggested they launch one. "We thought it was a great idea because we didn't know much about wine," said Mr. Bernstein, a retired chemical engineer. Added Mrs. Bernstein, a former schoolteacher: "It started out to be a light Sunday-evening supper. I hosted the first group with quiche and a salad and bread and pound cake. It was not enough food, we discovered. That's how it evolved into a big dinner."

Now they meet once a month except in July. The host couple chooses the wine and prepares dinner. The host pays for food but buys the wines from dues that members pay. They started with $10 per couple per meeting but are now at $20. They taste six wines per meeting. "We've gone to weddings of daughters; we went to the bridal showers. We've become very close," Mrs. Bernstein said. Several years ago, just before Christmas, one of the husbands died. The entire group attended his memorial service. Then his widow made a suggestion. "She said we should get a couple to join to replace them," said Mrs. Bernstein. "She said, 'You should take me off the list. You don't want me.' And we said, 'Yes, we do, and we'll help you when it's your turn.'" She remains an active member.

Memphis, Tennessee: The Buffet Group

While most groups we talked to had ten or fewer members, the one founded by Terry Moore, who does supply-chain management for International Paper in Memphis (he handles the logistics of getting the company's products to its customers), sometimes swells to around forty. "Sometimes I'll have my priest there or out-of-town guests. Sometimes French and German people who happen to be in town. It leads to good conversation." Six couples form the core of the group. People who attend each tasting are treated to tastes of twelve bottles of wine, grouped in three flights set up in three different rooms in the host's home. All bottles are bagged and numbered, and a buffet dinner is served, after which the wines are rated. The group meets every six to eight weeks, and the host supplies the wine and the food. Then they split the cost of the wine, with each person who comes kicking in a share. Some spouses serve as designated drivers. Contributions for the wine range from $15 to $75 per person, with $25 most typical. According to Mr. Moore, the purists in the group initially felt that the wines should be tasted with only bread and cheese, but his wife, Beth, is a gourmet cook, so they swayed the others. On occasion the Moores will host the core group, and they'll splurge on the wines, pairing them with each course. "Bottom line: we have a great time with some quality wines," said Mr. Moore.

San Francisco: The Wine-Bar Group

A group in San Francisco got its start at the famous London Wine Bar in 1990. Every Friday five friends met there to unwind with a bottle of wine. They so enjoyed tasting different wines together that they moved their wine feast to the Park Hyatt's restaurant, which allowed them to bring their own wines and charged them a corkage fee for opening and serving the wine. Over time, though, they discovered that they were tasting the same types of wines over and over again but "not expanding our tasting experience," one member, Russell Obana, told us. So they added an element of surprise, the bagged bottle. One tasting they called their "blind, bring something you have never tried before, and it better be French" tasting. Said Mr. Obana: "I have had nothing but great times sharing a glass of wine with friends." They still meet occasionally at the London Wine Bar, where it all started.

So, How Do You Do This?

Here's advice from Joyce Cekander, whose group in Frankfort, Illinois, is more than three decades old:

☙ Select people with the same degree of interest and commitment.

☙ Prior to starting, have some discussion about goals—to explore new areas, learn about the grapes, study countries, or other interests.

☙ Decide how often you will meet and how many people will be the maximum in the group.

☙ Have some idea of whether this is strictly tasting wine for wine's sake or social in nature. Along with that, talk about whether food is an integral part of the club.

☙ Decide how wine will be selected and purchased. "In our group, the host chooses the wine theme and purchases the wines, and then we each pay one-tenth of the total." She added: "The group can start at the ground level and grow together, learning and loving the taste of wines."

Here's some more advice from around the country:

From Boston: Start small, gathering at members' homes or whatever way people can do it. Members should not have to meet any kind of strict standard when they play host. It's fine to repeat a theme or come up with a variation on a theme such as "wines from wineries owned by women" or "wines from wineries in Sonoma that are owned by women," said Callie Crossley, a Diva.

From Columbia, Missouri: "Make sure that the more educated ones don't intimidate the novices and vice versa," said Margo Pettway, who started a group with her husband, Richard.

From Hartford, Connecticut: "You don't have to be an expert to enjoy the wine. You might do geographic areas, do a tasting of Italian wines," said Jane Booker. Added Colette Nakhoul: "Don't make the group too big, because you'll have scheduling problems and too many palates to suit."

From Houston: Schedule tastings at a reasonable time because some people have to commute, said Betty Jane Bernstein. She added: "You need people who are willing to put in a lot of work when it's their turn because the gourmet meals are quite elaborate. Some of the men use their computers to create wine-ranking sheets, and they help with the food preparation, too."

From Washington, D.C.: "Make sure you get a mix of people you enjoy, because, while the wine is the catalyst for meeting, it is much more fun to share with people you enjoy," said Tom Graham, a member of a group of six couples who have been tasting together for about three years. "Our name is CleVer Folks, although we always talk about changing it," Mr. Graham told us. "It stands for Cleveland Park (our neighborhood) Vertical Tasters (although we have yet to do a vertical tasting)."

Finally, This Advice from Us: There are as many ways to do this as there are wine-tasting groups. No one way is the "right" way. The primary piece of advice we'd give is simple: start slowly. No matter how much or how little anyone knows about wine, there's always some angst talking about it with other people. Will I seem stupid? Will I seem like a snob? Not only that, but all wine lovers have their own wine vocabularies, and it will take a while for everyone to speak the same language. We'd suggest simple tastings first, without fancy scoring sheets or speeches. You can always get more complex as time goes on, but, first, just concentrate on having a good time. Remember that this is ultimately about friendship and fun more than wine. Finally, be sure to have planned a safe way home. Your friends want to see you at the next get-together.

Here's how the folks at Joe Schmidt's retirement home did it. How did it work out? Let Mr. Schmidt—he and his wife, Helen, are in their mid-eighties and have been married for almost sixty years—tell you.

Most of our club members had not previously been wine enthusiasts. Most joined either to learn about wines or out of simple curiosity. We have a trea-surer, modest ($20) annual membership dues, and a $5 monthly attendee's tasting-party fee. At the tasting party, a volunteer is asked to be the next party host, set the time and date, provide the space, and also set the limit on the number of attendees who can be accommodated. Announcement of the date, location, and attendee limit of the next wine tasting is posted three weeks in advance with a sign-up sheet for the designated limit, on a "first come" basis. Additional places are provided on a "stand by" basis.

One person is designated wine host for the month. That person selects a theme and also is given a total wine budget for the month's meeting by the treasurer. It is up to the wine host to select, find, and buy the wines. The nor-mal selection is three different whites and three different reds. One or two volunteers are designated the "cheese hosts." In consultation with the wine host, they are responsible for selecting and buying several cheeses, crackers, and bread. The wine and the cheese hosts submit their bills to the treasurer for repayment. Fortunately, our dining room department furnishes, delivers, and picks up reasonably serviceable wineglasses, ice, water glasses, and slop buckets.

The wine host explains the theme, introduces each wine in turn, by generic type, if it is a blind tasting, and gives as much winery/vintner background as was collected. Each wine is presented; the attendees score the wine ac-cording to a sheet that includes appearance, aroma, taste, aftertaste, and overall impression. We have revised the score sheet several times, primarily to introduce a weighting factor and to clarify each item. Each attendee totals his own score for the wine under consideration. Score totals for each wine are indicated by a show of hands, usually accompanied by vocal exclamations at the high and low scores (getting louder as the tasting progresses!). Our recording secretary collects, tabulates, and averages the score results for each bottle of wine. At the conclusion, the secretary identifies the wine, if a blind tasting, gives its average totaled score, its cost, and the dealer from whom it was bought. Finally, all hands pitch in for a general cleanup, rinsing all glassware and readying them for dining room department pickup. Any extra bottles are sold to attendees at actual cost.

We have been operating for nearly three years quite happily. The only adjustment we have improvised a few times was, for example, when the wine host selected dessert wines. The cheeses were abruptly canceled, and we substituted tiny portions of chocolate-sauced crepes, cake, coated berries, poached pears. Another time the wine host insisted on substituting rare, thinly sliced duck breast to go with his Cahors. A couple of times the wine theme simply demanded food to show it off. But we have had to be careful that the monthly gatherings did not become more elaborate than originally planned.

Has it been worthwhile? Absolutely, YES! At first, Chardonnay was about the only wine most of the ladies would drink. A few wouldn't even try any of the reds. Now they are volunteering to have a turn at being wine host!

Passover

Sweet Wines, Sweet Memories—and a New Day

Ba-ruch A-tah Ado-noi E-lo-hei-nu Me-lech Ha-olom Bo-rei Pri Ha-ga-fen.
Blessed art thou, O Eternal, our God, King of the Universe, Creator of the fruit of the vine.—PRAYER RECITED FOR SHABBAT SERVICES AS WELL AS THE PASSOVER OBSERVANCE, DURING WHICH JEWS EVERYWHERE COMMEMORATE THEIR ANCESTORS' DELIVERANCE FROM BONDAGE IN EGYPT.

When John was growing up, Passover was his favorite Jewish holiday. Yom Kippur and Rosh Hashanah were more serious, and Hanukkah included presents and chocolate, but Passover was special. To begin with, there's the stirring story of deliverance—of the weak over the strong, good over evil. The service specifically includes children as an integral part: the youngest even gets to ask the four questions starting with "Why is this night different from all other nights?" What's more, Passover includes two nights of very special seder meals. Everything at the table is a symbol of something much larger, from the matzoh to the herbs. The whole family gets together, not just in fact but in spirit: the Passover Haggadah, or prayer book, that John's family used—and that we now use ourselves—is a 1923 copy of the Union Haggadah, passed down from earlier generations of his family. Passover was one of the two times in the entire year that his family used the formal dining room. Thanksgiving was the other.

Passover celebrates so many things—freedom of religion, life, family—and wine is central to the celebration. As our Haggadah explains: "Each participant in the service is expected to drink four cups of wine. Even the poorest of the poor who subsist on charity were enjoined to provide themselves with wine for the four cups." As John was taught at temple as a boy and as Dottie learned at conversion class, the four cups of wine represent four promises that God made to the Jews: I will bring you out; I will deliver you; I will redeem you; I will take you to be my people. There's even the prophet Elijah's cup of wine, waiting for him—an advocate for all who are disadvantaged—should he come in the open door. A glass of wine is set in front of every participant at the seder table. Children drink grape juice or something else symbolizing wine. Since the service marks the freeing of slaves, celebrants are commanded to drink some of their wine as they recline, a gesture of leisure. At some services, the fourth glass is consumed after this blessing from the Haggadah: "Blessed art thou, O Eternal, our God, King of the Universe, for the wine, and for the fruit of the vine, and for the produce of the field, and for that desirable, good, and spacious land which thou grantest our ancestors to inherit, to eat of its fruit, and be satisfied with its goodness."

For many of us, Passover was one of the very few times during the year when our parents drank wine and permitted the children to sip. The sweet purple liquid glistened in mothers' prettiest glasses, an enticing taste full of symbolism and mystery. For most families the wine of choice was a sweet wine made from Concord grapes, a native American variety. While its sweetness resonated with the celebration's message of a sweeter future in freedom, there's no religious reason the wine has to be sweet. So, we wondered, why were kosher wines sweet for so long? To answer that question, we talked to Rabbi Alan Litwak of Temple Sinai of North Dade, in North Miami Beach, Florida. Aside from his rabbinical training, we thought Rabbi Litwak might be helpful because he grew up just south of Napa Valley and enjoys wine. He does not restrict himself to enjoying only kosher wine. His explanation for why the traditional kosher wine was sweet tracks other accounts we had heard: "It had to do with the fact that Concord grapes were the only variety that were available for Jewish immigrants arriving in the New York area," he told us, "and because the grapes were highly acidic, the acidity had to be balanced with some sugar."

We also wondered why the traditional kosher wine that we grew up with was always red. For that we turned to the Orthodox Union, the world's largest kosher certification organization. There, Rabbi Menachem Genack, rabbinic administrator, said he had found two opinions based on the Talmud that declared that white wine cannot be used to say kiddush, the blessing said over wine or bread on the eve of the Sabbath or during a festival. He added: "The opinions say that white wine was not considered as good for libations at the temple." Rabbi Litwak has a different view. "Kiddush can be said over any 'fruit of the vine'—white, red, pink, alcoholic, or just plain grape juice. Drink something you like!"

Many Jews who otherwise don't keep kosher, like John's family, serve a kosher seder, and that includes kosher wine. The problem is that, since we all grew up with sweet kosher wine, too many people believe that all kosher wine is sweet. These days that is very, very far from the truth. Today, good kosher wines come in red, white, and rosé, dry and sweet, sparkling and still, and you don't have to be Jewish to enjoy them. They come from Israel, France, Chile, Italy, Australia, Argentina, South Africa, the United States, and many other countries, and they are not your grandfather's kosher wines. In our years of tasting kosher wines for our column, we've tried outstanding wines, among them fine Champagnes and Chardonnays, lovely Rieslings, flowery Pinot Grigios, stately Bordeaux, fine Cabernet Sauvignons, fun Beaujolais Nouveaux, fetching Chenin Blancs, and excellent wines made from Merlot, Pinot Noir, Cabernet Franc, Petite Sirah, Zinfandel, Barbera, Sangiovese, Gewürztraminer, Muscat, and more. All kosher. What does that mean? What makes a wine kosher? Well, it's complicated, but this is what experts at the Orthodox Union and kosher wine companies have told us: The process starts with special treatment and attention to cleanliness. *Kosher* is Hebrew for "fit" or "proper," according to Jewish dietary laws. Rabbis or their assistants supervise the wine's production from crush to bottling. Kosher wines are made with special enzymes and yeasts and fining agents—not animal by-products, like gelatin, for example—that clarify the wine. Often their front labels will sport an *O* with a *U* inside with a *P* near it. This is the stamp of the Orthodox Union and basically means there's no need to read the label further to learn whether the wine is kosher for Passover. The Orthodox Union says that essentially all kosher wines are kosher for Passover unless they've had unusual flavorings added to them that contain substances that are off-limits at Passover.

The word *mevushal* on the label means the wine can be handled by someone who is not Jewish and remain kosher. A mevushal wine is heated in seconds by flash pasteurization, with the temperature brought down quickly so as not to harm the wine. Some wineries do this to the unfermented white and blush juice; others do it to reds after fermentation. This can be important—just ask Jeff Weitzner of Jacksonville, Florida (John's hometown). We wrote about mevushal wine once, and that brought this note from Dr. Weitzner: "You saved my butt teaching me that kosher wasn't strictly kosher unless it was mevushal—for my daughter's wedding to an Orthodox Jew." He explained later: "As John knows, putting on a kosher wedding in Jacksonville is not easy, especially if you're a reform Jew and could not care less. We hired a local Orthodox rabbi to supervise, and my nightmare was that he would say, 'Jeff, we tried real hard to pull this off, and we're close, *but* I can't certify this as kosher' because of the wine. Fortunately, it was just a nightmare, and the reality was that the affair was a total success. The specific wines served were unimportant but were important in that they were proper for the occasion. My daughter and son-in-law are happily married and living in New York City."

Readers often ask us if the mevushal process harms the wine. In our own tastings—and we have tried many kosher wines—we have not found a pattern. Some mevushal wines taste better to us than nonmevushal and vice versa. In fact, in general, we have been so impressed with the quality of kosher wines that we now include them in our regular blind tastings, and they sometimes are among our very favorites. That's how much they've changed.

Here are some kosher wines among the more popular varietals. You can get just about any wine made kosher these days, but we'll focus here on the kinds of wine most people usually drink, from bubblies to white to red to dessert wines. For those produced outside of the United States, we've listed the countries they're from to give you some idea of the large universe of kosher wines available.

Yarden Vineyards Blanc de Blancs (Galil). Israel. Golden and honeyed, with languid bubbles. Deep, rich tastes. Classy and well made and bold enough to stand up to food. (Nonvintage; $26.99)

Nicolas Feuillatte Brut Champagne Brut. France. Kosher Champagne? You bet. Several of France's great Champagne houses make a certain amount of kosher bubbly. We really like this one year after year. It's classy and just about bursting with fruit and honeysuckle. Mouth-watering and full, with a long, elegant finish. (Nonvintage; $39.95)

Baron Herzog Wine Cellars Chenin Blanc (Clarksburg). Guava, mango, and passion fruit on the nose and a whole fruit bowl of flavors in the taste. Very pleasant, with some body. Chenin Blanc is a fine grape whose reputation has been hurt because of all of the generic white wine called *Chenin Blanc*. If you think Chenin Blanc means cheap, simple white wine, try this, a perennial favorite. (2002; $6.99)

Hagafen Cellars Johannisberg Riesling (Napa Valley). Charming and flowery, filled with tangerine and pineapple flavors, with a little spritz. Clean, fresh, and light. Very nice. (2002; $17.95)

Bartenura Pinot Grigio (Provincia di Pavia). Italy. Crisp, fruity, dry, and easy to drink, with pears and pineapples on the nose and in the taste. A lovely finish filled with minerals. Great as an aperitif, with fish or with fruit. (2002; $11.99)

Baron Herzog Wine Cellars Sauvignon Blanc (California). Floral, with very fresh lemon-lime tastes. Quite lively and exceptionally clean. (2002; $8.99)

Baron Herzog Wine Cellars Cabernet Sauvignon (California). Nice structure, good earth, and notably dry finish. Lovely, serious, and very drinkable, with some tastes of an expensive Bordeaux. Very classy, especially for the price. (2000; $14.39)

Golan Heights Winery Cabernet Sauvignon (Galilee). Israel. Almost like blackberry wine. No real structure, but a lovely mouthful of fruit, with some richness underneath. A bit grapey and maybe a hint sweet, but quite charming, with a very pleasant sweet-earth finish. (2000; $16.55)

Hagafen Cellars Cabernet Sauvignon (Napa Valley). Cherries, wood, and tobacco, with a long, oaky finish. Bordeauxlike structure. This is a very classy wine and always a good name to look for, especially in reds. (1999; $37.99)

Herzog Wine Cellars "Special Reserve" Cabernet Sauvignon (Alexander Valley). Edgy and controversial. Dottie finds cedar, spice, leather, and a chocolaty mouthfeel. John finds green pepper, but still enjoys it. This is always an interesting wine, but not everyone will like it. (1999; $36.29)

Weinstock Cellars Cabernet Sauvignon (California). Pillow-soft, with lovely cherrylike tastes. Cabernet for people who like Merlot. Soft and very pleasant. This was among our favorites in a tasting of inexpensive American Cabernets, both kosher and nonkosher. (2000; $11.80)

Backsberg Estate Chardonnay (Paarl). South Africa. For those looking for an "unoaked" Chardonnay. Crisp, refreshing, lemony, and filled with good fruit. Some mineral undertones to give it grounding. A great wine for company. Not only will they not believe it's kosher, they'll be surprised that it's from South Africa. (2001; $13.99)

Dalton Winery "Reserve" Chardonnay (Galilee). Israel. Interesting. Nicely spicy and so intense it seems to have a kick. The abundant fruit is tight yet soulful. Very clean and quite distinctive. (2000; $18.94.)

Teal Lake (Normans Wines) Chardonnay. Australia. Loads of ripe, luscious fruit—pineapple, mango, and tangerine—with nice acidity and a lovely fruit-oak balance. Slightly toasty with nice woody tastes. Many Australian Chardonnays have become boring; this most definitely is not. (2001; $12.99)

Yarden (Golan Heights Winery) Chardonnay (Galilee). Israel. Big and buttery, like a good old-fashioned California Chardonnay. Butterscotch, nutmeg, toast, and lots of body. Chewy, though it might taste a bit fat and a touch sweet with food. Yarden Chardonnay is always good to look for. (2000; $18.59)

Weinstock Cellars White Zinfandel (California). Cotton-candy nose. Clean and crisp, with a nice, kiwi tartness. Real wine, nicely fruity and always bracing. "It makes me smile. It feels like summer all of a sudden," Dottie said. Fresh, crisp, and bright. This has often been one of our favorites. (2002; $7.99)

Teal Lake Shiraz. Australia. Nice peppery nose—just what we want in a Shiraz—with some lilacs. This wine is a big success, fruity and peppery, with lots of fruit and some richness, yet soft enough for Merlot lovers. (2000; $10.99)

Carmel Valley Petite Sirah (Shomron). Israel. Just plain tasty. A bit grapey, with hints of earth and a nice little bite at the end. Creamy, comfortable, and yummy. Petite Sirah is usually associated with California—it's a red with real character and weight—so this is a nice surprise. (2000; $8.19)

Herzog Wine Cellars Late Harvest White Riesling (Monterey County). A perennial favorite. Low in alcohol and totally delightful, filled with exuberant tastes of peaches, apples, apricots, and very ripe grapes. Sweet yet light. Great after dinner. (2002; $18.99)

"Wine gladdens the heart. In our gladness, we see beyond the ugliness and misery which stain our world. Our eyes open to unnoticed grace, blessings till now unseen, and the promise of goodness we can bring to flower."

Jewish prayer

Restaurants

Indian, Chinese, and Hooters

Sign on the wall of a Clear Lake, Texas, restaurant, circa 1968:

Wines

1. Red

2. White

Please order by number —**STORY TOLD BY BILL PLANTE OF CBS NEWS**

Enjoying wine at restaurants should be one of life's joys, so it's impossible for us to talk about living well with wine without tackling the pervasive problem of Restaurant Wine Angst, or RWA. When things go well at a restaurant, this is how it's supposed to work: We were at Crabtree's Kittle House in Chappaqua, New York, just up the street from Hillary Clinton's proof-of-New-York-residency. In this posh neighborhood, the Kittle House is like a country inn, dignified, graceful, and relaxed at the same time. We'd describe the food as elegant American. It's friendly enough that even Media and Zoë enjoy going there. It has a seventy-thousand-bottle wine cellar and a massive wine list: more than two hundred pages featuring more than five thousand wines. The most amazing thing about it, to us, is that many of the wines, especially the older wines, are reasonably priced, although there are also some old treasures at nosebleed prices. It's clear that the people at the Kittle House see wine as an important part of every meal, not just a great profit center. One time in early 2003, we visited Kittle House to celebrate the new year with the girls and found even more to choose from: a list of thirty wines by the glass and half-glass. With all of this to choose from, what did we do? We looked for the unfamiliar, and something immediately leaped out at us: a Savennières from 1993. This is a wine from the Loire Valley of France, made from the Chenin Blanc grape, that we rarely see, either in stores or in restaurants, and we'd never seen one that old. This seemed like a very special experience. Here's the kicker: the bottle was $28.

Think about the wines you've bought for $28 at a restaurant. Pretty routine stuff, right? Well, we figured it would be hard to go wrong. We asked the sommelier about it, whether he thought the age would be a good thing or a bad thing. He said, "We'll find out." He brought the bottle from the cellar—it was the perfect temperature, not too cold—and, with our permission, took a small taste first. Then he poured it for us. It was delicious. "Light and very bright fruit balanced with some weight and minerals," we wrote. "Outrageously lively. No sense of age, but a real sense of weight. Perfect condition." Here is the bottom line: you don't have to be a wine expert to have a great experience like that. Outstanding wine experiences are awaiting you at many restaurants, and not just at places where you might expect to find them, like fancy French restaurants. Two of New York's more intriguing wine lists are at the Evergreen Café, a Chinese restaurant, and Sapphire, an Indian restaurant. Chinese? Indian?

We first dropped into Henry's Evergreen by accident. Dottie was at a doctor's appointment on the East Side of Manhattan, so John took the girls to a nearby McDonald's. On the way there, he passed a Chinese restaurant with a sign announcing a winemaker's dinner with wines from Grgich Cellars, one of California's venerable names. This was obviously interesting to us, so we made reservations. At the dinner we met Henry Leung, then the owner of the restaurant, and discovered his passion for wine—and about convincing the world that wine goes well with Chinese food. He told the gathering that when he was young he was assistant manager and maître d' at a well-known Chinese restaurant in Manhattan, David K, when his boss told him to look sharp because a famous restaurant critic would be in that night. When the critic sat down, Mr. Leung handed him the wine list—and the critic handed it right back. "Wine doesn't go with Chinese food," he snapped. "Bring me a Kirin beer." With that, Mr. Leung decided to dedicate his life to convincing people otherwise. We didn't identify ourselves at the dinner, but we called Mr. Leung later to chat. He told us he was so stung by the critic's remark that he started studying wine and the next year visited some of the great châteaux of France. Now he visits California wineries every year. When we talked to him recently for this book, he said his restaurant was hosting sold-out wine dinners every week. Not only had wine caught on at his restaurant, but diners were now bringing their own wine. "Some of them have pretty amazing cellars," he said. Mr. Leung said he charges a $10 corkage fee but waives it if someone also buys a wine from his list. Meanwhile, he dreams of opening yet another Chinese restaurant with a fine wine list, maybe even in California's wine country.

We first met Sunil Prakash by accident, too. We love Indian food, so we dropped into a pretty place near Lincoln Center called Sapphire. We asked for the wine list. We have learned not to expect much from wine lists at Indian restaurants—we guess most people drink cold beer with spicy food—but we were amazed. It was a small but very well-chosen list, full of interesting and reasonably priced wine. When we expressed some interest, Mr. Prakash dropped by, as though he'd been waiting his whole life for someone to ask about the wines. His enthusiasm was so charming that we became regulars. Mr. Prakash told us that, in the beginning, he had a "rough time" selling wine to the restaurant's customers and wine sales amounted to only about 3 percent of the evening's beverage receipts. "It was very difficult," he said. Then people began to trust his suggestions, and with a nice by-the-glass list, they could try wines with their dinners without investing in a whole bottle. Within a year of the restaurant's opening, Mr. Prakash said, wine sales rose to 20 percent of beverage sales each night. Think, he said: People usually don't drink beer with their dinner at home, so when they come to restaurants they are open to having wine. They just need some good selections. "Our food is flavorful, not chile-hot—except for some traditional hot dishes, and I would suggest something off-dry with those—so the wines go well with our dishes." For chicken tikka masala, the popular butter chicken dish, he suggests a Chardonnay without massive oak. For the chef's signature mussel appetizer, in which the shellfish is sautéed in onions, chile, crushed black pepper, and Marsala, he suggests a "dry, light New Zealand Sauvignon Blanc from the Marlborough region." For lamb dishes, he favors "light- to medium-weight reds." With some "fiery dishes," some whites, such as Puligny-Montrachet, "are big enough."

Mr. Prakash said he was first bitten by the wine bug when he was working in Austria at a school for hospitality management. For Christmas, his
boss gave him a wine book while other colleagues got fancy ink pens and
French silk scarves. From there his work took him to Munich, where his
fluency in German got a good workout and his taste for wine grew. His
company brought him back to Austria for a time and then sent him to
France, where he studied wine and received a formal diploma. From there
he came to the United States and Sapphire restaurant. By the way, the very
first time we went to Sapphire, we ordered a white Austrian wine called
Grüner Veltliner, which is a specialty of Austria but a wine we rarely see in
stores or at restaurants. It was so stunning—flavorful and filled with spices
and weight—that we called the importer the next day, found out where the
wine was sold, and bought a case. We had never done that before, and
we've never done it since. We still have a few bottles of that wine. Not only
is it getting better with age, but it always reminds us of the night we discovered Sapphire.

Restaurants with good wine lists don't have to be fancy, either. For one of
our columns in the *Wall Street Journal,* we compared the wine lists and service at America's top ten "dinnerhouse" chains, and we found a couple
of winners. (In the industry, a dinnerhouse is defined as a restaurant that
serves lunch and dinner, has a full bar, and where the check average is somewhere around the mid- to high teens per person.) It's true that most
treated wine shabbily. A waitress at Outback Steakhouse asked us why we
wanted a wine list. The drink menu at the Chili's we visited didn't even
mention wine, and when we insisted on a glass, we were brought a glass of
white Zinfandel that could best be described as tasting hairy. Our most unusual experience was at Hooters, where there was just one full-size wine by
the bottle: Dom Pérignon Champagne, which was part of the "Gourmet
Chicken Wing Dinner." For $150.05, diners get a bottle of Dom Pérignon
and 20 buffalo wings, which actually turned out to be a very tasty combination. (John later claimed he had lost his notes on our visit to Hooters, so we
had to return to try the combination again.) We found that the Olive Garden and Romano's Macaroni Grill are excellent destinations for wine, with
knowledgeable waiters, good lists, and an informal style that makes wine a
fun part of a meal. Olive Garden serves complimentary wine to people as

they wait in line on Friday and Saturday nights. Bottles are everywhere. The waiters show up at tables carrying one. There are interesting choices on its wine list, including Amarone, the special, raisiny red wine from Italy. At the Olive Garden in Tallahassee, Dottie was offered a taste of sparkling red, Lambrusco. Okay, so it wasn't terrific, but after shopping with Media for several hours, it was a welcome diversion and a very nice gesture that puts wine in its proper place as a welcoming, informal beverage.

In most American restaurants, wine sales average 20 percent of diners' bills, according to Ronn Wiegand, publisher of *Restaurant Wine,* a trade newsletter and consulting service based in Napa Valley. At expensive restaurants, he told us, wine is up to 40 percent of the total tab. As if the sometimes astonishing prices of wines weren't bad enough, people who order wine at restaurants often have to suffer through attendant rigmarole. Not only does all of this make ordering wine intimidating, and enjoying it a riskier proposition than need be, but all of the hoopla is generally unnecessary. One of our favorite restaurants for wine is Joe Allen in New York City's theater district. It has a short, well-chosen, and reasonably priced wine list. When you order a bottle, the waiter comes over, opens it, leaves it on the table, and says, "We just let you serve yourself." At that point you can pour the wine in your glass at your own pace and as much or as little as you like. This relaxed approach makes wine the simple beverage it should be.

So what is the antidote for RWA? First, you need to know how to manage the situation, starting with how to decode the wine list.

Decoding the Wine List

Over the years we've offered a great deal of advice on how to decode a wine list, which once brought this note from W. L. "Turk" White of Zionsville, Indiana:

> *"I appreciate your comments on how to navigate a wine list. Armed with those thoughts several years ago, I ordered a '97 Chalk Hill Chardonnay at a restaurant in Denver. It made the meal, without question. Last fall in Chicago on a warm weekend, we ordered an Oregon Pinot Gris we'd never*

seen. It was spectacular, and our waiter commented that we were lucky to get it. Apparently there were less than 150 cases made and the restaurant was lucky enough to have snagged one of them. Last spring in Scottsdale, visiting parents, we took off for a dinner by ourselves. Again following the "try something you've never seen before" advice, we had a Selene Sauvignon Blanc that burst out of the glass. I think wine lists are like good stories: each one has its own style. The best part is that it's a quiz with no wrong answers, just different ones.

We couldn't possibly have said that better ourselves. Here is our method, in ten easy steps.

1. Take your time. When the waiter asks for your selection, say matter-of-factly, "I'll need a few minutes." Don't think you'll look like a rube for demanding more time. Quite the opposite.

2. Decide on red or white, thus cutting the list in half. If we don't feel particularly "red" or "white" and so we're not sure which to order, we take a look at the menu to get a sense of whether we're more likely to order "red" food or "white" food. Remember, these traditional rules of food and wine pairings are steadily and delightfully morphing into imaginative marriages of tastes that defy the old rules, so order what you feel like, not what you think is "correct."

3. See what country or region most of the wines on the list come from. If most are, say, Italian, that's where the restaurant's heart is. Go with it. Be bold. We walked into a new restaurant in our neighborhood once and discovered that it was Peruvian. We had never had, or even seen, a wine from Peru, so we asked the waiter if they had any. He brightened. "We have one white and one red," he said. "Would you like to see them?" He then brought the bottles over, both from a winery called Tabernero, from the Chincha Valley. He explained that the white was made from Chenin Blanc, Sauvignon Blanc, and Chardonnay, while the red was half Merlot and half Malbec. We ordered the white. It was called Blanco de Blancos, and it was an unqualified success: crisp and clean, with some hints of mango and a definite grassy taste from the Sauvignon Blanc. It was fresh and easy to like, with some nice mineral undertones that kept the wine from being frivolous. While figures are fuzzy, maybe forty-five hundred cases of Peruvian wine are imported into the United States every year, which is probably about what big American wineries lose to evaporation each year. We felt so lucky to have tasted this wine.

In Sarasota, Florida, we dropped into a nice restaurant called the Bijou Café, a block from our hotel. The wine list was fine, but nothing special—until the last two pages. Those pages began with an explanation that the owner was from South Africa and had a special passion for South African wines. What followed was one page of whites and one of reds—all from South Africa. Even though we're familiar with South African wines—its signature wine is Pinotage, a very special, spicy red—most of these labels were new to us. We asked the owner for his advice (anonymously, of course) and ended up with a Cabernet Sauvignon from a winery whose name we wouldn't even try to pronounce: Boekenhoutskloof. It was expensive—$68—but it turned out to be the best South African wine we'd ever tasted. Our notes: "Like a big, well-made, and expensive Napa Valley red, but with lots of pepper on the nose. Intense, pure fruit, a little earthy. Doesn't taste alcoholic for such a big-fruited wine. Huge but not hard to drink. Cedar, eucalyptus. Incredible fruit but not sweet fruit, perfect with Dottie's super-rare steak." Man, those notes still "taste" good.

4. Nix the "showcase" wines, like the exorbitant "first growths" from Bordeaux and the cult wines from California. They're often there just for show or for people on expense accounts.

5. Decide what you're willing to spend—be a little flexible here—and ignore everything above that amount.

6. Eliminate everything you're already familiar with. This is key. Order wines at restaurants that you don't see in stores. Enjoy yourself. As a sommelier in North Carolina once told us: "We urge people to try something they've never tried before. That's what ends up making it fun. Remain open-minded." Don't limit yourself to California wine. Restaurants know that people are stuck in a California rut and penalize them for it with high prices. We sometimes see average California Chardonnay on lists that costs more than excellent Chablis from France, which is made from the Chardonnay grape. As a wine director from Ohio once told us: "Too many people stick with the big names of California. There are other great wines out there that you may not know a lot about but are wonderful. Be adventurous. Everybody knows California."

7. Avoid the second-cheapest wine on the list. We often find that the worst value on the wine list is the second-cheapest wine, because people are embarrassed to order the cheapest. Surprisingly, the best deal on the list is often the cheapest wine, which leads to . . .

8. Don't judge wine by the price. A $200 bottle might not be better than a $50 bottle. We once asked a sommelier from Michigan what was the biggest mistake diners make, and he said: "That's easy. Buying for the dollar amount, thinking that a $300 bottle is better than a $100 bottle." A wine director in Mississippi agreed, saying he had seen diners come in and pay $600 to $800 for a wine and leave three-quarters of it. Ouch! "I know they're thinking I probably would have enjoyed that $50 bottle more," he confided.

9. Pick two or three of the limited number of wines left and say to the waiter, "What can you tell me about these wines?" Chances are these will be interesting enough that the waiter will figure you know what you're talking about and then will call over someone who really does. Watch that person's eyes. When they light up as he or she is discussing a specific wine, order it.

10. Enjoy it. Maybe you'll really like it; maybe you won't. But it will surely be something new and different, and you chose it. If you like it, don't be shy about asking to take the empty bottle, or at least the label, home with you. How many times have you said to yourself later, "I wish I could remember what the wine was"? (Later, get the label off; see "Saving the Memories.")

One final thing: one of the greatest trends of the moment is that more and more restaurants are offering "tasting menus" and pairing a wine with each course for an additional charge. If you see this on a menu, by all means take advantage of it. Not only does it take all of the worry out of choosing a wine, but it's a very special way to taste several wines at one sitting—and some very special wine-food pairings. We once did this at a restaurant in Rutherford, California, called La Toque and had one of the greatest meals of our lives. One of the courses was a California Pinot Noir with monkfish with red-wine sauce, fava beans, and white asparagus. Pinot with monkfish? We would never have put them together—but it was simply outstanding. Later we called chef and owner Ken Frank and his sommelier, Scott Tracy. "Sometimes we're matching the wine to the meat or matching to the sauce," Mr. Frank told us. "Sometimes we'll make a match that works with parts of a dish. Sometimes one works with the whole thing and it just sings. Sometimes the wine brings out the best in the dish. Sometimes a wine and a food bring out the best in each other. Sometimes there are parallel tones and they're in perfect harmony." One pairing that pleased Mr. Tracy was sashimi of dayboat scallop with Japanese vegetable salad, paired with a dry Alsatian Riesling. Why? "I wanted some fruit here to balance the pickled vegetables and a bit of weight for the spice, and I knew it needed to finish dry to cut the sauce cleanly," he said. With this kind of thought behind wine-food pairings, why not let the experts handle this? Besides, you can take home what you learn from the experts and continue experimenting in your kitchen.

To BYOB or Not to BYOB?

We were at New York's Beacon restaurant, drinking a 1989 Château Montrose, an outstanding wine from a fine vintage. Considering the price of wine at restaurants, how could we afford such a magnificent bottle? We brought it ourselves, from our own cellar. We bought the wine years ago and waited for an appropriate occasion. Then we saw a little item about Beacon inviting people to bring their own bottle with them on any Sunday night—and waiving the usual $25 corkage, the fee charged by a restaurant to open and serve a wine that diners have brought.

In the midst of the recession in the restaurant industry in the early

2000s, many began looking for ways to get some butts in seats. One answer: BYOB. All over the country restaurants such as Beacon began having special BYOB nights, with no corkage fees. This is a wonderful thing, and not only because it means you can drink fine wine with great food at a more-reasonable price. The very mood of BYOB nights is special. As we were drinking our Montrose, for instance, the group next to us asked if we'd like to taste their 1983 Château Gruaud-Larose, which happens to be one of our all-time favorite Bordeaux wines. Would we like to? You bet. The wine, it turned out, belonged to Lester Brickman, a professor of law at Yeshiva University's Benjamin N. Cardozo School of Law. He was treating a group of out-of-town guests to this excellent wine and four others. They started with two bottles of 1991 Alsatian Riesling, then moved on to a 1992 white Burgundy with the seafood course, then on to the Gruaud-Larose that he shared with us and a 1991 red Burgundy, finishing the night with a 1977 Port. Wow. "The principal reason I went was that they waive their corkage fees on Sundays," he told us, but he's not averse to paying a corkage fee. In fact, he sees it as "a substantial selling point" for restaurants to permit patrons to bring their special wines. "Frankly," he explained. "I have a better cellar than most restaurants."

Every state has different laws concerning wine, and that includes bringing your own bottle to a restaurant. In some states this isn't allowed at all, but in other states it's encouraged. In New Jersey, for instance, many restaurants don't have wine licenses, and they encourage BYOB — reason enough to live in New Jersey. We love taking our own wine to restaurants. We have plenty of special bottles at home, but with two demanding girls, full-time jobs, and homework (for the kids and for us), we rarely get a chance to linger over them with a great meal. The ability to drink our fine wine with a restaurant's fine food, in a relaxed setting, is a marvelous thing. We have been taking our own wine to restaurants for years. In fact, we once grew so close to a fine Italian restaurant in Miami called La Bussola that we stored some of our own wine there and drank a bottle with the restaurant's owner from time to time.

Of course, not all restaurateurs are excited about this. When we asked Ralph Hersom, the wine director at New York's Le Cirque 2000, how he felt about diners bringing their own wine, he shot back: "Would you bring your own food?" Or, as a California restaurateur put it even more directly:

"Why not bring your own dead chicken and some carrots?" Le Cirque doesn't have a corkage fee because it doesn't think its guests need to bring their own wine. "We have over seven hundred wines on our list, and I like to think I've put together a wine list where there's something there for everyone," Mr. Hersom, who is both knowledgeable and enthusiastic about wine, told us. "I have a hundred wines that are $50 or less, plenty of very interesting wines from all over the world that are very reasonably priced." But, he added, "there have been times when we've made special arrangements for people who called ahead of time and explained that they have a special bottle that they'd like to open for a special occasion."

Napa Valley's famous French Laundry restaurant raised its corkage fee to $50. Yikes! Why? The restaurant says too many people were abusing its courtesy, many of them showing up with inexpensive bottles of wine bought earlier that day at one of the nearby wineries. The French Laundry won't even open any wine that a diner brings if it's on the restaurant's extensive wine list. Otherwise the restaurant says it will decant the wine diners bring and serve it in its Riedel glasses. "On a Friday night, with a third of your customers bringing in their own wine, even if you charge $30, you're not making up your cost," Laura Cunningham, the restaurant's general manager, told us. "I agree with corkage for one thing," Ms. Cunningham added. "If someone is celebrating a very special occasion or maybe they have a wine from their birth year. That's one thing. It's special." Even with the $50 corkage fee, she said, the number of people bringing in their own wines continues to grow.

We have never taken our own wine to a restaurant as fancy as Le Cirque or the French Laundry, largely because one reason we go to restaurants like that is their great wine lists. Restaurants often get limited-production wines that you'd never see in a wine shop. But we have brought our own to quite a few very good restaurants. Thinking about doing this yourself? Here are some guidelines that we've used for twenty-five years at restaurants that don't actively encourage BYOB. Also, don't forget that various state and local laws might affect this.

1. **Get to know the place first.** We've never taken our own wine to a restaurant we didn't know. Go at least once, and if it seems like the kind

of place that might be receptive—and, of course, the kind of place you'd like to go back to—then think about bringing your own bottle.

2. Consider the restaurant. If it's a fancy place with a great wine list, it's probably a bad idea to bring your own wine except under special circumstances.

3. Call ahead and ask if you can bring your own bottle and ask about the corkage fee. From the response, you'll get a sense of how the restaurant really feels about this. The corkage fee will tell you something, too. If it's high—it's impossible to say what the benchmark might be, but we'd get mighty nervous at around $25—our guess is that the restaurant doesn't favor the practice. "My favorite corkage policy was that of the late and lamented Ross' North Fork Restaurant in Long Island, New York. The policy was simple: $10 a bottle—or give John Ross a glass," Robert J. Reina of Douglaston, New York, an investment banker and teacher at the Art of Wine Seminars in New York, once told us.

4. Take something special. This is important. If you walk in with a widely available Merlot that you could have bought at the local wine shop on the way to the restaurant or something that's likely to be on the wine list, you're probably not going to be treated warmly. But if you have a bottle that is special in some way, the restaurant will likely be charmed. Even we might think about taking a wine from our birth year to a place like Le Cirque, but we'd call ahead first to ask if we could (to which they'd probably reply, correctly, "But 1951 was a terrible year"). "Bringing a bottle of Veuve Clicquot from the wine store around the corner is not too cool," John Fischer, assistant professor at the Culinary Institute of America in upstate New York, told us. "However, that bottle of Pommery Rosé that you have left over from your wedding would be nice to bring to your first anniversary dinner."

5. Have some of the restaurant's wine first. If it's just the two of you, consider having two glasses of the house wine or two glasses of Champagne while you study the menu. If there are four of you with a single bottle, perhaps order a bottle of the restaurant's wine first. This shows good faith.

6. Don't send it back! Hey, just kidding. But we are always amused when waiters pour us a taste of our own wine and stand back and wait for our approval. If we don't like it, what do we do? Spit it out, yell, "You call this wine?" and send it back?

7. Offer a glass to the waiter or sommelier or chef. Remember that the reason you have brought this wine is that it's special in some way. It's fun to share special wines, and the waiter, sommelier, or chef will appreciate your generosity (and they probably won't take more than a sip anyway).

8. Tip as though you had purchased a bottle from the wine list. The waiter is working just as hard opening and pouring that bottle as if you'd bought it there. If the restaurant seems to charge about $30 for a good bottle of wine, figure the tip based on your bill plus the $30 (or, say, $20 if you're paying a $10 corkage fee and want to figure the tip based on the two together).

And speaking of tipping . . .

Cork Sniffing, Tipping, etc.

We receive hundreds of questions about wine in restaurants, and there are no easy or definitive answers to any of them. We can simply tell you what we do, what has worked for us for three decades.

◌ **What do I do if they bring me a different vintage from the one I ordered?** It depends on whether you really care. If you were going to order the wine whatever the vintage, it doesn't matter. But sometimes it does matter. Maybe the listed wine was from a great year. Maybe you're looking for a young, fresh wine, and what you're offered is too old. This is one reason the waiter shows you the bottle before he opens it. We just say, "Oh, gosh, we really wanted the 2002. Do you have it? If not, can you bring back the wine list?" There are very pleasant, nonconfrontational ways to do this.

☾ **What do I do with the cork when the waiter or sommelier hands it to me?** Anything you want to. There is really no reason to smell the cork, since the wine itself is right in front of you and a smell of the wine will tell you more than the smell of the cork. But we smell it anyway because we like the way some corks smell—kind of like a winery. In other words, there is no reason to smell the cork—and no reason not to. More and more wines have plastic corks or screw tops; we do not recommend sniffing them.

☾ **What if the wine is too hot or too cold?** We find that most restaurants serve whites too cold and reds too warm. The whites are so frozen that we can barely taste them, and the reds are so hot that they're like bathwater. We almost always tell waiters just to leave the white on the table instead of dumping it into an ice bucket. When we drink it, we cup the bowl of the glass in our hands to warm the wine. We're also not shy about asking the waiter to put a red into an ice bucket for just a few minutes to get it down to "cellar temperature," which is about fifty-five degrees. If the waiter rolls his eyes at this request, just ignore him. You're paying for the wine, and you should have it the way you want it. Truth be told, you're also paying his tip at the end of the evening. You're in control here.

☾ **Should I really get smaller glasses just because I ordered a less expensive wine than the people at the next table?** We're surprised by how often we're asked this. To be sure, there are reasons why restaurants might appropriately serve different wines in different glasses. A fine young red Bordeaux, for instance, needs a big glass so it can breathe and open up, while an easy-drinking Merlot probably doesn't. A delightful, flowery Riesling is better in a smaller glass. We can also understand why restaurants feel that anyone who orders a very special, very expensive bottle of wine deserves the best glasses—as does the wine itself. At the same time, we worry that too often the size of the glass is determined by nothing more than the price of the wine and that diners who order inexpensive wines are penalized by being forced to drink out of small, cheap glasses. This almost seems designed to embarrass the diner for ordering an inexpensive wine. A larger, better glass makes any wine more of an event—as eating out should be—so we agree with diners who greet their small glasses with some skepticism. But if you feel offended, don't be shy about asking. There might be a very good reason why your wine is served in a particular glass, and the restaurant might have put a lot of thought into it.

◌ **When should I send a bottle back?** When there's something wrong with the wine. Of course, this can sometimes be a matter of debate. If the wine tastes or smells off, tell the waiter or sommelier. Yes, they are sometimes jerks about this, but not usually. Most would rather have you tell them than suffer in silence and never return. You shouldn't send a wine back just because you decide you don't like it.

◌ **Should I tip the sommelier?** We have no idea what is "correct" in this case, but we simply add the tip in one lump sum to the bill and figure the people in the restaurant will split it.

◌ **What is an appropriate tip on wine?** This is one of the biggies, and one of the most contentious wine questions we deal with. We add 15 percent or so to the entire bill, including the wine. We know some people feel you should tip the same for any bottle, figuring that the waiter works just as hard on a $15 bottle as on a $50 bottle. We figure a waiter works just as hard serving an entree of salmon as he would serving filet mignon, too, but we tip 15 percent regardless of how much the entree costs. We know, on the one hand, some people feel strongly that, considering the high markup on wine, a tip on the wine is superfluous. On the other hand, the standard markup on the food is pretty steep, too: 300 to 350 percent, according to an article in *Weekend Journal,* which also reported that the markup on salmon is often 900 percent. *SmartMoney* magazine reported that the markup on salads is often 1,500 percent, and we can't even imagine the markup on Coca-Cola or bottled water. Our feeling is that if a restaurant charges too much for wine, the appropriate response is to order an inexpensive wine and never return to the restaurant—not to penalize the waiter. Which leads to the mother of all restaurant wine questions:

ℭ **What is an appropriate markup?** We want a restaurant to have an interesting inventory of wine, to store it well, and to have a knowledgeable staff that serves it in appropriate glasses. We know all of that effort costs money. Many restaurants do none of that and still charge ridiculous prices for wine. It's not just the money that bothers us, but the message. Restaurants that want us to enjoy ourselves consider wine part of that enjoyment and keep prices reasonable. According to Mr. Wiegand at *Restaurant Wine,* in casual restaurants it's "pretty common" to charge three times their cost for wine. At dinnerhouse and fine-dining restaurants, it's "generally" two to two and a half times their cost for better wines and three times for inexpensive wines. For the costliest top 20 percent of wines, he told us, the price restaurants charge is "moving toward retail," a trend he said he has noticed over the past ten years. Indeed, in talking to restaurateurs and others, we've found that about three times their cost is a sort of benchmark—not an average, but a general round figure they talk about. Personally, when we see wines on the list for much more than double the retail price, we get nervous. However, if we know the retail price—that is, if we've seen the wine at a store down the street—we'll probably avoid it anyway, but that does tell us something about the kind of place we're patronizing.

Our advice, in any case, is to order something you've never seen before, because restaurants often get stuff that's not sold in retail outlets. If you can't get the wine elsewhere, the issue of markup becomes far less relevant. (Restaurants and wineries are well aware that high markups drive diners crazy. Gallo, which is a brilliant marketing machine, makes a restaurant-only wine called Copperidge, which tastes just like many of its other low-priced offerings. Why is it available only at restaurants? Gallo explains on its website that these are "varietal wines with brand name popularity, but without the retail price comparison.")

One of our favorite places to drink wine was Windows on the World in the World Trade Center, where the great wine list was reasonably priced. Kevin Zraly was wine director for the restaurant when it was created by Joe Baum and Alan Lewis. He said those men, now deceased, felt the proper markup was two times what they paid for the wine plus $1. Today, he said, "there are no rules. It comes down to the size of the restaurant, the location of the restaurant, the cost of the entrees." He believes in "progressive pricing," having a higher markup for a lower-priced wine than a higher-priced wine. That idea has really caught on, especially at better restaurants. Mr. Zraly, by the way, told us he never spends more than $50 on a wine at a restaurant. Why? "I'm not willing to pay the markup that restaurants must charge," he said. Besides, he added, "I can get a perfectly good wine for under $50."

Wine Bars

Finally, a word about wine bars. Let's just put our cards right on the table here: we love wine bars. When we were young, wine bars were hot. We remember the first one we went to: the London Wine Bar in San Francisco, which bills itself as the nation's first. As budding wine lovers, we couldn't believe what we'd fallen into: a bar with a seemingly endless supply of different wines, many of which we'd never seen before, that we could taste in small amounts with a bartender who was as passionate about this as we were. That bartender is still there. His name is Gary Locke, and he has seen it all. Since Mr. Locke arrived at the Wine Bar in 1976, he has seen fads come and go, but he said the "general dynamic" of his clientele stays the same: "We have a pretty solid core of regulars." The wine bar's inventory today fluctuates on a seasonal basis from eight hundred to twelve hundred wines. There are several ways to taste: by the half-glass, by the glass, or by the flight (a flight is a group of wines that have something in common). There are three or four different lists that change with different frequencies. One list has samplers and flights of the really good stuff. "These wines tend to be more upper-end, fairly expensive wines that people don't normally have access to," Mr. Locke said. The London Wine Bar is able to snag a few cases of these small-production wines because its well-heeled clientele, from the financial district and law firms that surround it, "is exactly the kind of demographic that wineries want," he said. If you really like a wine, the wine bar is happy to sell you a bottle. It also serves a light lunch with salads, pastas, cheeses, and pâtés, "nothing very fancy," he said, and while it doesn't serve dinner, it does offer an appetizer menu.

After our first visit to the London Wine Bar in the 1970s, wine bars seemed to disappear, only to reappear in the eighties. We were living on the Upper West Side of Manhattan then, and a little place called Stephen's opened, down a couple of steps on a side street. Near overheated Columbus Avenue, this was an oasis of calm and elegance, where we sat and tasted so many different wines that we never could have tried if we had to buy whole bottles.

It wasn't just New York: one of our readers mistily recalled a wine bar in Anchorage, Alaska, that came and went in the 1980s. Before we knew it, Stephen's was gone, replaced by a Chinese restaurant. We left New York in the mid-eighties, and by the time we got back, in 1990, wine bars were pretty much gone. Oh, sure, some places were called "wine bars," but they were more about cigarettes and "real" drinks than wine. Well, they're back. In fact, they're so "in" that even faux wine bars are back, too—places that are essentially bars with a couple of open wine bottles. To us, that's not a wine bar. But there are real wine bars, too. In New York they range from the understated bistro feel of Le Bateau Ivre to the fancy Morrell in Rockefeller Center, which has a great location, interesting wines in pristine condition, really nice glasses, and knowledgeable servers.

New York's Artisanal restaurant is best known for its awesome selection of cheeses, but it also has 150 wines by the glass—and not your everyday wines, either. Have you ever had a Swiss white? Well, on one visit, they were offering a flight of three Swiss whites, all made from the Chasselas grape and all from the 1998 vintage. Total price: $12.50. Chasselas, which is a specialty of Switzerland, is somewhat neutral, so it takes on all sorts of the characteristics of its terroir and winemaker. The differences among these three were fascinating, and experiencing them against each other gave us a good idea what this wine is all about. A very lengthy list isn't as important, though, as a well-chosen one. In New York's trendy meatpacking district, Ara Wine Bar is a very chic spot with a list of about forty wines, each one carefully chosen. With the help of the relaxed people behind the bar, you can have a tour of the entire wine world on that list.

In Boston, Les Zygomates has dozens of wines by the glass. Readers have suggested wine bars all over the country: Postino in Phoenix, 33 in St. Louis; Carpe Vino in Auburn, California; Cesare's in Stillwater, Minnesota;

Chesapeake Wine Co. in Baltimore; Grapeseed American Bistro and Wine Bar in Bethesda, Maryland; Noble Rot in Portland, Oregon; Bistro Lepic Wine Bar in Georgetown. We asked Dan Macdonald, the outstanding wine and food editor of the *Florida Times-Union* in John's hometown of Jacksonville, Florida, if he had a favorite wine bar there, and he wrote back: "The Grotto, on San Marco Boulevard, ranks as the best tasting experience in town. There's an extensive by-the-glass menu. Customers have the choice of two-ounce, six-ounce, and half-bottle servings. The six-ounce pours range in price from $5.50 to $10 with an occasional special wine by the glass for sometimes closer to $20. The store has bottles for sale at retail prices—no restaurant markup. Bottles can be purchased to drink there or to take home to enjoy over dinner that evening. The Thursday night tastings kick off the unofficial weekend for young Jacksonville professionals." John grew up near San Marco Boulevard, and, trust us, Jacksonville back then had nothing like that.

On a visit to New Orleans, we dropped into a new wine bar called the Wine Loft (we happened to see it next to Emeril's), pulled up to the bar, and were immediately impressed by the excitement of the people pouring. They offered us a flight of Sauvignon Blanc–based wines and put a piece of paper in front of us explaining what we were tasting: a white Bordeaux, a Sancerre, and a New Zealand Sauvignon Blanc. Cost of the flight: $8, a small price to pay for such a fascinating tour of the wine world. When we left, they insisted we take our leftover wine with us in plastic cups. So on Bourbon Street, during college basketball's Final Four, surrounded by college kids with plastic cups of beer, there we were, feeling very much a part of the scene with our leftover Midnight Cellars Zinfandel, a small-production wine we'd never seen before.

In Atlanta, which has a particularly vibrant wine culture, there are a number of choices, such as the hip and very pretty Vinocity, which offers more than seventy wines by the glass. At a little place called Toulouse, we found wine bar heaven. One of the great things about any good wine bar is the ability to taste different wines of the same type against each other. By tasting three or four Chardonnays or Merlots or Sauvignon Blancs against each other, you really can detect and appreciate how different they are. That's what wine bars are all about—that and, of course, simply having fun.

Toulouse offered more than sixty wines by the glass and explained on the menu that they'd open any bottle on the list if we ordered two glasses of it. The menu also explained that wines by the glass were about a quarter of a bottle, or about six ounces, and they were priced accordingly. We decided to taste all four by-the-glass Zinfandels on the list. We told our waitress, who had no idea we were wine writers, that we'd like to do that, and she replied, "Would you like a splash of each first so you could tell which you'd like to order a glass of?" We told her that, really, that wasn't necessary, but she insisted. She came back with four glasses, each with a "splash" of Zinfandel. She told us to decide which we liked best and she'd get a glass of it. The splashes were free.

To us, the key to a wine bar isn't just the selection but the staff. They need to be expert enough to be relaxed and wise enough to understand who wants to talk about wine and who wants to be left alone. Another key is that the opened bottles need to be cared for carefully or poured out. We've been to too many "wine bars" where the wines seemed to have been open forever. If the people behind the counter are having a good time, chances are you will, too. *Wine bar* might sound intimidating, a place where snobs hang around and talk about the pros and cons of malolactic fermentation, but we'd urge you to give one a try at your earliest convenience. Here are some tips for how to make the most of your experience:

> **1. Take someone with you.** It's much more fun if you can taste with someone. Then you can try more and compare notes. Wine bars are a great place to take a date.

> **2. Before you sit, make sure it's really a wine bar.** Are there plenty of bottles everywhere, many of them open? Or just plenty of liquor and a few bottles of wine standing up with corks in them? (Some wine bars even have fancy systems that keep gas pumped into the bottles to preserve them, a good sign that this is the real deal.)

> **3. Sit at the bar** instead of at a table if you can and if you're just there for the wine. This will be more fun if you can schmooze with the bartender. If you want to eat something, some bars have special bar-food menus with small bites of this and that.

4. Look at the list of wines by the glass. Note whether there are two sizes of wines by the glass. Many offer pours and whole glasses. Go with the pour, since that means you can try more wines without overdoing it.

5. Look for flights of wines (ask about this if it's not noted on the wine list). Sometimes you can taste three or four American Chardonnays against each other or four different wines made from the Merlot grape but from different countries. If not, make your own flight by ordering, say, all four of the by-the-glass Cabernets on the list. At Artisanal, we once tasted three Pinot Noirs—one from Australia, one from France, and one from California. The winner, to our surprise: Australia. That was loads of fun for $12.50.

6. Be adventurous. This is a fine opportunity to try something new without having to pay for a whole bottle.

7. Go from white to red. Because you're at a wine bar, you'll likely have several different wines. As in any tasting, go from lighter wines to heavier wines, from white to red. It's hard to taste a light, fruity white after a meaty red. So focus on whites when you first sit down.

8. Don't be shy about taking notes, even if it's just to give each one a star or two. You don't want to forget which is your favorite.

9. If the wine tastes bad to you, suggest in a nice way to the pourer that perhaps it has been open too long and offer him a taste. It sometimes happens that that last glass of wine in the bottle has sat too long. Good establishments often will open a fresh bottle for you.

10. Don't hesitate to ask to see the label again of the one you like best. You might want to buy it, and you want to know for sure what it is.

11. Talk with the bartender. Don't feel like you need to be a wine expert. Just say, "Gee, I really like that." Good bartenders know how to talk to people, whether at a wine bar or at Mickey's Tavern. Don't be surprised if the bartender pours you some freebies that he or she wants you to taste.

12. Ask if anything is available that's not on the list. Sometimes wine bars have tastings for their staffs to determine what new stuff they'll be offering. If you're lucky, there might be something great that's open but not yet on the list. Sometimes there are special wines that they offer only to regulars. In any event, we've rarely been to a wine bar that didn't have something special under the counter.

"I recently opened a wine bar in Southlake, Texas, called Into the Glass. We have ninety-five by the taste or glass. Our mission is to have fun with wine and to eliminate the pretentiousness that surrounds the industry. Our slogan: 'Don't overthink it, just drink it!'"

Wayne Turner

Weddings

"It Worked Because of the Wine"

"My biggest questions are (a) how much wine should we figure for each guest—this is by far the biggie; (b) assuming we wanted to have both a red and a white, what are some safe but not boring choices; (c) what price range should we be thinking about where we could get something nice without further blowing an already decimated budget?" —**MARK NADLER, ST. CHARLES, ILLINOIS**

When we were married in Dottie's family's backyard in 1979, we knew we wanted to serve Taittinger Brut "La Française" Champagne, because it was the first real Champagne we had ever had and we had fallen in love with it on a cross-country train trip. We also knew that we wanted more Champagne than our guests could possibly drink. Our eighteen bottles for seventeen people did the trick. Of all of the occasions to celebrate with wine, weddings and anniversaries are unique in the way they embody your dearest hopes for the future and your appreciation of today. They reflect the new path you have started on and your happiness as you mark your progress on that path every year. What you serve at your wedding will always be special to you, an instant connection to powerful memories of a day filled with love and family and friends. The wines you share in your annual ritual that commemorates that day also resonate in a deeply personal way. Here's how to have more fun with wedding wines than you might expect.

The Wine Shower

"My friend is getting married, and she and her fiancé already have all the china, towels, and pots and pans that they'll ever need in their new life together. So a group of us is throwing her a 'wine shower' because we think people can always use more fine wine in their lives."

Molly Guthrey Millett, St. Paul, Minnesota

What a great idea. Ms. Millett, a feature writer at the *St. Paul Pioneer Press,* and Sue Campbell, the features editor, were trying to figure out something special to do for their friend Ellen Thompson. As Ms. Thompson told us: "I'm forty-one years old, so there were not a lot of things for my house that I didn't own." Added Ms. Campbell: "It's not like they needed anything. So we thought, okay, what would they want, what would they enjoy, what can we do to help launch them in their relationship that is meaningful?"

Ms. Campbell and Ms. Millett decided to throw a wine shower and invited eight women. The bride is a graphic artist for the newspaper, and her groom, Randall, works for Minnesota Public Radio and sings and plays violin in a band. They knew two things about Ms. Thomson's wine preferences. "Ellen loves everything French," Ms. Millett told us, but she isn't fond of Champagne. Otherwise there were no limits. They could buy the couple anything. Because the betrothed are artistic types, some looked for attractive, unusual labels, some for pretty bottles. Everything was gift wrapped. Most of the guests gave the happy couple French wines, but Ms. Millett decided to go another way. "I like to support local wines," she explained, so she gave them a dessert wine from a local winery, Alexis Bailey of Hastings, Minnesota. "It came in a really cool blue bottle," Ms. Millett said, and the wine apparently was such a big hit the couple bought more of it when they returned from their wedding in Scotland and served it to visiting French musicians. In all, the newlyweds received fifteen bottles of wine, mostly reds, with little tags attached telling them who they were from. "I thought they might last a while, but they were gone in no time," the happy bride said. The wine shower, she said, was a huge success: "No embarrassing negligees."

Wine Registries

"We strongly encourage you to consider your presence at our wedding the best gift you could possibly give us. If you feel completely compelled to get us something, we have a wine registry (we've registered for the wine we like to drink). The shop is Atlas Liquors in Medford. Please make sure to provide your name to Atlas when you order so the bottle is marked with your name—that way we can toast you when we drink it."

A note from Christine Schmidt and Andrew Schmitt of Winchester,
Massachusetts, to everyone invited to their wedding

Engaged couples used to register for "necessities" like china and silver. Now they register for all sorts of things. Even Home Depot plugs itself as a good place for wedding gifts. Here's a better idea: wine registries are a great way to stock the wine rack you'll be setting up for your new life together. That's what the Schmitts did. "We're in our thirties, and at this point in our lives we had the china and silverware we needed or wanted," Christine explained. As they were planning their wedding, they read one of our columns in which we suggested a wine registry, and it really rang a bell. They went to three wine shops before they found one that was willing to give it a shot. "We made an appointment with the buyer and toured the store with him, picking out an assortment of wines we'd like to try." Ultimately, the gifts they received this way allowed them to stock "a nice little cellar with over a hundred bottles, which was a real treat for us," Christine told us on the telephone while holding four-month-old Anton, born two years later. "This was a really nice way to sample wines from all different areas and regions and in all different price ranges."

The idea of a wine registry was new then, so there were some glitches along the way (not to mention that some of their older friends felt a little squeamish giving them wine instead of things they considered longer lasting, like a comforter). Now more and more wine stores and on-line purveyors are offering this service, often at no extra charge. They work pretty much the way other wedding registries work, but instead of picking out dishes or silverware that you'd like your friends to give you, you talk to a wine merchant about the wines you like or would like to try. The merchant will need your wedding date and some of your preferences in wines so that when your friends call the store they'll have an idea what you would like. Or you can be adventurous. Tell them to surprise you. The merchant might ask what foods you like to eat and what you like about the wines that you've enjoyed to help guide your friends' choices. Some merchants will send along the wines with food-pairing suggestions and tips for when you should open the wine or how long it can age. When the bottles come with the giver's name attached, leave that on so you can think about that person when you open the bottle. We've kept notes on every bottle we've shared over our thirty years together because each one is a treasured memory of our shared life.

If you're a guest and the newlyweds haven't set up a registry, think about giving wine as a gift. Personally, we often give a case of sparkling wine with a note that says, "Don't save these. Make every day of your marriage a celebration." We hear from readers all the time about how important wine presents have been to them. Consider this, from Daniel R. Katz of New York City:

> *"When my wife and I were married several years ago, we were given a bottle of Château Haut-Brion and told that we should open it on our ten-year anniversary. We loved the gift. It was a thoughtful, one-of-a-kind, lasting present. And it was something we could look forward to enjoying for a long time. Since then, I have given several friends wine as wedding gifts. It is a lot of fun to work with a wine salesperson on picking the right bottles. I like to choose three: one to open on the first-year anniversary, one to open after five, and one on the tenth anniversary. Of course, there are always jokes about whether the wine will last longer than the marriage and who gets the bottles if it doesn't work out. But the bottom line is that wine makes one of the greatest wedding gifts out there and is definitely one of the more enjoyable gifts to purchase."*

We once received this note from Tom Dever of New York City: "Rather than get a standard wedding gift that is likely soon forgotten by the couple—I'm a single guy so I cannot speak from experience—I decided that it would be more interesting and special if I were to get the couples three bottles of wine." He wanted to give his newlywed friends three wines to be enjoyed at the same intervals that Mr. Katz chose—on the first, fifth, and tenth anniversaries—and he asked our advice. We suggested Bordeaux for the first anniversary because it's so very special and elegant that it makes any celebration that much more memorable. We thought Zinfandel would be fun for the fifth anniversary because of the wine's bold vibrancy, its zesty spirit. While a good Zinfandel should possess a serious structure, it should also have a certain wild lustiness, as you would hope their marriage would have at that point. We liked the idea of a Sauternes for their tenth year together because these wines are sweet, as you hope the years have been for them. One benefit of those three is that all of them come in a wide range of prices. Sauternes can be so pricey, in fact, that you might consider buying a half-bottle.

Mr. Dever told us later that he has given that wedding present to three couples so far, with excellent results—"overwhelming," in fact. Two couples told him that having the wine around spurred them to learn more about the wines and "opened them to the world of wine." The third couple told him that now, instead of grabbing something from the shelf of a wine store, they read about wine and discuss what they want to try. "Not to toot my own horn, but the gift seems to have opened them up and allowed them to develop a greater appreciation for wine," Mr. Dever told us, adding: "It also guarantees that you will be in their thoughts, if only in passing, on those benchmark days of their lives."

Selecting Your Wedding Wines

Choosing the wines for your wedding doesn't have to be a chore. You can make it an excuse for a party. This is a good time to get married, at least in terms of wine. There are so many choices, something good to fit every budget. Some people want to go with a sure thing— Chardonnay for the white and Merlot for the red, things they know their friends already like. Others want to introduce their friends to some of their special favorites, wines off the beaten path. Here's a critical first point: when you are choosing the venue for your wedding, be sure to ask questions about wine. Some hotels force you to order the wines from their own overpriced, mediocre list or will charge you an outrageous per-bottle corkage fee. Even some caterers might be resistant to letting you choose your own wines. The wines at your wedding are important; make sure you have as much freedom to choose them as possible. Don't put this off. You don't want to discover any unpleasant constraints at the last minute.

Now for the big choice: which wines? This can be a great deal more fun than you think. Since you're already planning, you have plenty of time for this important task. Do this:

- Tell the groom and his friends to choose the red.
- Tell the bride and her friends to choose the white.
- Tell the parents (who, after all in many cases, are footing the bill) to choose the bubbly.

Here's how to do it. First, figure out what your total budget is for wine and then break it down, deciding how much you'd like to spend on the white and the red and the bubbly. Then buy, say, six of the same kind of wine around the same price. Put them all in bags and number them. Then have everybody in that group taste all six. Don't make this too serious. Don't worry about a different glass for each or "palate cleansers" or taking extensive notes about bouquets and hints of brambles. Just relax, throw in some casual dishes, and sip. At some point it will be clear which is the favorite wine. It will probably be the first bottle to empty. Not only will you have chosen the wine for your wedding, but you will have started off the wedding preparations right. Now you're probably saying to yourself: "Wait a minute. We're not really choosing wines here. We're having little parties." Well, yep, you got us. But you'll also choose a wine that you and your friends like, not just something chosen by a caterer, a wine merchant, or a hotel. That will make the wine more special.

We know that Mr. Nadler is right that there are three basic questions brides, grooms, and their families want answered when planning wine for a wedding: how much to buy, what to buy, and how much to pay. So here are some answers:

How Much Wine to Buy? It depends on whether you have an open bar or are serving wine with dinner, how long the festivities will last, what other beverages you're serving, whether your friends are serious partiers, and so on. Are the guests mostly beer-drinking twenty-somethings? Is there a sit-down dinner? There are so many variables. Bill Parkinson of Harvard, Massachusetts, once wrote to ask us this: "We have a daughter-in-law-to-be who would like French Champagne at her wedding. Could you give us some advice?" Mr. Parkinson tried some of our suggestions and let his son Dougald's fiancée, Janet, choose Heidsieck Monopole Blue Top Brut. The wedding was held in an apple orchard that the Parkinsons own. "Those who wanted a fizzy drink, but not Champagne, drank Harvard's locally grown, sparkling apple juice," which was made from some of the apples grown in the family's orchard, Mr. Parkinson, a physicist and astronomer, told us. It was a big hit— such a big hit, in fact, that the guests drank more cider than Champagne. Who woulda guessed? That's why it's so hard to decide how much wine to order.

If pressed to the wall, our answer would be: too much. It's better to have wine left over than not to have enough. If you figure a half-bottle per person, which is about three glasses, you should be fine. If you are serving Champagne before and after and then red and white with food, plan on a half-bottle per person of the bubbly and a half-bottle per person of the red and white together. Not that people will drink that much wine, but you can't be sure which wine they'll drink, so you need plenty. See if you can find a merchant who will accept returns of unopened bottles (this isn't legal in some states). You can certainly find a use for the leftovers—as gifts to some special people as they leave the wedding, as wines for the honeymoon, or to stock the happy couple's first cellar together.

What Wines Should You Have That Won't Break a Bank That's Surely Already Broken? For the bubbly, look at our recommendations in "New Year's Eve." For your red and white, we suggest a Merlot and a Chardonnay. Yes, we know that, to some extent, they are clichés, but pretty much everybody likes them, so you can't really go wrong. What you're looking for is something that's easy to drink, pleasant, and likable. You also want something that's so reasonably priced that you can pour it liberally without worrying about the bill. Sure, many Merlots and Chardonnays are obvious and boring, but not all of them. Here are some reliable names that are widely available. All of these cost under $20, and many can be found for less than $10. This also means you can order more than you think you'll need without worrying too much about massive waste. Plus, you might be lucky enough to get discounts because you're buying so much (merchants often offer a 15 percent discount on cases, and perhaps you could bargain for more on a larger order). Our notes are based on tastings of the 2001 or 2002 vintages, but we're recommending these because we find them reliable year after year.

Some Reliable Chardonnays for Your Wedding

Beringer Vineyards Founders' Estate (California). The lovely nose, with plenty of toast and honey, will immediately make guests predisposed to like it. The taste is round and pleasant, with some sweet, woody tastes, but nice acids for food, too.

Bogle Vineyards (California). Nicely acidic and crisp, with real fruit tastes. Tastes classy and expensive, with a lovely balance of flavors. If you don't tell people what it cost—sometimes as low as $6.99— they'll never know.

Cambria "Katherine's Chardonnay" (Santa Maria Valley). It costs more than the others—closer to $20—but it tastes like it cost even more. It's classy, austere, and a bit flinty, with nice toast, good fruit, vibrant acids, and excellent balance. Especially if you're spending a lot on the food—lobster, for instance—this is the way to go.

Edna Valley Vineyard "Paragon" (Edna Valley). Bright pineapple and Key-lime flavors, with some soulful woody tastes, especially on the finish.

Hahn Estates (Monterey). Edgier than the others, with more unexpected tastes and real character. Spicy and a bit herbal.

La Crema (Sonoma Coast). Really good fruit, ripe and tasty. Plenty of nutmeg, but well balanced, with nice restraint.

R. H. Phillips Vineyard (Dunnigan Hills). Plain-old good wine, with buttery mouthfeel and no edges. Seamless good fruit. If you go with this, get even more than you had planned, because it will go quickly.

Some Reliable Merlots for Your Wedding

Beringer Vineyards Founders' Estate (California). Rich, fruity nose, with tobacco, cedar, and some sweet cream. Roasted, toasted, creamy, and fruity. Plump, with a blackberry, woody finish. An exuberant wine for an exuberant wedding.

Benziger Family Winery (Sonoma County). Rich, with some stature. Plenty of fruit, but also some weight. This would be good with more serious, somewhat heavier food.

Bogle Vineyards (California). Blueberries, blackberries, and wood on the nose, but enough restraint that it's not just a fruit bomb. Lovely. This is good for people who like Merlot (because it's soft and easy), but also for people who don't (because it's not flat and sweet). Acids, cream, and plenty of fruit in nice balance. Really winning.

There are times when a $9.99 bottle of wine simply can't be beat. Ask Krista and Brandon Caldwell of Los Angeles about that. The longtime friends exchanged vows on July 28, 2002, in the Grand Canyon—on a narrow spit of land that jutted out over the canyon. Gulp! The groom, who is an independent software designer and also a pilot, chef, personal trainer, message therapist, and tailor—he made his bride's wedding dress—had traveled the country many times, usually on a motorcycle. "The Grand Canyon," he told us, "has been a particular inspiration to me. It says that the hand of God is here. Look at the beauty and the grandeur. There's something about the scale of it. It's humbling." He proposed while they were on the trail near Yosemite Falls one night in January. "We were on our backs looking at the stars, near the falls," he said. "I didn't know it at the time, but she was so overcome with the beauty of it that she was sobbing silently. My heart was moved by how beautiful the stars and the trees were and by how much my love for her matches that, and I asked her to marry me. There was silence. Dead silence. So I said, 'Krista?' and she said, 'What? I'm sorry.' She hadn't heard a word of it. She hadn't heard over the sound of the falls. Then, of course, she said yes."

When it came time to get married, the Grand Canyon it was. After the service, which brought together friends and family from all over the country, they had a reception at the park's historic El Tovar Lodge, where a caterer served a sparkler that somehow didn't make a dent in their consciousness. They don't remember it at all. It was on the second night of their married life, after they had moved from the lodge to the campground, amid family and friends, that they had the wine they still remember. The Park Service grocery store had a small selection of wine, including a Cabernet Sauvignon from Meridian, which is a value-priced winery owned by giant Beringer Blass Wine Estates. It looked interesting, so Krista's dad, Thomas Whitaker, bought several bottles. The groom cooked chili—over a campfire, even—enough, he said, "to feed the whole campground." The Meridian was simply wonderful, and the wedding party quickly cleaned the store out of it. It is a wine that Mr. and Mrs. Caldwell, and their entire wedding party, will never forget.

We had our own wedding crises that we still remember: a big storm the night before, a tiff over seating assignments for dinner, a last-minute carpet dyeing ("Mom, you're going to dye the carpet *now?*"). All these years later, those momentary crises make us smile, and we smile even more broadly when we remember Dottie's mother's lamb, our tears of happiness, and how great that Taittinger tasted right out of the ice in the birdbath. Things will work out fine, and when they do, this is what it's like: we once received a letter from J. Mark Lambright of Dallas, asking for advice about his daughter Candice's wedding. We offered some pointers and later asked both of them how it went.

SHE SAYS: *"Having my dad in charge of the selections was a wonderful distraction for him during all of the wedding planning. He received some helpful advice from other father-of-the-bride friends to stick to the rules of the 'three Ss'—sit down, shut up, and shell out. He was also told to think of a wedding as buying a Mercedes and then immediately driving it off a cliff. He took this advice to heart and only checked in to make sure that everyone was happy with the plans. Being able to pick out the wine and Champagne not only gave him the chance to be creative and have some fun, but definitely helped me out. We had a very traditional wedding, with about 90 percent of the guests coming in from out of town. The family and friends who arrived early were involved in many different tastings throughout the week. All of the guests were given cards to rank the wines. (This let my dad combine his two favorites: wine and computer spreadsheets to choose the favorites.) This was not only fun for everyone, but allowed more time than the wedding and the Sunday brunch that followed for everyone to meet each other. It also allowed us to have a nice, relaxing time several nights before the wedding, which was priceless. The tastings also left me with memories I will cherish my whole life."*

HE SAYS: *"What I decided to do was have a little fun out of it and at the same time get some feedback out of a kind of disparate group. Some were wine connoisseurs and some weren't. I bought some reds and whites and handed the participants spreadsheets and asked them to rate the wines one through five, with five being their favorite. What I found was that everybody had a great time doing it. And one of the interesting things for me was some people were tasting Chardonnays and saying 'Hey, this one tastes different from that one.' The wines that the group selected were not my personal favorites. The Chardonnay was one that was a little sweeter than what I preferred. And the interesting thing was it won hands-down among the group. The red was a Merlot. It was my favorite of the Merlots, but if I had chosen the wines, I would have picked a Cabernet, just because I prefer it. But it didn't matter. We got lots of compliments on it. People talked about the wines at the wedding. It went over real well. It was a lovely wedding and it worked because of the wine."*

Anniversaries

Celebrating Your Own Special Vintage

"Our thirty-fifth wedding anniversary is coming up this November, and I was wondering if there are any 1966 red wines or Champagnes available with which to celebrate our long and wonderful relationship." **—THOMAS WHITAKER, OMAHA, NEBRASKA**

"She was a blind date. Some friends of mine were moving, and I was throwing a farewell party for them. They had been telling me about this gal who lived a hundred miles away, so I invited her to the party. She was from Eugene, Oregon, and she was coming to the party in Portland and was going to stay with her aunt. She got off the bus, and she called her friends, and there was no answer. No one was available to take her to her aunt's. So she called me, and I was close to the bus station, so I went. I walked into the bus station, and it was one of those things. There was this gorgeous, tall, thin woman standing there, and as I walked by to the dispatcher's office to have her paged, I thought, That is really something. So he announced her name, and here she comes walking out there, this gorgeous woman. We met in February and were married in November. It's been an extra-special marriage."

There you have it, from Thomas Whitaker, on how he met his wife, Lorraine, in 1966. What wine could possibly match such a special occasion? Well, Mr. Whitaker (father of Krista in the previous chapter, proving that romance runs in families) came to the right place with his question, because we're experts on anniversaries. We met in 1973, and we always celebrate that day. We were married in 1979, and we always celebrate that day, too. We also usually celebrate the anniversary of our first date (a Bob Dylan concert).

In fact, when the *Today* show celebrated its fiftieth anniversary in 2002, we were the ones they called to find an appropriate wine from 1952 and open it on air. This took some work. To us, the best bet—especially since they were footing the bill—was a fine Bordeaux in a big bottle. Large bottles age more gracefully, and good Bordeaux can age for a very long time. It seemed to us that a Port or a fine dessert wine, both of which also age well, would be too precious (especially for a morning show), and a Champagne might be flat, which would be depressing *and* bad television. So we went to one of our favorite books, *The Great Vintage Wine Book* by Michael Broadbent, and found that 1952 was a pretty good year, with wines that were "rather stern and unyielding," which is good news for a wine that we want to drink at the half-century mark. Among the great wines of Bordeaux, Château Latour is known as the "biggest" and toughest, so that seemed like a good bet to us. Mr. Broadbent said he last tasted it in 1980 and it "will last for decades." Another good sign. We looked around at various wine stores across the country that specialized in old wines, found one that had it in stock and would deliver to New York, and ordered it.

When the big day came, we waited in the green room with our bottle. John opened it while we waited—with an old bottle, it's possible that opening it might be ugly, with the cork breaking apart or refusing to budge at all. We also wanted to smell the wine to make sure that it wasn't vinegar. If it was, we'd already decided that John would run out, find any wine store, and refill the bottle with anything else. As it happened, the cork came out beautifully and the wine smelled heavenly.

The anniversary show was a big event, with all sorts of famous people there. When John went to use the bathroom, he stood in line between Tony Bennett and Bryant Gumbel, and how often does that happen? Jane Pauley dropped into the green room to say hello to everyone. Suddenly, with just moments left in the show, which was running late, they came to get us and the wine. Everyone had been gathered—Katie Couric, Al Roker, and all of the current hosts, along with a big cast of alumni, from Florence Henderson, Barbara Walters, and Hugh Downs to Gene Shalit, Joe Garagiola, Tom Brokaw, and Edwin Newman. We'd been told we'd serve the wine on air, but they were running out of time, so as soon as we stepped onto the set during a commercial, Katie Couric grabbed the bottle and poured giant portions, emptying the bottle before she got to half the people assembled. Then, those with wine had to quickly pour some into the empty glasses of the people next to them so that everyone would have something to toast with. As they counted down the final seconds of the commercial, a large, tiered white cake with yellow roses on it was wheeled onto the set. Finally, there we all were, wine in hand, ready to go "live" again. "Now we want to close this morning with a magnum of a very special wine, Château Latour 1952 — oui oui oui," Ms. Couric announced. She had told us during the break that we would have time for one sentence. She introduced us, nodded, and we both went blank for a second. Finally snapping to, John said, "This is a 1952 Château Latour—great year for TV, not a great year for wine, except this one." Everybody laughed, but the truth is that John, along with everyone else, was immediately upstaged when the chimp they'd invited—a stand-in for the famous J. Fred Muggs, who used to be on the show—lunged at Gene Shalit's glass and then the magnum. Clearly, he knew a great thing when he smelled it, because the wine truly was magnificent.

So, how do you do this? How do you find just the right wine from just the right vintage? First, this important note: how you do this and the thought you put into it matters just as much, probably more, than the wine itself. In 1979, Jack Tierney was a high school teacher. Cheri Tierney had just moved with her parents from Maryland to Naperville, Illinois, and was living with them. Mr. Tierney and some of the guys he knew would meet at Houlihan's now and then, to relax after work. One night, when a friend couldn't go with him, he went by himself. He looked around and didn't see anyone he knew and was about to leave when it happened. "As I was going to leave, I spotted an acquaintance, and when I went to say hello, he was talking to two young ladies. One of them was Cheri. Three and a half years later, we got married," Mr. Tierney told us. "Things happen for a reason. I believe that that was the only opportunity I would have had to meet her. We had no friends in common. We didn't work together. We wouldn't have met otherwise."

Mr. Tierney is now a busy guy running training programs for Morgan Stanley, but he makes time for romance. When he and Cheri were on their first cruise, the ship docked in Key West for several hours, and they fell in love with that quirky outpost of civilization. So they vowed to return. For their twentieth anniversary, they left the kids with their grandparents, rented a convertible in Miami, and drove to Key West over that ribbon of concrete, the Overseas Highway, a 110-mile-long stretch of U.S. 1 that connects the mainland to the southernmost islands. "We just had each other and nobody else," he told us. Mr. Tierney had bought his wife a platinum ("symbol for twenty years") ring with three diamonds and planned to surprise her with it over dinner. He also arranged for his wine shop to ship a bottle of 1982 Chateau Montelena Cabernet Sauvignon, one of California's finest wines, to their hotel. Cabernet Sauvignon is Cheri's favorite type of wine. Once in Key West, Mr. Tierney made reservations at a restaurant and asked if he could bring his special bottle. When the big night came, they walked into the restaurant and found their bottle awaiting them at a table under the stars. The server opened the wine and poured a taste for him. She then poured each of them a glass and left. "I told my wife, 'Before you drink this, close your eyes.' At this point I pulled the little ring box from my pocket and opened it up in front of her and told her to open her eyes. I told her 'Happy Anniversary.' She loved the ring, and we toasted with the wine. This was our second honeymoon. I had such high expectations for this trip, and it fulfilled all my expectations."

Of course, you might want to create new memories with a very special wine from a more recent year, in which case we'd suggest a great Champagne such as Dom Pérignon (see "New Year's Eve"), a very fine French "first growth" such as Château Lafite Rothschild, or one of California's famous wines, such as Opus One. Also, don't forget that the best wine for this occasion might just be a wine that wouldn't seem very special to anyone else but is special to you and your spouse because it holds special memories. Heck, if we could find another bottle of Always Elvis, a cheap Italian white we opened thirty years ago and have been joking about ever since, we'd open it for an anniversary in a second. All that said, many people really want to get an anniversary wine from a specific year. Here's how to do it:

 Plan early. This will take some time. Not only that, but if you order the wine from someplace distant, which is likely, it should sit for at least a few days to calm down after its journey.

℀ **Do some homework.** Michael Broadbent's book (now updated as *Michael Broadbent's Vintage Wine*) is great, if you happen to own it, but there are all sorts of vintage guides and tasting notes available on the Internet (see, for instance, winespectator.com and wineloverspage.com). These might give you some idea what to look for or what to avoid, although—as our Latour showed—good wines are made even in vintages that aren't great. Be flexible. Don't decide that you simply must have a French wine, because maybe your year was a terrible one in France but great for Barolo in Italy, for instance.

℀ **Think red.** Some white wines age beautifully for a very long time, and we've had thirty-year-old Champagnes that were terrific. They are good options if you drink only white. But, overall, your chances are better with a fine red. Port and some dessert wines, such as Sauternes, get better and better with age, so if you and your loved one like Port or Sauternes, that's great. But most people are looking for a dry wine to have with dinner, which takes us back to red.

℀ **Be prepared to spend real money.** You're almost surely going to have to spend hundreds of dollars on a wine that's twenty or thirty years old and still good. Hey, we're not happy about that either, but it's a fact.

℀ **Look far afield.** Most wine stores will not have old wines, but there are stores that specialize in them. Various big auction houses routinely auction old wines, but usually as part of larger lots. There are many auction sites on the Internet. We'd rather deal with a real store, even if it costs more, especially when we're dealing with an old wine to be used for a special occasion. Take a look at 2020wines.com and MarinWineCellar.com. The first is where we got the 1952 Latour, and the second is where we got a 1974 Cabernet to celebrate one of our own anniversaries. Wineaccess.com and Wine-Searcher.com are quite useful, too. We don't endorse those or recommend them over any others, and there are dozens out there, but those sites might give you some idea how this works and what's out there and for how much.

℀ **Keep in mind** that interstate shipping laws are archaic, so not every place can send everywhere.

☙ **Make a call and talk.** This isn't a time to be shy. You need to have a serious talk with wine merchants about what might still be a good wine. Explain why it's so important. They will work with you to make this a special occasion, though there are never any guarantees in wine. Be sure to ask about the "fill," which means how high the wine comes into the neck of the bottle. The lower the fill, the more air that's gotten to the wine, and that's a bad thing. The fill is so important that fancy auction catalogs note how high the fill is of every old bottle. It's not foolproof, of course, but this does give some indication of how well the wine has been stored and what kind of shape it's in. In any case, if you say to the merchant, "How's the fill?" he'll figure you know what you're doing.

☙ **Send it express.** Once you have bought the wine, pay for overnight delivery. The wine is bound to be old and fragile, and you don't want it to sit around in cold or heat.

☙ **When you open it, follow our advice on old wines** in "Open That Bottle Night."

☙ **Make a toast.** Before you take the first sip, make a nice toast to your loved one and seal it with a kiss. If the wine isn't as great as you had hoped, be happy that your marriage has stood the test of time better than the wine. If the wine is great, you and your spouse will have even more to be thankful for.

We're not the only ones who think this is a great idea. We have an endorsement from a higher authority. The Rev. Rob Eller-Isaacs and his wife, the Rev. Janne Eller-Isaacs, perform a wine ceremony as "a central liturgy" within the wedding ceremonies they perform at United Church–Unitarian in St. Paul, Minnesota. "It began with developing the wine ceremony as a way to acknowledge family. And being of Jewish heritage myself, I thought about breaking the glass and using that symbol as a way to say that when people marry one another, they become, at their best, more effective instruments of love and a healing of the world's brokenness," the Rev. Rob Eller-Isaacs told us. "It strikes me that if there is anything that I can offer as a way of continuing the symbols that reflect that moment of commitment, I should offer it.

"So I ask in the wedding interview, 'Do you drink wine on a regular basis? Is it a central part of your life?'" If they say yes, then he says, "Well, if you can afford it, I would suggest that you buy a case or more of something that a good wine dealer tells you will lie down and age for forty years or more. And then, on very special occasions, not just once a year, open it and use it in a liturgical way," some public demonstration of devotion. The first bottle should be consumed during the wedding ceremony, he said, and thereafter for "each really significant turning" in the couple's life, as a way to renew the vows and celebrate their commitment. The Rev. Eller-Isaacs said he has been suggesting that couples do this for twenty years, and occasionally he'll hear back from those who have taken his grape advice. "Once in a while," he said, "someone gives us a bottle by way of thank you."

Why should the wine be something that will be good after forty years? "Because I don't know of any wine that stays decent much longer than that. And forty years is a pretty solid marriage," the Rev. Eller-Isaacs told us. "If they need to buy a different vintage after that, that's fine."

The Fourth
of July Perfect Summer
Wines (Even, Shhhh, Chilled Reds)

"We live outside of Denver, Colorado, in an area where the houses have a bit of room around them. Every year for the Fourth, we have a multigeneration party of our children and grandchildren and some old friends with their children and grandchildren, plus a few extra families who don't have family here in the Denver area. We set up a cold buffet and have tables and chairs out on the grass, and the grandchildren run around, play, and eat on blankets whenever they get hungry. We watch the sun set over the Rockies while we eat, and when it is dark enough, we climb up on the roof to watch the fireworks from all the communities around us. This year we had a very informal tasting of white jug wines you have recommended for summer drinking. It was wonderful fun for all of us and an easy way for new friends to feel a part of the group." —JULIA SECOR, CHERRY HILLS VILLAGE, COLORADO

What wine pairs perfectly with the Fourth of July and with summer in general—with hamburgers and hot dogs, fireworks and friends? Matching food and wine isn't just about the tastes. It's about the mood, the occasion, and, yes, even the weather. Summer is all about easy living, lazy days, fun, and pure enjoyment. The wines you drink when the temperature is rising should reflect the same easygoing, fun spirit.

Every city has its own seasonal traditions, including events that you look forward to from year to year. For us it's the series of free summer concerts in Central Park, two each by the Metropolitan Opera and the New York Philharmonic. Thousands of people spread across the Great Lawn, almost everyone with a substantial picnic feast and a bottle or two of wine.

We've seen everything from dinners emerging from brown paper bags to fancy-schmancy catered affairs complete with linen tablecloths and ornate silver ice buckets filled with Champagne. New Yorkers do have style. We have been attending these concerts for years, since we were young and it was just the two of us. Then, after we became four and Media and Zoë were toddlers, we'd take them, pushing their double stroller into the park with our picnic bags hanging from the stroller's handles. Now, past fifty and with aching backs, we walk over to the Great Lawn with Media and Zoë and a shopping cart filled with our food and wine.

One night the New York Philharmonic was performing a concert of Leonard Bernstein music on the day that the U.S. Postal Service issued its Bernstein stamp. We put together an elegant picnic dinner from a nearby deli—grilled eggplant wrapped around ricotta cheese was its centerpiece—and headed to Central Park with the girls. Just as we picked up the night's programs and reached the Great Lawn, some raindrops fell, so we ducked under a large tree and spread out our blankets. To our surprise, we'd sat right in the middle of the world's biggest swarm of fireflies. As dusk arrived, we looked over at the girls, and their heads were ringed by fireflies, like perfect little halos. Although the rain never came in earnest, we didn't leave our idyllic refuge under that majestic tree with its enchanted colony of fireflies. What wine could possibly match such a perfect summer night? A white wine from the Loire Valley of France. On that night it was Sancerre, crisp and mouth-watering. But it also could have been Muscadet or Vouvray. They're vibrant, light, refreshing, great with food, and outstanding bargains, often under $10. Hard to beat that.

Now is a particularly good time to try wines of the Loire, because new ones, from various areas of the region, are showing up all the time. Quincy, Savennières, Ménétou-Salon—these are names we had rarely seen on shelves until the past few years, and they tend to be well priced because they're new to most people. Some excellent reds are made in the Loire—we especially like Chinon, from the Cabernet Franc grape—and there are some outstanding sweet wines, too, but dry, crisp whites are truly the region's specialty. We tend to stick to the old standbys, Muscadet, Sancerre, and Vouvray, because they're three of the world's most consistently satisfying white wines.

Muscadet usually costs less than $10 at stores and often around $6.99. At restaurants, especially seafood restaurants, it's frequently one of the least expensive bottles on the wine list, and we rarely pass up an opportunity to try it. Muscadet, which is made from a grape called Melon de Bourgogne, tends to be better with seafood than American Chardonnay because it's leaner and nicely acidic. It's a highly drinkable, fun wine, with subtle, fruity tastes and a kind of cloudy mustiness that gives it special character and depth. Young and fresh, it comes alive with food from salads—of seafood, chicken, or lentils—to grilled vegetables and poached, grilled, or fried fish dishes.

Sancerre, which tends to cost more than Muscadet, is made from the Sauvignon Blanc grape. We're all familiar with that grape these days. American Sauvignon Blanc is the second-most-popular white varietal in the United States (after Chardonnay, of course). Look for R. H. Phillips, Kunde, Geyser Peak, and Groth. Crisp, juicy, fresh Sauvignon Blanc is a specialty of New Zealand (look for Babich, Brancott, Cloudy Bay, Goldwater, and Villa Maria), and outstanding Sauvignon Blanc is arriving in greater quantities every day from Chile and South Africa. These are Sauvignon Blancs with extraordinary varietal character—tastes of fresh-mown grass and a mouth-popping lemon-lime zestiness. Well, think of Sancerre as the more mature, more urbane French cousin of those wines. It, too, has grassy tastes, with zesty lime flavors bursting all around it, but Sancerre has an undertone of earth and minerals that gives it grounding and a certain seriousness that can make the wine a fun and delicious experience. This is our all-time favorite summer picnic wine, not in small part because no matter what the weather, it reminds us of sunshine and happy times.

Vouvray is made from the Chenin Blanc grape. Chenin Blanc really is a noble grape—seriously, folks—but it got a rotten reputation in the United States because it was used by many jug-wine producers to mean "cheap white wine." Try a Vouvray; you won't cringe the next time you hear "Chenin Blanc." It's juicy and tart and reminds us of crisp green apples. Pair Vouvray with cold roast pork—perhaps vitello tonnato, the Italian classic of veal with a tuna sauce—for a real treat.

Here are some reliable producers of Muscadet, Sancerre, and Vouvray. When you buy Muscadet, look for Sèvre-et-Maine on the label (that's an area) and *sur lie,* which means the wine sat in its sediment for a time, giving it added complexity (the Muscadets that follow are all Sèvre-et-Maine *sur lie*). On a Vouvray label, *sec* means that it's dry and *demi-sec* that it's a bit sweet. Muscadet is often under $10; Sancerre is usually between $10 and $20; and Vouvray is $7 to $15. Younger is better. These tasting notes are from the 2001 vintage; buy the youngest you see.

Some Loire Whites

Château de la Chesnaie Muscadet. Always reliable. Nicely acidic, with lovely, highly drinkable fruit. Some intensity and weight, really mouth filling. Dottie calls it "an earthy lemon sorbet."

Château du Cléray Muscadet. Lovely flavors, fresh and clean, with some hints of melon. A fuller, richer, more complex taste than some. This stands up nicely to any kind of fried fish or seafood.

Marquis de Goulaine Muscadet. This is the Muscadet that made us fall in love with Muscadet many years ago, and it's still our favorite. Plenty of fruit and plenty of minerals. Nicely acidic. So clean and refreshing that it's like a splash of cold water on your face on a hot day.

Archambault Domaine de la Perrière Sancerre. Crisp and seriously mouth-popping. Alive with fruit flavors, but without as much taste of minerals and weight as some others.

La Poussie Sancerre. Like a cleansing explosion of lime in your mouth. Vibrant and easy to drink. Great with a fleshy fish.

Lucien Crochet Sancerre. Crisp, fresh, and lovely, with good lemon-lime fruit but also some weight and minerals. Serious wine yet light on its feet.

Champalou "La Cuvée des Fondreaux" Vouvray. Always pleasant and filled with mouthwatering acids and fruits—kiwifruit, lychee, pineapple, and more. A complete wine, with earth, fruit, minerals, mouthfeel, and depth.

Domaine des Aubuisières "Cuvée des Silex" (Bernard Fouquet) Vouvray. Tart, clean, and juicy, with lots of citrus and pineapple taste, yet light. Like a green-apple sorbet. All the right notes. Great with pork and awesome with an onion tart.

Henry de Fontenay Vouvray. Extremely refreshing, with all of the flavors in nice balance. Plenty of tangerines and other just-picked citrus flavors.

Michel Picard Vouvray. Bright, with pineapple, lemon, and all sorts of citrus. Really lovely, with a long, lemony finish, but lighter than we'd expect.

Rémy Pannier Vouvray. Green-tinged, with a great nose, filled with life. Lemons, flowers, minerals, and slate on the nose and in the mouth. It sparkles.

Hamburger and Hot Dog Wines

"My question is what to serve with a basic hot dog and hamburger cookout. In the past we've had a yummy, inexpensive Rosé d'Anjou, which is a favorite summer wine of mine, but I was considering branching out. Our constant quest is to get the best wine we can find for under $10 a bottle, and we're giddy if we find something we like for closer to $6 or $7."

Lauren Keller, Kalamazoo, Michigan

Most of the time our summer meals aren't in Central Park and don't include grilled eggplant wrapped around ricotta cheese. Most of the time, instead, we're having hamburgers, hot dogs, or grilled chicken or fish, maybe by the pool. As Ms. Keller points out, rosé wines are great for summer. As she also points out, few people want to spend big bucks on simple summer wines. Our own feeling is that there should be a place for wine in that big tub of ice at your feet, right there along with the twelve different kinds of beer.

SPANISH ROSÉ

Fine-wine grapes have colorless juice; the purple skins give red wines their color. Rosé wines are made by leaving the clear juice in contact with the dark skins for just a short time (except in Champagne, where most pink bubbly is made by blending a little red wine with the white wine, but that's another story—see "Valentine's Day"). In the best rosés, this doesn't just add color but something more. When we buy a rosé, we're looking for a wine that will be perfect for a summer picnic—refreshing, dry, and light, with some of the body of a red and the easy drinkability of a light white. Too many Americans think of rosé wines as sweet and simple because those of us of a certain age grew up with Mateus and Lancers, the simple, inexpensive Portuguese rosés in the cool bottles. Also, Americans tend to drink American wine, and many rosés made in the United States are, well, sweet and simple. There are exceptions, of course, rosé wines with real character. Look for Toad Hollow "Eye of the Toad," Baron Herzog Rosé of Cabernet Sauvignon, Bonny Doon Vin Gris de Cigare, Iron Horse Rosé de Pinot Noir, and Robert Sinskey Vin Gris of Pinot Noir. Especially be on the lookout for small-production rosé from smaller wineries, such as Beckmen Vineyards Grenache Rosé and Gargiulo Vineyards Rosato di Sangiovese.

France produces some outstanding rosé wines. Our very favorite rosé, for instance, is Château Grande Cassagne from Costières de Nîmes in the Languedoc region. Ms. Keller is right about Rosé d'Anjou. Not only that, but excellent rosés are arriving in the United States these days from Greece, Italy, and many other countries, made from grapes ranging from Cabernet Sauvignon to Xynomavro. If you really want to see what's possible with rosé, be a little adventurous and try one you've never seen, maybe from a country you never associated with rosé. Spain, for instance. Spanish wines are coming on strong these days, from good old Rioja to extraordinary Ribera del Duero and many others. Getting more attention, amid the crush of all of these Spanish wines, are rosés, often made from the Garnacha grape, which is the Spanish name for Grenache. To us, they are the most consistently satisfying rosés on the shelves, and they usually cost under $10.

Unlike the flabby, simple rosés most of us grew up with, good rosé has enough acid to make it a good food wine and enough tannin—from the red grape skins — to give it a little bit of backbone. This is what we enjoy about rosés from Spain. They're refreshing enough to drink at the beach, well balanced enough to enjoy with a fine picnic, and interesting enough to think about — if you really want to. It's impossible to know which Spanish rosé you might find at your store. As long as it's young and fresh, it'll be hard to go wrong. Here are four rosés from Spain that we've enjoyed year after year. Our tasting notes on them (all from the 2001 vintage except the Vega Sindoa, from the 2002 vintage) will give you some idea why we enjoy these wines so much. These are good with all kinds of summer foods: poached salmon, chicken curry, even barbecued ribs. Most of these cost less than $10.

Vega Sindoa, Bodegas Nekeas (Navarra). Our favorite. It's tart, clean, and crisp, with a very serious nose, good acids, and a hint of tannin for structure. Beautifully balanced and surprisingly austere for a rosé. Anyone who thinks rosé can't be "real wine" needs to taste this. It's real wine, proud to be pink.

Enate Rosado (Somontano). This has a lovely, deep cranberry color. It's filled with lively, fresh fruit, with hints of strawberries and a nice tartness. It has plenty of zingy acids to make it great with roast chicken, hamburgers, or hearty bean casseroles.

Gran Feudo, Bodegas Julián Chivite (Navarra). Easy, pleasant, and crisp, with an earthy fruit taste. This is lighter bodied than most, making it particularly delightful and maybe the best of the bunch to sip by itself.

Marqués de Cáceres (Rioja). A deep blush color, with a little bit of effervescence, almost like a pink sparkler. It seems a bit sweet, but it's so pleasant, friendly, and vibrant that it hardly matters. Perfect for that big tub of ice filled with summer drinks.

WHITE ZINFANDEL

In the Introduction, we wrote about Warrant Officer La'Quitta Joseph, who dreamed of white Zinfandel while serving in the army on the front lines of the war in Iraq. White Zinfandel is particularly appropriate for the

Fourth of July because, as we mentioned in the Thanksgiving chapter, Zinfandel is a special American grape. Until the 1970s, Zinfandel was red, just red. American winemakers had a great deal of fun with real Zinfandel, making Portlike late-harvest Zinfandels, zesty hamburger Zinfandels, and classy, structured Zinfandels. Then Sutter Home popularized white Zinfandel, which is made like other rosés with the colorless juice left in contact with the dark grape skins for just enough time to develop a blush color. Sutter Home left it slightly sweet and made a fortune with it. White Zinfandel was the single most popular "varietal" wine in the U.S. until 1994, when it was overtaken by Chardonnay. Over the years, we have found most white Zinfandel sweet and simple, but not all of them.

Here's our message to Ms. Joseph and to all Americans—and there are millions of them—who like white Zin: don't be embarrassed about what you like. At the same time, don't think you have to settle for adult Kool-Aid just because you're drinking a simple, inexpensive pink wine. Some white Zinfandels are better than others. Be sure to get the youngest you can find. All of these will cost less than $10. By the way, when we last caught up with Ms. Joseph, she had returned to Fort Benning, Georgia, and was about to leave for a three-year assignment in Hawaii and probably more service in Kuwait. During her return to the States, she visited her first winery, St. James Winery in Missouri, and she stretched a bit, growing fond of red Zinfandel, the real thing. "I really like the taste of it," she told us.

De Loach Vineyards (California). Our favorite, year after year. Refreshing, fruity, and not too sweet, with a nice lemony kick. Crisp. It's so clean it almost tastes like a good white wine. We've always felt that this white Zinfandel, uniquely, could be included in a tasting of fine rosés from around the world. Good with summer foods. Unfortunately, De Loach, like quite a few California wineries, filed for bankruptcy in 2003, and its name, inventory, and some of its vineyards were sold. Its new owners say they will continue to produce De Loach white Zinfandel. (2001)

Ernest & Julio Gallo "Twin Valley Vineyards" (California). Simple and somewhat sweet—it tastes and even looks something like cranberry juice—but it's so clean and pleasant that it's hard not to like, especially because it's only about $4 or $5. (2002)

Montevina Wines (Amador County). Very pink. Light, pleasant, and clean. Refreshing, though it doesn't have much real-fruit taste. (2001)

Vendange Wine Cellars (California). Like a very pleasant fruit wine. Quite fresh but a little thick, with charming flavors. Chill well. Dottie felt that if this were frozen, it would make a really good sorbet. (2001)

Weinstock Cellars (California). Always good. Cotton-candy nose, but a makes-you-smile wine, with lemony tartness and real fruit. Crisp and bright, with interesting kiwi and lemon tastes. Quite fresh, with real fruit." Kosher (2002)

PINOT GRIGIO/PINOT GRIS

Think back, way back—to, say, 1990. Way back then, can you imagine anyone pulling a bottle of Italian Pinot Grigio out of the ice-filled tub in the backyard? The rise of this wine in the American marketplace has been stunning. In 2001, Pinot Grigio became the most popular imported wine in the United States, and it did this in the face of a surge in red-wine drinking in America. Pinot Grigio is a grape, the same grape as Pinot Gris, which is grown in many parts of the world, but Italy made Pinot Grigio famous, with pleasant quaffing wines, especially from the regions of Friuli-Venezia Giulia and Trentino–Alto Adige. For many people, Pinot Grigio became an antidote to heavy, slightly sweet, and ponderous Chardonnays. Indeed, Pinot Grigio can be a great summer wine, but too many have become lemon bombs, highly acidic and devoid of fruit flavors. There's no reason you have to settle for that. There are some Italian Pinot Grigios on shelves that have real fruit and real taste and are genuinely fun to drink.

American winemakers, naturally, have rushed to get on the Pinot Grigio bandwagon, though their wines are sometimes called Pinot Grigio and sometimes Pinot Gris (especially in Oregon). In general, we have found that

American wines labeled Pinot Gris are heavier and fuller than American wines labeled Pinot Grigio. A really good Pinot Gris has a little bit of the weight, mouthfeel, and earthiness of a red wine with a lively, sometimes prickly taste that offers the excitement of a good summer white. Some remind us of melons, tangerines, and apples, with an interesting earthy taste that adds character and complexity. The wines from Oregon, especially, seem better designed for food than by-the-glass sipping. Those called Pinot Grigio seem designed to compete head-on with the wines of Italy, light and easy.

Here are some good Italian Pinot Grigios and American Pinot Gris/ Pinot Grigios. The Italians tend to cluster around $10, while the Americans are often a few dollars more. Buy them young.

ITALIAN PINOT GRIGIO

Borgo Magredo (Friuli Grave). Crisp and slightly lemony, with hints of minerals and melons that give it interesting complexity and layers of flavor. (2001)

Ca'Montini "L'Aristocratico" (Trentino). We like this every year. It's quite ripe, with fruit-bowl flavors. Clean, refreshing, and simply delightful and easy to drink. (2002)

Conte Placido (Delle Venezie). Nice minerals, not overly acidic, with very ripe fruit and a little melon. This is more than just a nice quaff. It's fruity instead of lemony, with a fullness about it. (2002)

Forchir (Friuli Grave). Real wine with real taste. Full of layered fruit, especially melons, yet restrained and almost austere. This is not just a lemony concoction, but a wine of some weight and gravitas—a surprise. (2001)

Frattina (Lison-Pramaggiore). Perfumed and attractively fruity. Quite round, with a lovely, tart finish and a bit of weight. (2002)

Pasqua "Vigneti del Sole" (Delle Venezie). Crisp, fruity, and refreshing, with some serious "stuff" in the finish. A nice hint of minerals gives it grounding. (2002)

Peter Zemmer (Alto Adige). A reliable name to look for. Tastes like good fruit, with harmonious acids. Excellent with food. (2002)

Ruffino "Lumina del Borgo" (Venezia Giulia). Nicely fruity and fun, with a little weight and a hint of earth to give it extra texture. (2001)

AMERICAN PINOT GRIS

Adelsheim Vineyard Pinot Gris (Oregon). Always a fine name in Oregon wine. This is prickly and dry, rich with melon fruit but with an elegant restraint. (2001)

Estancia Estates Pinot Grigio (California). Some nice minerals and good fruit, with tastes of melons, pineapple, and other tropical fruits. No real depth, but fun and easy to drink. Chill well; it gets crisper as it gets colder. (2003)

Firesteed Cellars Pinot Gris (Oregon). Reliable and reasonably priced. A very attractive honeydew-melon nose. The taste is almost chewy with fruit, but with plenty of rich earth, too. It tastes like ripe grapes, and layers of minerals and earth give it a special complexity. Perfect pitch. (2000)

Gallo of Sonoma Pinot Gris "Reserve" (Sonoma Coast). Lovely, lively grape tastes. Clean, vibrant fruit, with some minerals at the back. (2001)

J Wine Co. Pinot Gris (Russian River Valley). Light and summery, like Pinot Grigio: Exuberantly fruity, with a riot of fruit flavors and nice mouthfeel and weight. Not much nuance, but utterly charming. (2002)

Rancho Zabaco Winery Pinot Gris "Reserve" (Sonoma Coast). Melon flavors and a real brightness that makes it stand out. (2001)

Sokol Blosser Winery (Willamette Valley). Refreshing and tart. It has real character and vibrant tastes. Always a good name to look for in Oregon wine. (2000)

JUG WHITE

Jug wines. Makes you sort of grimace and smile at the same time, doesn't it? Maybe that's because many of us have had jug wines that seemed to leave a bad taste in our mouths for days—and many of us have had jug wines that were charming, whether at a barbecue on a hot day, a picnic table in Italy, or, as in our case, the long-lost Greek restaurant down a few steps on MacDougal Street in Greenwich Village. We'd order a carafe of wine and a large plate of mixed appetizers as our only course. The lone waitress would go into the back and fill a carafe from a giant bottle of anonymous Greek wine. It couldn't have been better.

People have different definitions of jug wines. It's not the size of the bottle alone, because many of the world's greatest wines come in big bottles (although, of course, those aren't called jugs, but "large-format bottles"). Some wine-industry experts consider a jug wine anything that costs less than $3 for 750 milliliters, a regular-size bottle. Some people define jug wines as generic wines, such as "American Chablis," as opposed to wine with any varietal designation such as Chardonnay. We once conducted a tasting of jug wines and decided to define jug wines broadly as any wine that cost $7.99 or less for a 1.5-liter bottle (equal to two regular bottles) or the equivalent price for an even larger bottle. We chose $7.99 because that was the point at which we could find enough for a broad tasting. We understand that some people say a wine must be cheaper than that to really qualify as a jug wine, and some consider even more expensive wines jug wines. One man's jug is another man's magnum. The fifty we bought came from all over the world—France, Italy, Bulgaria, and other countries. Most were from California. Despite the different labels, many of the California jug wines are made by the same three giant companies: Gallo (Carlo Rossi, Livingston, Gossamer Bay, among others), the Wine Group, which is best known for Franzia (also Glen Ellen, Corbett Canyon, Foxhorn), and Canandaigua (Inglenook, Nathanson Creek, Vendange, and many more). We bought wines with varietal designations and with names that mean absolutely nothing, such as "Rhine Wine" and "American Chablis." It's not at all clear what is really in these wines, and we weren't reassured by labels for Carlo Rossi Chablis and Rhine that said in red letters, "100% grape wine." Our bar was simply this: if we were hosting a summer barbecue and inviting the neighborhood, which of these wines would be good enough to serve to that large number of friends?

Too often, the wines simply lacked any taste of actual grapes. They tasted mostly like oily lemon water, perhaps with a little sugar thrown in. We understand that these are made in industrial quantities—we imagined many of them waiting to be bottled in big tanks in New Jersey that we previously thought held oil—but even wine made in bulk can be made with some care. They should taste good. Too many of these didn't. We'd certainly avoid Chardonnay, especially from the United States. The ones we sampled were almost uniformly lacking in taste, though we did like a Chilean Chardonnay from Concha y Toro, which had real character. The French whites we tasted were also uniformly disappointing. Overall, the best type of wine in this tasting was Sauvignon Blanc, and we'd urge you to gravitate to that varietal when you look for a jug wine. These were our favorites, and here's the bottom line: even jug wines should taste like wine, like they came from real fruit. In an era of wine surplus, there are good deals even on inexpensive wine. Don't settle for less than good wine, at any price.

Sutter Home Winery "Signature" Sauvignon Blanc (California). Our favorite. Vibrant, fresh nose. Real wine. Pleasant and easy to drink, with some varietal character. It's light, but quite refreshing, with some lemony acids. Clean, a little juicy, and mouthwatering. (2001)

Concha y Toro "Frontera" Chardonnay (Valle Central, Chile). Nicely made, with a hint of green pepper and some crispness. Much drier than most. In a universe of sweet jug wines, this stands out as special. (2001)

Ernest & Julio Gallo "Twin Valley Vineyards" Sauvignon Blanc (California). Pretty nice nose, with some peaches and grass. Creamy, a bit like a junior Chardonnay. A bit sweet, but pleasant and easy to drink, with enough acids for food. (Nonvintage)

Livingston Cellars Chablis Blanc (California). "Chablis Blanc" can mean anything, but in this case, fortunately, it means a pretty good wine: grapey and slightly sweet, but easy-to-drink, with hints of kiwi, grapefruit, and peaches. Light and pleasant, and it tastes like grapes. (Nonvintage)

Nathanson Creek Cellars Sauvignon Blanc (California). Pleasant and clean, with a hint of varietal taste. Easy to sip. Well chilled at the beach, this would be a winner, and it would also be good with some food, like cold pork or anything with pesto. (2000)

CHILLED REDS

Even in summer, some people prefer red wines, and, to be honest, that's what we prefer with grilled hamburgers, even on the hottest days, although many reds are too challenging for the dog days, and room temperature is just too darn hot during the summer. That's when we turn to chilled reds. There, we've said it: "chilled reds." If you think it's gauche to drink chilled red wine, think again. Stephen Brook, in his book *Bordeaux: People, Power and Politics,* recalls a giant event in Bordeaux: "In September 2000 the Fête des Vendanges was held at Château La Louvière, a splendid neoclassical pile in the Pessac-Léognan district. The festivities began towards the end of a very hot Saturday afternoon. . . . Amidst this beauty and grandeur, we took our places and were served by hundreds of waiters streaming out of five separate kitchens at the same moment. And how did the team of 150 sommeliers manage to serve dozens of magnums of red La Louvière suitably chilled for the warm evening?" If chilled reds are good enough for a fine red at the château itself, they're certainly good enough for our patio.

Here are some wines that are terrific for summer if they're chilled. We don't mean ice cold, but three or four hours in the refrigerator—putting their temperature somewhere below cellar temperature—will make them more refreshing summer beverages. If they get too cold, big deal; in the heat, they will warm up quickly enough. The types of reds that work best for us at cooler temperatures are those with berrylike fruitiness and youth. Think about how a just-picked wild blackberry or raspberry tastes on a hot summer day. The juice of the berries is light and pure and exuberantly fresh, bursting with flavor.

Beaujolais. Beaujolais is our all-time favorite summer red because it makes no demands on us—it's simple and easy. It goes with a wide variety of summer foods, from salads to ribs, but it's also good as a sipping wine. It can be served at various temperatures, too. It's hard to beat the ubiquitous Georges Duboeuf Beaujolais-Villages, which is particularly fetching when chilled on a hot day—and it usually costs about $7.

Rioja. When we lived in Miami, where it's always hot, we drank a great deal of Rioja, from Spain. Its fairly light body makes it especially good on a hot day, and it can take a little chill. It tends to be vibrant, sometimes tart, and pretty spicy in its own right—that's one reason it takes well to chilling—and it can make summer meals fun. There are great, expensive Riojas (and we'd never serve those below cellar temperature), but for summer fun, we prefer the less expensive, widely available Riojas such as Marqués de Riscal, which often costs around $10. For a more complete list, see "Thanksgiving."

Lighter Pinot Noir. There are few better pairings on a hot summer day than cold poached salmon and a cool, light Pinot Noir, especially a fruity one from Oregon. Many Pinots are weighty and very serious. We avoid those in the summer. But the lighter ones are better when it's hot, and they also happen to cost less. Some to look for: Clos du Bois and Napa Ridge (our two most consistent favorites), Echelon, Erath, Firesteed, Kendall-Jackson, Meridian.

Shiraz. The idea of a cold Shiraz—the big, chewy, peppery wine of Australia—does not sound very attractive, we admit. But less expensive, less weighty Shiraz, such as Yellow Tail and Banrock Station, are quite good cold, especially with a very rare hamburger from the grill. Chilling focuses the wine's ripe-berry fruit into a winning, makes-you-smile summer drink. Some other names: Black Opal, Bulletin Place, Lindemans "Bin 50."

And for Elegant Summer Parties

Finally, we know that summer is not entirely about simplicity. Sometimes summer means a fancy, outdoor Gatsbyesque party. For that you want something elegant and special. What to do? Our advice is to go with a white Bordeaux. While Bordeaux is best known for its great reds, a good deal of white wine is made there, too. Much of it is simple and undistinguished, but some is unique and delicious. Here's how to find a good one: Look for a white from Graves (pronounced Grahv) or, even more specifically, Pessac-Léognan (Pess-sac Lay-own-yawn). The wines have a complex combination of character and drinkability. They're generally made by blending Sauvignon Blanc and Sémillon. These are traditional blending partners; the Sauvignon Blanc adds life, juiciness, and excitement, while the Sémillon adds weight and seriousness. These wines are filled with tastes of minerals and all sorts of fruit, with a clean, lingering finish. They also get better as they warm, so they'll be fine as they warm outside during the party. Fine white Bordeaux wines improve as they age, so don't worry about the vintage. These will generally cost less than $25, but they're not very popular, so sometimes wine stores will sell them at great prices. One wine to look for is Blanc de Lynch-Bages, the white wine from the famous Château Lynch-Bages. It's not from Graves, but it's our very favorite white Bordeaux. It usually costs more than $25, but if you see it, grab it. Here are our notes from the 2001: "Lychee and kiwi. Bright, fruity, acidic yet almost dusty quality. Walks the right line down every taste, with no taste more obvious than another. Minerals, fruit, an elegant taste that's both crisp and bold, both filled with fruit yet quite serious, easy to drink yet also majestic. Endless finish, with many fruits, from grapefruit to apricot. Complex and earthy. Sweet-tart, with an almost bright shock of fruit. Smoky and a great counterweight to chilled lobster or scallops." Ready for a white Bordeaux? Here are some to look for from Graves:

Benjamin de Vieux Château Gaubert (Graves). Nutmeg nose. Light yet fruity, with lemon-nutmeg tastes. A bit of alcohol on the finish. (2001)

Château Carbonnieux (Pessac-Léognan). A perennial favorite and one of the more widely available Graves, so you should be able to get a couple of cases of this for the event. It's golden. There's earth, minerals, and lemon and melon in the very luscious nose. The taste is just as good, but nicely restrained. Classy wine. (1999)

Château Coucheroy (Pessac-Léognan). Jazzy, herbal, and fresh, with a little bit of brown sugar, custardlike tastes to give it some weight. This is a serious white wine—and we see it for $9.99 from time to time, which is a steal. (2001)

Château La Louvière (Pessac-Léognan). Intense and nicely lemony. Toasty and filled with fruit. Lovely and elegant. It reminds us a bit of a very light crème brûlée. (2000)

Château Olivier (Pessac-Léognan). Rich and classy, with some butterscotch and lemon. Mouth coating and complex, yet easy to drink on a hot day. (1998)

Clos Floridene (Graves). Bursting with pears, lemons, kiwi, and lychee, with an underpinning of minerals and real richness. Dottie calls this "a fancy white, suitable for a fancy dinner." Beautifully made and serious. This would be a real treat for anyone who likes wine. (1998)

Château Bouscaut (Pessac-Léognan). Very serious wine, sweet with fruit yet with weight and character. Clean and vibrant, but its extra weight and complexity—with caramel and almond tastes—make it a bit edgy and maybe just a little bit risky for the dinner party. (1998)

Vacations

Trains, Planes, Ships— and Disney World

"It was October 1999, the last evening of a weeklong Rhine cruise that was a once-in-a-lifetime trip that I took my father on. During the previous couple of days we had just sampled some remarkable German wines. I asked the waiter on the ship that night for their best red wine so that I could cap off a memorable week with my aging father with a truly memorable wine. I naturally expected French, but they instead suggested a German red wine from Assmannshausen because it had just come in, and told me to trust them. And at just that moment as we were rounding the bend on the Rhine River, a big sign on a hillside that said Assmannshausen came into view. I figured that this was definitely a sign to try the wine, so we did. We were both astounded with the flavor. I was pleased that I had succeeded better than I had thought in procuring a very memorable wine for my father. Indeed, we ordered it several more times the following week during our continued travels, and each time we had the same feeling of quiet satisfaction as we sipped the wine. This wine occupies a special place in my heart. I have never found it again." —JOHN VESTER, WESTPORT, CONNECTICUT

Vacations can be a treacherous time for wine drinking. You're often in unfamiliar places, at the mercy of unfamiliar wine shops and restaurants with strange lists and sometimes even stranger customs. Bizarre things can happen. We were once at Walt Disney World at one of those "character dinners" where Goofy and Pluto and their cohorts drop by the table to play with the kids. We ordered a nice bottle of Chardonnay, which was sitting on the table when Mickey Mouse came by, jovial as ever. As Mickey signed Media and Zoë's autograph books, John got up and prepared to snap a picture. Suddenly, Mickey began waving his arms furiously at John. Since Mickey doesn't speak, we had no idea what was going on. Finally, an assistant ran over and explained that Mickey could not be pictured in a photograph with wine. To this day, one of our very favorite pictures from a vacation is our photo of Mickey frantically waving his arms at John and trying to block the view of the wine.

And get this one: John was once flying on Continental Airlines from Newark to San Diego. The airline somehow lost his reservation and, to make it up to him, gave him a seat in first class. Hmmm, John thought, free wine, and not the stuff in the tiny screwcap bottles that they apparently store above the engine. After the plane took off, a flight attendant asked if John would like something to drink. After the bruising battle to get on the plane, John said that he'd love a glass of red wine. The flight attendant disappeared for a long time, and John heard all sorts of commotion in the galley. Finally, another flight attendant came out. "We're so sorry," she said, "but they forgot to give us a corkscrew. We can't open the bottle." Then referring to the first flight attendant, she said, "He just broke a bottle trying to get it open for you." John asked to see the bottle anyway, hoping it would be something bad, but, unfortunately, it was a very good Cabernet Sauvignon from Australia called Deakin Estate. (For the record, the Federal Aviation Administration says passengers may drink only wine that is served by flight attendants. The regulations are silent about who brings the wine aboard.)

Despite all of this, we hear all the time from people like Mr. Vester who have had the greatest wines of their lives on vacation. One reason for this, we figure, is simply that they're relaxed on vacation. They're open to new experiences and everything seems better—the water is bluer, the food is more delicious, the people nicer. Still, there are ways to increase the chance that you'll have a memorable wine experience on your next vacation, whether you're on a cruise, a train, or a plane. Here are some lessons we have learned on cruises, on trains, on trips to Disney World—and that our readers have learned all over the world.

1: Do Your Homework

We don't overplan our vacations. The whole point of a vacation, after all, is relaxation and getting away from schedules and must-dos. But a small amount of planning can make a big difference in your wine experiences. When we were taking a cruise that stopped in Puerto Rico many years ago, we simply asked a friend from Puerto Rico where we could go to lunch that might have a good wine list. He recommended a place called Alioli, and we still remember it vividly. Dottie had the best squid-ink black pasta she has ever had, there were rich ladies-who-lunch all around us who were fascinating to watch, and we had two bottles—we were young—of an outstanding Saint-Véran from France.

These days, the Internet is an excellent tool to help with preparations. Planning for a Disney cruise with Media and Zoë, we saw that we had a stop in Nassau for one evening. We don't think of Nassau as a natural wine destination, and we wouldn't expect to have a transcendent wine experience in the Bahamas. Great fun in the sun, yes, but not great wine. Still, we went to a search engine and plugged in "wine and Nassau and Bahamas." The third item that showed up was graycliff.com, which said that the Graycliff Hotel in Nassau had the largest wine cellar in the Caribbean, more than 180,000 bottles. It added: "If you're looking for something special, chances are it's here," noting, for instance, "1911 Latour at $3,100." To be honest, we're never looking for a $3,100 bottle of wine, but, still, we figured this stop alone would make the whole trip worthwhile. We made reservations.

When the time came, we left the ship and went into central Nassau, where Dottie supervised Media's shopping for clothes and Zoë's searching for a carved coconut head of a pirate with an eye patch and a bandana. With them launched, John dropped by the Graycliff to check out the wine list before dinner (always a good idea, if time permits, when you're going to a restaurant with a big list). The wine list! It was eighty-four pages long, with a table of contents and an index. There were wines going back to the mid–nineteenth century, treasures like a 1961 Krug Champagne ($690) and an 1875 Château d'Yquem ($17,500). The prices for less lofty wines, too, were awesome, with few bottles listed under $100. At the restaurant that night, we met the very knowledgeable sommelier, Garry Parks. John surprised

Dottie with the wine he had chosen earlier: "R," the hard-to-find dry white wine made by Château Rieussec, the great producer of Sauternes, the dessert wine. This was from the 1983 vintage and was $84. It seemed like it would be a good aperitif—lovely and light and probably too old to stand up to food. We don't often see old white Bordeaux, so it was a treat. To us, as white Bordeaux wines get older, they acquire a certain quiet majesty. "R" is made from the same kind of grapes that make sweet Sauternes, primarily Sauvignon Blanc and Sémillon. The wine was terrific—clearly old, with hints of caramel, which made its kinship to Sauternes that much clearer. Although dry, it had the same soulful fruit tastes, the same kind of weight. "Voluptuous and rich," we wrote in our notes during dinner. "Sensuous, with lots of earth, grapefruit, star fruit, and wood." It was the kind of wine we could taste for a long time in our throats because it left a lingering cloud of taste.

We followed this with a 1989 Chablis Grand Cru Les Clos from Moreau, for $98. We don't often see Chablis that old, and since this was a fine year from a fine producer, we figured it would be in good shape. Bad news: It was in such great shape that it hadn't aged nearly enough for our taste. It was light and crisp, with traditional Chablis steeliness, minerals, and lemon. It no longer had its youthful zest but hadn't yet developed the depth that we expected age would bring. Amazing. Was it great with the stone crab claws? You bet. This meal, and the wines, turned a short stop on a cruise into an experience we will always remember.

2: BYOB

E specially if you are going on a trip that will keep you confined for some time, such as a train or a cruise, carefully pack some bottles of wine into your luggage. We have been traveling on long-distance Amtrak trains since the bedrooms were those marvelous Art Deco sardine cans, all shiny metal, with fold-up sinks in the bathroom. In 1979, we honeymooned on a train. It's important to carry on plenty of your own wine—we always take Champagne—along with a big ice bucket. Similarly, when we take cruises, we always pack some wine into our suitcases. Some ships have excellent wine lists, but when we're sitting on the porch at night when it's a little chilly or during the day when it's hot, we want a special wine of our own. Marc Lerner, a podiatrist from Red Bank, New Jersey, has been a serious wine collector since 1977, and he has an excellent cellar. When he took a cruise on a Celebrity ship, he had read that he could bring special bottles aboard. So he and his wife, Emily, took along to share with their three grown sons at dinner—get this—a 1982 Château Pichon-Lalande, a 1983 Château Lafite Rothschild, and a 1989 Château Pichon-Baron. They paid a corkage fee of $12 for each bottle. "The boys are into wine as much as we are, and we all looked forward to them with great anticipation," Dr. Lerner told us. How were they? Fabulous. Are you surprised?

Luis C. Ortega, manager of corporate beverage service for Celebrity Cruises, told us that while the company prefers that vacationers purchase its wines, it's happy to open their special bottles for $12 and has no established limit to the number of those special wines people may bring aboard. Bob Midyette, manager of Fleet Beverage Operations for Royal Caribbean International's nineteen cruise ships, said that Royal Caribbean limits the number of bottles diners can bring to the table to one or two for the duration of the cruise and typically requests that the wines be items that Royal Caribbean does not carry. Its corkage fee is also $12 per bottle.

Bob Dickinson, president and CEO of Carnival Cruise Lines and a renowned lover and collector of wine, told us he welcomes passengers who want to bring special bottles with them aboard the cruise line's twenty ships. "I know from my hobby how much people who are into wine really love it. I'm in the happiness business. People enjoy a week or two away from the madding crowd. Frequently people will pick a date for a cruise to celebrate a birthday, an anniversary, whatever." He added: "We're just trying to promote the idea that you can go on a cruise vacation, and you shouldn't have to suffer if you enjoy drinking rare wines or are used to drinking older wines." Carnival's corkage fee is $10. On the Disney Cruise Line, the corkage fee is $15.

Even if you don't take along a suitcase full of wine on a ship or a train, think about taking along one single bottle to open as soon as you reach your cabin or your hotel room. If your wine is white, get some ice right away, plop the bottle into the bucket, add water, and, ten minutes later, open it up. If it's red, just open and pour. The plain old water glasses will be fine, and the wine will really make you feel like you're on vacation. (Ideally, pack the wine in your carry-on. That way, if your bags are late or lost, you'll have the wine when you want it most, cooling your heels until things get right.) The first time we went to Disney World with Media and Zoë, we took along a bottle of Château Montrose 1979, a fine Bordeaux. As soon as we could, we opened the bottle, stood on the balcony overlooking the Magic Kingdom, felt the warm Florida breeze, and sipped under the stars. To this day, it's one of the best bottles of wine we've ever tasted. Was it the wine or the moment? Who cares?

3: Expand Your Definition of "Local Wine"

It's a cliché, of course, that wherever you are, you should drink the local wine. That's true, whether it's Tuscany or North Carolina, but we mean something broader than that. Many wines available in one place aren't available in another, and that's "local" enough for us. We love visiting the Inner Harbor in Baltimore, and we often end up at Phillips, a huge, crowded, touristy restaurant that always has some nice wine surprise. Way back in 1998, the special wine of the day was James River White from Williamsburg Winery for $16.95. Our waiter, Jim, shocked that we knew that Williamsburg Winery is in Virginia, said: "Look, if you like that, you've got to try their Chardonnay." The Chardonnay, a 1994 for $21.95, wasn't quite big enough for our taste, but it was beautifully made and likely perfect for people who like their Chardonnays more restrained. In the next few years, Virginia wines became all the rage, but we were ahead of the curve because of that dinner. (And, of course, we've also enjoyed wines from Maryland, such as Boordy.)

In the Bahamas on one of our cruises, we hoped to get some wine for our cabin, but the selection in the downtown shops was awful. We dropped into the then-new Atlantis resort on Paradise Island, which was quite empty. There was a little wine shop nearby, so we checked it out. To our surprise, the shop was filled with fascinating wines from South Africa. Why? Because, it turned out, the developer of Atlantis was from South Africa. We picked up a sparkling wine called Graham Beck Brut and a Chenin Blanc—which is called Steen in South Africa—from a large winery called KWV. The Steen was delightful—it tasted very much like an inexpensive German wine, flowery, simple, and fun—and the Brut was outstanding. Blind, we might have guessed it was French, with a real hint of chalky soil. It was delicious on our porch.

Remember that local doesn't just mean local wine but local wine experiences. For instance, if you're from Missouri, check out a wine bar in New York, as Deborah Maltby of Liberty, Missouri, did:

"A few weeks ago my family was staying in a hotel on the East Side of New York City for a short vacation, and at dinnertime one evening we wandered into a wine bar, Le Bateau Ivre on 51st Street. We like to make dinner out of a series of small plates, whether tapas or mezes, or, in this case, mostly tartines. We also like to try a few wines by the glass. When I wanted a dry white wine, the server brought a wonderful Chablis which just exploded in my mouth. I still haven't seen any Chablis here. I'll look in Kansas City."

4: Look Around

John's father loved to fish but never actually caught anything. For Christmas one year, we gave him a cartoon that showed a man in a boat, his line in the water. The water all around his boat is dense with fish—except for a blank space around his hook. Wine is like that. There is probably really good wine all around you, but you have to be willing to spend just a little bit of time looking for it. Disney World is a great example. We first visited Disney World in February 1974, and we now take Media and Zoë every year. So we are qualified to say this: there are great wine experiences waiting for you at Disney World—but you have to look for them. First the bad news: Disney World's basic "family dining" places have short wine lists with routine wines that are quite overpriced. The Cape May Café at the Yacht and Beach Club, for instance, has eighteen wines on its wine list—simple stuff that's way overpriced. Kendall-Jackson Chardonnay costs $36.00 a bottle, or $7.75 a glass. This is really a shame for a place that has an outstanding seafood buffet that cries out for a good glass of Chablis from France. But then there is the California Grill atop the Contemporary, with a very fine list—or rather, lists. The regular list has almost 100 wines, some quite unusual, and just about all of them are also available by the glass for one-fourth the price of a bottle. There's a reserve list with almost 100 more wines, really expensive and rare stuff, available only by the bottle.

Disney World says it has more sommeliers than any other company in the world, almost three hundred. Including the Disney Cruise Line, Disney World sells one *million* bottles of wine a year. We called John Blazon, manager of Beverage Standards for Walt Disney World, to talk about this. "In 1995, the California Grill jump-started our wine program by focusing on the dining experience to include wine, and it was well received," he told us. Disney World has fifty-two full-service table restaurants. For the restaurants there's a core 250-bottle wine list that's created from research on what's selling. "We look at sales figures and stay close to the trends," Mr. Blazon said. "When Pinot Grigio is pushing against Chardonnay, we understand that and are there to support it. We do it with blind tastings, with full support of suppliers, in October." All of the restaurants except the ten fanciest have to create their wine list from the core 250 bottles. The other ten—such as the California Grill and Jiko at Animal Kingdom, which has an all-South African list—can choose up to 40 percent of their wines from outside the core list. Because Disney World sells so much wine, wineries are eager to get on its lists, which means that some of its restaurants have all sorts of wines that we've never seen before. Some years ago, we spied something at the California Grill called Mason Sauvignon Blanc from California that was new to us. We loved it. Before long, Mason became quite famous, and once again, we were ahead of the game.

5: Don't Bring Preconceptions

If you are in Atlanta and there is a wine from Georgia on the list, don't skip it because you assume it's bad. If you were visiting Umbria, you'd try an Umbrian wine, right? Don't assume that your cruise ship has bad wine or is ripping you off. Celebrity Cruises, for instance, has a fun, broad, and eclectic wine list. Its regular list, which is standard for all nine of its ships, includes wines from France, Italy, Spain, California, Germany, Australia, Chile, and Greece. It includes nonalcoholic wines, dessert wines, and Port as well. There's also a reserve or extended list and a "rare vintage" wine list for the ships' specialty restaurants, plus an abbreviated list for the cruise lines' casual dining restaurants.

Aboard Royal Caribbean International's ship *Serenade of the Seas,* which we checked out for a few hours when it was docked in New York, there's a vibrant culture of wine. There's a Champagne bar, an elegant, welcoming space anchored by a gigantic bottle of Champagne specially made by Perrier-Jouët. (All but two ships have Champagne bars.) On a table outside the main casual dining area, stewards stand beside a table with wines that guests can order ahead of time so that when they enter the dining room the wines are waiting on the table. The wine list is interesting and approachable, with the wines by the bottle and by the glass carefully categorized according to varietal and style, including sections on "other whites" and "other reds," and dessert, kosher, and nonalcoholic wines. Prices are similar to those in landlocked restaurants, and, as with lists everywhere, diners are punished for refusing to leave their comfort zone: Kendall-Jackson Chardonnay, for instance, is $42, while more interesting, more unusual wines from all over the world are less (personally, the first thing we'd try is the Fairview Sauvignon Blanc from South Africa for $27).

The specialty restaurants, Chops and Portofino, have a good selection of high-end wines, from big names in California Cabernets to greats from Tuscany to top-drawer wines from Bordeaux. We wondered how wines are kept aboard a ship, so we peeked. In the temperature-controlled storage areas of the ship, there are two rooms, one for red wines and liquor and a cooler one for white wines and beer. Terrance D'Souza, the cellar master, showed us cases of wines from all over the world. He brought over his "baby" and carefully unwrapped the purple tissue paper covering it to unveil a 1993 Château Lafite Rothschild. There were cases of Opus One, the cult wine produced by the partnership of Robert Mondavi and the Rothschild family, legendary winemakers in France. In the room for white wines were cases of Giesen Sauvignon Blanc from New Zealand—we love that—and loads of different varietals from Coppola and Beringer. And, of course, white Zinfandel. "We could float this ship on white Zinfandel," Mr. Midyette told us. Way in the back, Mr. D'Souza leaned down to pat a stack of cases of Dom Pérignon. He explained that he doesn't keep a lot of the best stuff around because the vibrations aboard the ship cause breakage; they restock constantly.

Walking around this ship, we felt a strong sense that the cruise planners connect wine with being in the vacation mode. If they make it easy for people to have wine, people will. Even in the theater, each chair has a glass holder for people who want to sip while they watch a show. Before the show starts, waiters and waitresses even come around to take drink orders. Mr. Midyette told us Royal Caribbean's average ship offers a selection of 140 to 200 wines. Royal Caribbean's lists are amended "to include more European wines when we deploy ships to Europe, and we will include some popular northwestern selections when we deploy to Alaska and Canada." Royal Caribbean's huge ships *Navigator of the Seas* and *Mariner of the Seas* both have a wine bar called Vintages where guests can pay for a weeklong series of wine classes and special experiences, including an interactive game called "Wine Survivor." The game challenges guests to answer wine questions or per-form tasks that may be considered intimidating to the wine novice—open-ing a bottle of wine or Champagne, what to do with the cork, identifying the appellation of a wine, selecting a wine from the dining room wine list that complements a particular entree, pronouncing the names of wines cor-rectly, or distinguishing wines through blind tasting. The winner gets a bot-tle of wine and a "survivor" certificate. The selections include wines from all over the world, and we must say that we wish restaurants on land had such user-friendly lists. The list is carefully presented, with simple yet not patronizing descriptions of wines and grapes. The wines are offered by the bottle, by the glass, and by the two-ounce pour.

The wine list on Carnival, the world's largest cruise line, is interesting and well organized, helping diners by grouping wines under headings like "light, dry white wines," "blush and lightly sweet white wines," "light, fruitier red wines," "medium-bodied red wines," "full-bodied red wines," and so on. Some lists sport subheads like "From sweet to dry," or "Fruity with fewer tannins to full-bodied with heavier tannins." The wines are from all over the world, and the prices range from under $20 to $350. Carnival's wines-by-the-glass list has 32 selections on it, from Champagnes to dessert wines, and the regular list has 137 wines, including a selection of nonalcoholic wines. Like Royal Caribbean, Carnival tailors some wine lists to certain regions.

The Disney ships, the *Wonder* and the *Magic,* have a regular list, with wines that range from $22 for a white Zinfandel to a $70 Pomerol to a $170 Champagne; and a reserve list, with prices that range from $39 for a Zinfandel to $69 for a New Zealand Sauvignon Blanc to $399 for a famous Bordeaux. The lists feature wines from California, France, Italy, Germany, Australia, New Zealand, Hungary, Canada, Portugal, and Chile—not to mention Fess Parker's 100 Years of Magic Chardonnay for $38 in honor of the 100th anniversary of Walt Disney's birth (yes, that's Daniel Boone and Davy Crockett. He owns a winery in Santa Barbara County). Disney also offers passengers wine packages, one bottle for every night of their cruise from a special selection of wines. What a great idea. Imagine choosing your wines early in the trip and having them waiting for you every night at dinner. No muss, no fuss—no wine lists.

It's not just cruise ships. Even on trains, there are often very interesting wines and fun experiences. During one of our trips, on the *Southwest Chief* from Chicago to Los Angeles, several interesting wines were on the list. At dinner, with a perfectly done slab of baked fish and a pork chop in a cream sauce, we had an excellent Wild Horse Pinot Blanc from California (a good buy at $20) that our waiter opened with a flourish. "I don't get to do much wine service," he explained. In the club car, there was a very pleasant Castoro Cellars Cabernet Sauvignon ($5.50 for a half-bottle) from California. Brian Rosenwald, superintendent of passenger service for about half the system's trains and overseer of wine service for most of its trains, told us that wine sales doubled systemwide after the company retooled its lists in 2001, and sales continue to grow. With Amtrak eyeing its bottom line, the trains now offer wines only in the half-bottle size, which cuts down on waste and breakage but also limits the selection. Still, there's fun to be had: on one of our favorite trains, the *California Zephyr,* from Chicago to the San Francisco area, Mr. Rosenwald is taking advantage of the fact that wine is made in every state. At the train station in Palisade, the heart of Colorado's wine region, wineries have been invited to come aboard and conduct free wine tastings for passengers. "Our goal is to get all of them on,"

Mr. Rosenwald said. "Certainly very few people have had these wines, and the wineries have an opportunity to pour their wines for a fairly broad national and international customer base."

After the free tastings, passengers can buy the wines in the train's lounge and dining car. These tastings on the *Zephyr* are free and open to all adult passengers and usually are conducted in the dining car between lunch and dinner. Sometimes so many people are interested in the tastings that the staff conducts two shifts. Mr. Rosenwald wishes he could do the same thing with the wineries in Texas, as trains pass through that huge state. Heck, he'd like to have free tastings on all long-distance routes, particularly those that draw large numbers of leisure travelers, people who enjoy the experience of a train trip and aren't in a hurry.

The fabled *Coast Starlight*, which runs down the scenic West Coast—an absolutely beautiful ride—has a separate first-class lounge that seats fifty people. For that line, only sleeping-car passengers are invited to the complimentary tastings, Mr. Rosenwald said, adding, "I wish I had separate cars for all of the trains. We could have winemaker dinners." Travelers so loved a Riesling from Gainey Vineyard in Santa Barbara in a free tasting on the *Coast Starlight* a few years ago that Amtrak ended up selling ninety-one cases of it in one month, a record. Amtrak "welcomes customers who bring their own bottles because we know that it's often in association with a special occasion, so our corkage fee is zero," Mr. Rosenwald said. If you're traveling in a private bedroom and have brought your own wine, Amtrak is happy to provide ice buckets and glassware. We can confirm this from our own experience: on several trains, the only time the porter ever saw us was when he brought us food and ice and took away our empty Champagne bottles.

6: Don't Settle for What You See

Many places have special wines that aren't on the list. Sometimes there's a different list, a second compilation of treasures. It might be called the *reserve list* or be known by another name. Sometimes special wines are being saved under the counter for anyone interested enough to ask. Sometimes the list just hasn't been updated yet to reflect new additions. Especially in wine regions, both in the United States and overseas, it seems like there's always something native that only the locals know to ask for.

> *"In 1986 my wife and I took a one-week vacation in Provence, which was designed to permit us to eat in great restaurants. The first night was at L'Auberge du Père Bise and the second at L'Oustau de Beaumaniere in Baux. The night after we ate at Oustau we went to a small but excellent restaurant in Baux called La Riboto de Taven. After much discussion over the wine list, the sommelier suggested we try a special Côtes-du-Rhône, made by a friend or relative, which was not on the list. It was Château Fonsalette made by J. Reynaud. It was spectacular and, along with the very friendly people in the restaurant, made it a very special and memorable evening. My wife passed away in 1997, and so when I find it, I get a goose-bumps feeling as I re- member our great times together and especially one special night in Provence."*
>
> James K. Leslie, Chevy Chase, Maryland

7: Trust the Waiter

> *"We were living on St. Thomas, U.S. Virgin Islands. While a paradise to tourists, living and working on such a tiny island can sure put you through the grinder (not to mention the three hurricanes we survived in the two-year period in which we lived on the island). So we decided to get off the rock and recharge our batteries over a long weekend by taking in the various paradors of Puerto Rico. Paradors are government-sponsored B&Bs. They typically are in historically significant buildings and have a family-run feel about them. Our favorite was an old coffee plantation in the central mountains in a small town called Jayuya. It is here that my wife and I discovered Santa Helena Cabernet Sauvignon Seleccion del Directorio (Chile). It was recommended by our waiter in the parador's dining room. It was so good we had two bottles that night, as well as the next (even had them save a label for us). I remember the wine as filling*

*my mouth with black cherries and vanilla and as being an incredible
complement to the steak and pork we had each night. It really rejuvenated
our spirits. Ever since leaving Puerto Rico, I've been searching for that
wine."*

Shawn Russell, Atlanta

Yes, we know that waiters don't always steer you in the right direction. We
remember once dining at a restaurant in Italy and asking for any local wine.
The waiter brought us a wine from the other side of Italy. Well, we guess it
was local over there! Still, we have heard from readers again and again
about outstanding wine experiences because they were willing to let the
waiter be their guide, and we'd still recommend that—especially if you
can't really read the list.

8: Avoid the Usual; Take Risks

You probably do things on vacation you don't normally do—eat a
new kind of food, go scuba diving, take off your bikini top (well,
maybe not). You should have some fun with wine, too, by taking some
risks. On a hot day in Nassau, the girls were so exhausted by noon after
shopping for coconut heads, wrap skirts with fringes, and straw bags that
we walked into the first restaurant we saw, which turned out to be Greek.
That's right: we had Greek food for lunch in the Bahamas. The wine list
was spare, but there was a white we'd never seen before for $35, so we or-
dered it. Out swooshed a man with a strange-looking flask. "You've chosen
a great wine!" he enthused. "It's made by monks!" The wine, Agioritikos,
from the Tsantali winery, was quite good, and unusual—which is just what
we're looking for on vacation: to find and enjoy the unfamiliar. The Agioritikos had an interesting combination of crispness and a bit of musky
weight that made it pretty darn good with lamb and with a big Greek salad
piled high with great feta cheese. When we returned home, we looked up
the wine and, sure enough, it really is unusual and it really is made by
monks.

9: Love the One You're With

It's impossible for us to separate how a wine tastes from the circumstances under which we are drinking it. Anthony's, a restaurant on Paradise Island, had forty-five different rums — and three wines. This is the islands, the waitress explained. So we ordered "a bottle of the white," and out came a Glen Ellen Chardonnay, from California, a simple, common $7 bottle (for which we paid $18). But you know what? On a steamy night in the Bahamas, with spicy jerked chicken, grilled shrimp, and spare ribs, it was delicious — cold, crisp, refreshing, and informal. We can't imagine that any wine could have tasted better.

10: Prepare for Your Return

As Frank Sinatra sang, "It's very nice to go trav'ling, but it's oh so nice to come home." (Of course, he also sang, "It's very nice to just wander the camel route to Iraq.") You're bound to be both tired and excited — and maybe even a little vexed from some aspect of your travel — when you return home. That's why it's so important to have put a nice bottle of Champagne in the refrigerator before you left. Think about coming back and having a cold glass of bubbly waiting for you. Unpack later.

Visiting American Wineries | Should You Rinse the Glass?

"At Milat Vineyards in St. Helena, we nearly tripped over the Milats' big, dozing dog on our way through the front door. Mike Milat, one of the proprietors, gave us a warm greeting and, after pouring his wines for us, took us on a personal tour of the winemaking facilities. He helped Lumi climb into one of their big stainless-steel vats—beware their 2002 vintage!" —ERIC AND LUMI MCCLURE, NEW YORK CITY

B ack in 1997, before we were writing our column, the *Wall Street Journal* began producing a few pages of features that would later grow into *Weekend Journal.* Our bosses said they'd pay travel expenses for anyone who came up with a good feature about travel. We were going on a little family trip to a country inn in New Marlborough, Massachusetts, anyway, so we made this story proposal to our bosses: We'll take our trip just as we planned. We'll make no arrangements to see a winery or try to locate one beforehand. We'll see whether we accidentally run into a winery and, if we do, we'll write about it—and you'll pay for the trip. It seemed a good bet. Small, family-owned wineries are sprouting up all over the country. Wine is now made in more than three thousand wineries in all fifty states. If you're in Atlanta or Dallas or even Pleasantville, New York, just flip open the Yellow Pages, look under *Wineries* and you'll be surprised. We even once happened into now-shuttered Lafayette Vineyards in Tallahassee, Florida, which made, among many other wines, one called Blanc du Bois. On the North Fork of Long Island, there were no wineries open to the public until 1977; there were twelve when we first visited the North Fork in 1991; now there are more than twenty.

We felt confident, too, because of our accidental wine tourism on our previous trip, one winter earlier. Back then, in Connecticut, we saw a small sign that pointed to DiGrazia Vineyards. When we called later that day, the man who answered asked when we would like to visit—he said something about hospital rounds—and set up an appointment. An hour later we were sitting in a little winery with Dr. Paul DiGrazia, a longtime gynecologist who always dreamed of making wine. At some point he began living his dream, making wine in his garage—literally—in Brookfield. By the time we met him, Dr. DiGrazia had made wine into a profitable side business, producing about five thousand cases a year of everything from Honey Blush, a wine made without sulfites, to a "white port" called White Magnolia, selling 80 percent of it from his winery and the rest in wine shops throughout Connecticut.

Meeting people like Dr. DiGrazia—or, as the McClures discovered, Mr. Milat—is at least half the fun of visiting wineries. For almost thirty years we have arrived at wineries unannounced—and without letting on that we're journalists—and been greeted with smiles and much wine. That's because winemakers really enjoy pouring their creations and talking about them with people who actually care. So many of our fondest vacation memories surround wineries and winemakers: tasting bubblies with the late, great Hanns Kornell in Napa; watching hummingbirds in the backyard with Dorothy Nichelini; talking about hand-painted bottles with Pat Pugliese in Long Island; talking with Judy Jordan at J Vineyards & Winery in Sonoma about pairing wines and food and balancing work and family. At F. Teldeschi Winery in Sonoma, Dan Teldeschi, the owner-winemaker, could have talked to us all day about his powerful Zinfandels. No one beats the indefatigable, white-haired Jim Prager, at Prager Winery and Port Works in Napa, for wowing visitors with tales, tall and otherwise.

We were thinking about experiences like these in 1997 as we drove all the way to Massachusetts without seeing a single winery. Sadly, we headed back toward New York City empty-handed, concluding that our experiment was a bust—and, of course, bummed out because we'd have to pay for the trip ourselves. We pulled off the highway to get hamburgers for the kids, then took a wrong turn getting back on the road. Suddenly, looming before us was a billboard: "Discover Millbrook Vineyards & Winery." Fifteen minutes later we were driving up a hill, on a dirt road flanked by vines of various ages, toward a beautiful, modern winery. It was built there because its owner—John Dyson, former deputy mayor in New York City mayor Rudolph Giuliani's administration—has a house across the street. Mr. Dyson and his brother-in-law had been experimenting with growing grapes at another location when the property, an old dairy farm, was put on the block. Rather than have an unwanted development across the street, Mr. Dyson bought it and built the winery. The first grapes were planted in 1980, and the first wines were sold in 1985. Today Millbrook makes fifteen thousand cases a year, and more than twenty thousand people visit the winery.

Anastasia Smith, the sales manager then, answered the bell. Inside was an array of wines that you would rarely, if ever, see outside the winery. For instance, there was an incredible 1991 Sangiovese. That's the grape from which Chianti is made, but it's hardly grown at all in New York state—in fact, Millbrook stopped growing it there after that vintage. Ms. Smith answered our questions about the winery's library wines—the old stuff—and then asked us, her only visitors at the time, if we would like to taste some of the newer wines. While our girls read the children's books that the winery kept on hand, we tasted six wines (including two Chardonnays from the same vintage but made differently) and bought far more than we had planned—about two cases' worth. One of the great pleasures of visiting a winery is buying wines that you will likely never see anywhere else and remembering the visit as you drink the wine later. With our two cases safely in the trunk, the kids chased some geese outside as a farmhand passed by on a tractor and waved. And the *Journal* paid our expenses as promised. Aha!

Here's the point: there are wineries all around you, and they are great places to visit. Don't be shy! So our first advice to you would simply be: think of all of America as wine country. Most states now have a thriving wine tourism industry, and many have "wine trails." Even a quick search on the Internet will likely give you a very enticing list of wineries in your area. To get an idea of what's out there, take a look at these sites:

pennsylvaniawine.com/wineries
winesnw.com
ctwine.com
liwines.com
visitwinstonsalem.com/site/winetrails/winetrails.html
texaswinetrail.com
travelenvoy.com/wine/associations.htm

Those are just examples. There are links like that for wine areas all over the country. Visiting your own local winemaker is great fun, and we can't urge you strongly enough to do it. We also understand that, for most people, *wine country* really does mean Napa and Sonoma, the epicenter of wine tourism in the United States. More than ten million people go there for wine tourism every year, and one of the questions we're asked most frequently is which wineries there are fun to drop in on. Let's say this first: you don't want to go anywhere we'd recommend. We mean it. The very best wineries to visit are the little, undiscovered ones, the ones you find yourself. Don't you take special pride in that little restaurant around the corner that no one else knows about? Well, that little winery around the corner can be your own discovery, too.

We have been visiting Napa and Sonoma for almost three decades, back when great pioneers still poured their own wines behind the counter. The first place we visited was Robert Mondavi Winery. But we've also visited scores of little wineries and visited with dozens of winemakers. Napa and Sonoma are marvelous places to visit. The scenery is beautiful, and the same weather that's great for grapes is great for vacationers, too: warm enough to swim during the day and cool enough for a fire at night. Napa and Sonoma also are becoming major destinations for great food (for more about one fine restaurant, La Toque in Rutherford, see "Restaurants"). A visit to wine country also allows you to see and taste the latest trends in wine—not to mention wines that otherwise you'd never see. At Gundlach Bundschu Winery, for instance, we once found a wine called Kleinberger that, we were told, is a German grape type that isn't even used much in Germany anymore. We bought a chilled bottle and drank it right there, with lunch, at the winery's picnic tables, and—no surprise—it was delightful.

Almost all wineries sell wines in tasting rooms that you can't get anywhere else—and, in some cases, ones that are truly irreplaceable: the last Charbono that Villa Helena ever made (the vines have been pulled up), the late-harvest Chardonnay that Simi couldn't re-create, and a Cale Cellars Chardonnay that will never be made again because the winemakers retired to Florida.

There are two kinds of wine tourism in Napa and Sonoma: with crowds and without. We prefer without, although most people, for some reason, prefer with—and, indeed, if you have never been to a winery before, you might be most comfortable visiting some of the larger wineries such as Beringer, Mondavi, and Sebastiani. That's where we started ourselves, more than a quarter-century ago. Things have changed a great deal since then. Many wineries are owned by big companies now, so fewer owners or wine-makers can be found pouring their wines these days. Tasting rooms have become profit centers—everyone seems to be building a newer, bigger, better one—and some wineries seem as focused on arranging weddings and selling T-shirts and caps as making Cabernet. Small, quirky wineries are harder to find, though delightfully personal ones, such as Van Der Heyden and Casa Nuestra in Napa and Deux Amis in Sonoma, continue the tradition.

Not long ago, almost all tastings were free. Now most wineries charge, especially in Napa, and it's a little complicated. At many places there are levels of tasting: say, free for regular wines, $5 for more special wines, and $7.50 for reserve wines; or $5 for a basic tasting and $2 each for reserve wines. At too many wineries, pushy salespeople offer to sell wine futures—"better get them now!"—and nearly every place seems to have a heavily promoted wine club. These things tend to be flexible, depending on how interested you really seem to be. Some wineries "forget" about the fee if you're friendly and curious. Many have poured extra stuff for us that wasn't on the tasting list because we were genuinely interested in the wines.

Here are some tips, both from our many years of visiting wineries and from some people we know who have worked behind the bars at tasting rooms for years. The quotations are from them—tasting-room personnel and winery owners who pour their wines for visitors in four different states. These are people who have seen it all. As one told us: "There are three types of people I have seen who visit wineries. One is the wine snob, who is out to prove to himself that no matter what you make, he will not like it. The second type is basically a guy out on a first or second date who has just read a wine book and wants to impress her with all of his great wine knowledge, and he uses all of the terms out of context. And you just sort of chuckle and go on and figure that she'll figure that out after a while. The other 98 percent are people who are just out to have a good time and find something they like."

These tips focus on Napa and Sonoma, but most of them are universal:

ﾟ **Can't decide between Napa and Sonoma? Napa is much easier.** It's smaller and more accustomed to wine tourism. It's easy to visit one winery after another. Sonoma is far more spread out, and therefore it's harder to visit many wineries quickly. But Sonoma wineries tend to be more relaxed and less crowded.

ﾟ **Plan ahead.** You want to spend your time at wineries, not on the road. That means you need to identify clusters of wineries that are open to the public. Free winery maps are available all over wine country. There are also many guide books. If you are visiting a different wine region, refer to the kind of websites noted earlier, which often have a great deal of tourist information.

ﾟ **Try not to do too much in one day.** We're wine professionals, and even we find that six tasting rooms in a day is our limit. At that point our palates get really tired. As a tasting-room manager told us: "Don't do more than three tasting rooms. You'll enjoy it more. Have lunch and do one other thing, maybe visit a farm stand, someplace other than the wineries."

ﾟ **Have a designated driver** or hire a car. You will likely drink more than you think you will.

ﾟ **Start early.** Most wineries open at 10:00 and get more and more crowded as the day goes on. We know wine in the morning doesn't sound very attractive, but this is when you're most likely to have the kind of personal, interactive visit to a tasting room you're hoping for.

ﾟ **If you choose Sonoma,** you might want to start at Dry Creek Vineyard. It's a nice place to visit, and it's near several other welcoming wineries.

☙ **If you choose Napa,** get off of crowded Highway 29 at some point and take the Silverado Trail instead, where the wineries tend to be less crowded.

☙ **Many wineries are open only by appointment.** It's not that they're unfriendly; they may be small and not have the staff to welcome a constant stream of visitors. If there is a wine you really love and you'd like to see where it's made but it's by appointment only, call or write ahead. Otherwise our advice is not to visit wineries by appointment. We find it cramps our style to know we have to be at a certain place at a certain time. Plus, visits by appointment generally take longer; it's hard to taste and run. There are so many wineries to visit without an appointment that it's really not necessary.

☙ **Try to avoid weekends,** which are crowded.

☙ **Think small.** In general, unless you're new to this, avoid the big, commercial, crowded places. There are far more intimate, more memorable experiences awaiting you at smaller places.

☙ **Be considerate.** If you do go to a small winery and meet the owner or winemaker, remember that these are busy people, and although they enjoy meeting you, there are many tasks and chores at a working winery. Unless you're invited, don't spend the rest of the afternoon with them.

☙ **If there is a bus in the parking lot, come back later.**

☙ **Don't be shy about walking out.** If you walk in and no one cares whether you're there or not, leave. We do. There are so many other wineries where you'll be genuinely welcomed. You can visit only so many wineries in a day anyway; why waste your time?

☙ **If you have kids with you, ask if there are any pets.** Many wineries have delightful pets that love kids. Otherwise, tasting rooms can be awfully boring for children. Some tasting rooms have coloring books, videos, and other things to help entertain kids—which makes sense to us, since it means Mom and Dad will stick around longer and maybe buy wine—but that's still unusual.

◌ **Relax.** The people behind the counter are generally nice people. They're not there to make you feel intimidated; quite the opposite. As one winery owner said: "You're drinking old fruit juice, that's all."

◌ **Be bold!** When you enter a tasting room, you will probably be handed a tasting menu and told how many wines you can sample for how much money. Try things you have never tried before or, say, try the regular Chardonnay against the reserve Chardonnay. Try Malbec or even a red dessert wine. "Explore and judge for yourself. None of my medals are hanging in the tasting room. I don't want someone walking out of my winery with a wine because it won a medal because someone else liked it," one winery owner told us.

◌ **Don't bring preconceptions.** You might not think you like dessert wines, for instance, but if the winery is very proud of its own, give it a try. You have little to lose—and your mind might be changed forever. Everybody has different tastes, so be prepared not to like some of the wines. But don't close off the possibility of tasting them just because you think you might not like them.

◌ **Taste, don't drink.** You will be tasting many different wines. Try to have just a sip of each, or else you will have more than you really want. This is especially a problem at the first couple of stops. Ron Kurtz of Spring, Texas, wrote us that he had a marvelous time visiting wine country but added: "Biggest mistake: tasting seven wines at Geyser Peak at our first stop, 10:30 Sunday morning. Sure glad that Pezzi King had a pleasant picnic area so I could fully enjoy my nap later that afternoon."

◌ **Rinse?** You will likely be given one tasting glass. Should you rinse it between tastes? This is a controversial question. We don't rinse between tastes of the same kind of wine—white to white or red to red—because we figure the water will be more damaging to the taste than the previous wine. We rinse when we go from white to red and then from red to dessert wines.

◌ **Nibble?** Many tasting rooms offer little crackers to munch between glasses of wine. We don't, largely for the same reason we don't rinse, but others feel strongly that this is a good idea. Your choice. In any event, if you have children, it's not a bad idea to ask the pourers if they have crackers. It gives kids something to do. To make sure the children have something to snack on, think about packing your own.

 Ask questions. Don't feel like you need to ask expert questions ("Were your vines head-pruned?"). Just ask questions that naturally come to your mind ("How do you make this rosé?"). Said one tasting-room pro: "The best way to enjoy wine is to let us help you. To learn, try something you're maybe not used to. My only reason to be here is to explain our particular wines or talk about wines in general or talk about how wine and food go together. We love to talk about wine, to share the experience." Remember that there are no stupid questions—although, okay, we'll admit that pourers in tasting rooms do have some funny stories. Said one: "I was doing a tour, and we were down in the barrel cellar, and I had one gentleman ask, 'How long does the wine stay in caskets?' I told him they're both used for aging, but for two different purposes."

 Don't be embarrassed about having a sip and pouring out the rest, either because you don't like the wine or because you don't want to overimbibe. If you don't do this, you might be sorry. That's what those buckets are for. We guess you could actually spit into those buckets, but we've never seen anyone do it. (Hey, we're professional wine spitters, but we'd never do it in a tasting room. Instead, we either just smell the wine or take very small sips.)

 Enjoy the whole experience, not just the wine. Go beyond the tasting room; look at the vineyard. Go out and look at it and enjoy the environment. Be a part of the whole scene, not just the tasting room.

 You don't have to buy anything. Don't feel pressured to do so, but if you've had a fun tasting with a friendly person—especially the winemaker or an owner—it's a nice gesture. In any case, be careful how much you buy, especially if you're on vacation. Many people, including us, have found that a bottle here and a bottle there adds up to far more to carry back than we expected, and many wineries will not ship to most states because of restrictive local laws. If you have to carry the wine back, you can buy Styrofoam wine carriers at packaging stores and check them with your luggage. We're not guaranteeing anything, but we've never had a bottle break. Also—and don't tell anyone we told you this—there are shipping stores in wine country that specialize in figuring out how to ship your wine home even if you're not supposed to. Ask around and you'll find out who and where they are. Fortunately, some of those restrictive laws are being challenged and changed.

ᶜᵉ **Have a picnic.** One way to get rid of some of that wine is to have it for a picnic right there at the winery. Many wineries have lovely picnic areas. Get some sandwiches at a local deli, buy a bottle at the winery, borrow a couple of glasses, and enjoy.

ᶜᵉ **Don't leave the wine in the hot car** while you visit other wineries. The wine in that bottle is a cherished memory, and you don't want to cook it. After several purchases, double back to your hotel, if it's possible, and stow the wine there.

ᶜᵉ **Finally, and perhaps most important: don't do this to get drunk.** It is gross and rude to have had too much to drink at a tasting room and destroys the experience for everyone else. This is obviously a major issue if you're driving, but some tasting-room veterans tell us that the biggest problems come from people who have hired a limo with a driver, because that makes them feel empowered to drink too much. Don't. As one tasting-room veteran told us: "The only really horrendous negative trend I see is people trying to treat tasting rooms like bars."

Specific Wineries

Readers and friends always ask us for names of specific wineries to visit in Napa and Sonoma. We're nervous about this because it's impossible to know when or where you will have a good time. Not only that, but wineries come and go, tasting room personnel come and go, and ownership changes so often that who knows what tomorrow will bring. By the time you read this, there will surely be new wineries that will offer memorable experiences, while some of those below might be sold, closed, or just completely different. Here are some places we always recommend to friends when they're going to Napa and Sonoma.

NAPA

Milat Vineyards. It's tiny and makes charming wines, and there always seems to be a Milat behind the counter to talk about wines and winemaking.

Napa Cellars. This small, ten thousand-case winery is one of the first you'll encounter on Highway 29, and we have loved its Chardonnay. Its wines are sold primarily at the winery.

Dutch Henry Winery. It's essentially just a rustic garage with a man who loves talking about his wines. The Pinot Noir is excellent.

Sullivan Vineyards. Great wines and great people. This is very informal, and if you want to really fall in love with visiting wine country, you'll want to spend a few minutes here. Readers who have visited always write us that they had a very memorable time. Awesome reds.

Clos Pegase Winery. It's so fancy that we were skeptical, especially because it seems to be more about artwork and money than wine. But the guy behind the counter was passionate about the wines, which were uniformly good. And the art was fascinating.

Freemark Abbey Winery. We were so enthusiastic about the wines at this old standby that the man behind the counter kept opening new ones to compare. When he suggested that we pair Viognier with Gorgonzola cheese, he just seemed to float away—exactly the kind of experience we love in a tasting room.

SONOMA

Dry Creek Vineyard. Proof that even a busy tasting room can be a load of fun. The whites are particularly good.

Geyser Peak Winery. It's a beautiful setting, and the tasting includes several small-production varietals that most people never get to taste. The winery says it opens these wines to introduce people to something different, and the tasting-room personnel seem to be having fun doing it.

J Wine Company. Wonderful. A $10 tasting includes four wines, including a bubbly, and a delicious little appetizer designed to pair with each (Pinot Gris with smoked salmon tartare, for instance).

F. Teldeschi Winery. Dan Teldeschi was pouring inky Zinfandels going back to 1994 when we were there, and he likes to see your face when you try them. A throwback to how it used to be. Just don't say the words *white Zinfandel.*

Wellington Vineyards. Just barely off busy Highway 12, Wellington quietly makes excellent Rhône varietals, such as an outstanding Syrah. We'd just left a crowded winery and ended up at Wellington, alone. When we asked about the Syrah, the winemaker came out to explain how he'd made it.

Christopher Creek Winery and *Limerick Lane Cellars.* We list these together because they're neighbors on the same short road. Both are small and friendly and have great reds—Syrah and Petite Sirah at Christopher Creek, Zinfandel at Limerick Lane. The winemaker at Limerick Lane got off a forklift to pour his wines and gave us restaurant suggestions. We have heard more raves about visiting these two wineries—both the experience and the wine—than most others.

Family Wineries of Sonoma Valley. There are more and more "tasting rooms" that are nowhere near the wineries, and generally we avoid these because they can be sterile and commercial. This little room is different. Seven small wineries offer their wines here—you can sample quite a few, and there's no charge—and we found knowledgeable family members from two wineries behind the counter. The wines, all small production, are excellent.

The Wine Room. Just down the road from Family Wineries, this is a tasting room for five more small wineries you've probably never heard of. Be prepared for some unusual tastes and keep in mind that the guy in the torn jeans who's hanging around is probably a wine-maker or the owner of one of the wineries. The crackers and spreads are good, too, and the tastings are free.

ONE DAY IN NAPA

We are often asked: "I am going to San Francisco and I want to take a day trip to Napa. Where should I go?" So we actually did this ourselves, timing and mapping a one-day excursion. Ready? Here's how we'd do it. First, if it's a weekend, skip it. Every place will be crowded and the traffic will be so bad that it's unlikely you'll have a very satisfying time. If you have no choice, set out early, hit a couple of places, then head back. (All of this assumes, once more, that you have hired a car or have a designated driver.)

Leave yourself about ninety minutes to get to Napa from San Francisco. Get to Napa around 11:00 A.M. and head onto Highway 29, the main drag through the valley. One of the first places you'll see is Napa Cellars. Stop there. It'll get your trip started right. Head back north on Highway 29 for four miles to Galleron Road and turn right. Go to Sullivan Winery. Get back on 29 and go one mile north to Milat Winery.

It should be noon or after so you have a choice to make. If you're hungry right now, get back on 29 north for just about a half-mile to V. Sattui for lunch. If you can wait, drive right past Sattui to Louis Martini. This is a fairly large winery (now owned by Gallo), but it has such a special place in California history that we always go there to pay homage. Not only that, but the tasting room staff seems to be having a good time. The wines have a special honest earthiness to them that seems very traditional and warm to us, and the winery has the same feel. This is important: if you're there in late spring or early summer, you must buy a bottle of Martini's Moscato Amabile. It's a slightly sweet, slightly sparkling wine that's sold only at the winery, must stay refrigerated, and should be drunk immediately upon purchase. It's one of the most delightful wines around. Buy it and find someplace to drink it right away—at a picnic table or on a blanket in a nearby vineyard.

It's definitely time for lunch. V. Sattui is, indeed, a tourist spot, with dozens of different wines—some of them quite good—scores of different cheeses, and hordes of visitors. But it's a charming stop nonetheless. You

can taste a number of wines for free, then buy the one you want to drink at
a picnic table outside (we'd advise a light, very fresh white if it's hot outside). Get some cheese and a sandwich. They'll open the bottle for you,
give you a couple of plastic cups, and point you to the picnic area. Thus fortified, head back north on 29. It's getting late. Keep driving north. You'll see
all sorts of wineries you recognize, like Beringer, and less familiar wineries,
like Folie à Deux. Any one of them would be a fun stop. Since time's a factor,
however, just keep driving all the way up, almost to downtown Calistoga. Finally, about eight miles from Sattui, you'll see Stonegate Winery. The reds
are particularly good.

It's time to head back to San Francisco. Go over to the Silverado Trail,
the much less crowded road that parallels 29. At the trail, turn right, head-
ing south. The valley will look wholly different from this road. The wineries are less crowded and a bit harder to find. The valley spreads even more
beautifully before you. Once again, you'll pass well-known and new names.
If you have the time, drop in. If you're running out of time, keep driving. In
twenty-one miles—and you'll have to look sharp—you will see the perfect
place to end your day, Regusci Winery, on the left. It's a gorgeous spot, and
the valley looks beautiful from its windows. Not only that, but we think
they have some of the best undiscovered wines in California. The Merlot is
stunning. Get back on the Silverado Trail and then make a right back over
to 29.

It's possible to be even more methodical than this. We once offered
some advice on a day in wine country to Dan Cook of Clarkston, Michigan, and asked him to get back to us about how it went. Turns out that, in a
single long day, he visited both Napa and Sonoma, stopping first for coffee
and some local intelligence just outside of Sonoma, then dropping into
three wineries in Sonoma, driving across Alexander Valley to Napa, visiting
another winery and then having dinner. "By this time," he told us, "we were
honestly a little 'wined out,' so I had a cold draft beer."

The other side of the coin is offered by Ray I. Scroggins of Watertown,
Wisconsin. He also wrote to ask what to do with just one day in wine country, and we asked him, too, to get back to us. "We've found that 'less is
more,'" he told us. "The temptation is always to see too many wineries. For
anyone who has just one day (as we usually do), I'd suggest finding one win-

ery that has a tour (if that is what you want) and then picking a couple for tasting. We have found that we are better off choosing one establishment, buying a bottle or two, and picking up some bread, cheese, sausage, etc., to have an impromptu picnic. It never works that well for us to carry wine back, so we've decided to consume and enjoy."

We certainly can't argue with that.

Touring Foreign Wine Regions | The Universal Language of Wine

"We are going to France in two weeks. The trip is designed so that we can visit wine regions. We are driving. The problem is we don't speak French! We have read in many books that the wine-tasting etiquette in France is quite different from what you would expect to see in California, and that it is almost necessary to speak French if you want to visit some off-the-beaten-path wineries. So my question is: how do we approach this? I remember reading in one of your columns that you had gone to German wineries and you don't speak German. I would love to hear your advice." **—KLARA B. ISKOZ, CAMBRIDGE, MASSACHUSETTS**

Many people are nervous about visiting wineries in their own states, not to mention those in Napa and Sonoma. But if untold treasures and adventures await you a couple hours' drive from your front door, imagine what great experiences and tastes you can enjoy during your travels to wineries in other countries.

When wine lovers think about visiting wineries in another country, France is usually where they make their first pilgrimage. That's what we did in 1983. At the time, our top priority was to conceive our daughter Media. Our second priority was to make sure that when we did that, we would have splendid wines coursing through our veins. That's pretty much the extent of our ambition for that trip, and we had a lovely time even though, alas, we did not conceive Media until many years later. The trip was otherwise a huge success. We don't like to make too many plans when we travel other than having hotel reservations (we feel better knowing where we're sleeping).

That leaves us room for spur-of-the-moment detours and spontaneous flights of fancy, like the time we walked into the woods in Burgundy and had a picnic near a brook with sandwiches and a Chablis we'd just bought. We're also not multilingual. John studied Latin for many years, but that's not very useful at wineries, and Dottie studied some French long ago, in high school and college. What we've learned is that it doesn't really matter if you can't speak the local language. We have heard from so many people over the years who had the greatest experiences visiting wineries overseas, whether or not they had any language skills, appointments, or contacts. We'll introduce you to some throughout this chapter.

Alsace, France

Jeff Bloom and Cindi Cohen, Vienna, Virginia

Alsace is a fantastic area for a wine lover to visit. The Wine Road (Route du Vin) runs roughly between the two major cities, from Strasbourg in the north to near Colmar in the south. In between, it winds through pictur-esque villages, including a few medieval walled towns, surrounded by rolling hillsides filled with incredibly even rows of vines. The Wine Road is filled with signs for wineries open for tasting, some names familiar to Americans and some too small to export. The tasting experience is very different from what one would come across in American (particularly California) wineries. Even those wineries with actual tasting rooms rarely have a tasting list of what they are pouring. Instead, they will open whatever you would like to taste. This is even the situation in a place like Hugel, a fairly large producer with a tasting room in the middle of Riquewihr, one of the more touristy villages. It's sometimes difficult not to feel guilty about asking your host to open some of his finer wines, but nobody ever seems to mind, and that is clearly the norm.

Americans are something of a rarity in Alsace, with most of the tourists coming from France and Germany. As a result, there is limited English spoken in many of the tasting rooms and restaurants, even at some of the larger producers. People are very warm and welcoming, however, and we've never had a problem communicating. Without appointment, we have been able to stop in and taste at such producers as J. B. Adam, Lucien Albrecht, Paul

Blanck, Marcel Deiss, Hugel, Kuentz-Bas, Domaine Schlumberger, and Pierre Sparr. The winery staff people seem genuinely pleased that you've taken the time to visit and are interested in their wines. At Paul Blanck, in Kientzheim, for example, we spent a bit of time trying a number of different wines and talking about the vineyards and the recent vintages with a member of the staff. We bought two bottles of relatively inexpensive wines, and he threw in a third, a Muscat we hadn't tried, because "I know you will like it."

For our second trip to a wine region overseas, we chose Italy. The Italian language is Greek to us, so for that trip Dottie memorized three sentences: "Could we taste your wine and perhaps buy a bottle?" "Can you take two for dinner at 8:00?" and "Where is the bathroom?" We're sure she garbled the language badly, but you know what? Wine has its own way of facilitating understanding, and we've found that people everywhere generally appreciate the effort you make. In Tuscany, we were told that anyone who put a bottle of wine out by the road or displayed the sign of the black rooster—the sign of the official association of Chianti Classico producers—was advertising that you could stop in and buy a bottle. So we did. These were tiny wineries, essentially homes where people made some wine. The people spoke little English and couldn't have been nicer. Their wines were impressive and uniformly inexpensive.

Rioja, Spain

Carol and Tom Manchester, Rancho Palos Verdes, California

We looked at websites and read a book called Rioja and Its Wines, *by Ron Scarborough, published by Survival Books Limited. After identifying the places we wanted to visit, we then got on the web and found sites for many of them. We contacted some of them by e-mail and some by fax (mostly in English, but a Spanish-speaking friend at work helped with one bodega) and assembled an itinerary.*

Bodegas Martínez Lacuesta is right on a main street in Haro, in the heart of Rioja, hidden behind a high wall and a large gate. We were greeted by Señor Luis Martínez Lacuesta (their first harvest was in 1895 and done by his grandfather's brother), who apologized for his English (which was fine) and took us on a tour of his extensive bodega. He explained the bodega system, where the wines are stored until they're ready to drink, and he selected a 1991 Reserva from the family stash for us to taste. The tasting room, in fact, was his family's dining room. As he poured the wine, we could smell garlic and anchovies cooking in the nearby kitchen. We asked to buy some 1987 Grand Reserva. He said there were a few bottles of the 1980 left, which was a better vintage, and we could have it for the same price. It was delicious, and we still have one left.

In 2001, our company asked us to conduct a tasting for some important people in Frankfurt. We're big fans of German wines, but we had never been to Germany, and we don't speak a word of German. We looked on a map—geography has never been one of our strengths—and saw that Frankfurt was near the Rhine River, home of some of the world's greatest wines. We figured we'd spend a couple of days in the Rheingau region, see the mighty Rhine, and then drive back to Frankfurt for our speech. We made hotel reservations but made no advance plans with wineries and, as always, didn't tell anyone that we were wine writers. Here was the first eye opener: the Rheingau is closer to the airport in Frankfurt than Napa is to San Francisco. Even with our terrible sense of direction—we couldn't get out of the parking lot in our rental car and circled the airport three times— we were on the Rhine in just forty minutes. The Rheingau is as easy to navigate as Napa, too, with one main road going right through the region. The wine road even has signs: "Rheingauer Riesling Route."

The Rheingau region—the other famous region is Mosel-Saar-Ruwer— is pretty small, but it's home to more than a thousand wineries, and it's beautiful, hilly and green, and filled with history. Some say that Charlemagne ordered the first vines planted there. Riesling is the great grape of the region. It seemed as though every house we passed in this picturesque region was 'Weingut' this or that—tiny wineries we'd never heard of and whose wines, in most cases, never get to America. On our way to our hotel, we passed a delightful-looking restaurant in Hattenheim, along a narrow, curving street, and decided we'd go there our first night. After parking almost on the sidewalk—the street was really narrow—we entered the restaurant and were shown to our table, just beyond a happy party of diners with a dog snoozing under their table. Other diners turned to look at us and smile, but no one spoke much English, and we were impressed by how really foreign German sounds. We had a marvelous time ordering the specialties of the house. On the wine list was something we'd never seen before, so we tried it. It was a Kabinett Trocken (Oestricher Doosberg) 1999 from Peter Jakob Kühn, a winery right near our hotel. The wine was dry yet flowery, very young, and with an unmistakable taste of minerals that gave it stature and complexity. It seemed to have little body but, at the same time, was peppery, with bold tastes. We called the winery the next day and asked if we could drop by. Mrs. Kühn said sure, come on over, and we did, pulling into a driveway on what looked like a familiar suburban street of neat homes. A slight, dark-haired, energetic-looking woman, Mrs. Kühn led us into a tasting area just off her kitchen and poured us several wines.

In some ways, visiting wineries in other countries is easier than visiting those in the United States. Winemakers don't expect you to be familiar with their winery, and there's no pressure to talk winespeak because, in any case, you often aren't even speaking the same language. As it happened, Mr. Kühn was there, but in his laboratory—concerned, his wife said, that his English was not good enough. He needn't have worried. His wines spoke well for him. Indeed, what the winemakers want most is to convert you, to introduce you to something that you will love, never forget, and tell your friends about. They're happy to sell you a bottle or two of wine, of course, but their main mission is to convince you that the wines of their region are the best in the world. If you're respectful and willing to give the wines a chance, you'll have a good time.

As we were leaving, we asked Mrs. Kühn whether they made a red wine. "Would you like to try one?" she asked. She left the room and came back a few minutes later with a wine called Pur Pur, which is made primarily from Spätburgunder, Germany's name for Pinot Noir. She explained that the winery has been in the family for generations, but when she and her husband took charge, the first thing they did was plant some red grapes—their contribution to its history. When she poured it, the room filled with smells of chocolate and blackberries. We had come to the Rheingau to drink Riesling, but this was the most remarkable wine we tasted.

Slovenia

Dr. John E. Morrison, Denver, Colorado

I'm a pediatric anesthesiologist on a Fulbright Fellowship at the University Medical Center, Ljubljana, Slovenia. Slovenia, a lovely, small country bordering Italy and Austria on the north—the site of Hemingway's A Farewell to Arms—is proud of its wines. The vineyards nearer Italy tend to produce more reds than whites, while the eastern area of the country around Ptuj produces primarily white wines. The larger distributors and growers' wines are available throughout the country, with wine-tasting rooms at the vineyards. Smaller vineyards are found throughout the country within a ninety-minute drive from the central capital, Ljubljana, in any direction. Fortunately, one does not need to be fluent in Slovene to converse easily with local winegrowers; their warmth, humor, and pride in their wines make visits pleasant and rewarding.

Hungary

Mark O'Malley, Brussels

I am an American ex-pat in Brussels. I spent the weekend in Budapest and stumbled into the 12th annual Budapest International Wine Festival by accident. On Sunday they had a fantastic wine exhibition and fair at Buda Castle that featured about fifty Hungarian wineries, all offering tastings for prices ranging from 25 cents to $1. As you would expect, some were okay, some pretty good, and, at least surprisingly to me, some were very good. As you would expect, the Tokaji and other sweet wines were the biggest part of the show, but they had a surprising number of more traditional choices (Pinot Noir, Cabernet Franc, and Cabernet Sauvignon) that also were quite good. If you find yourself in that part of the world during early September, you might want to stop by for a visit.

We never got over that red wine from Germany. How often do you see red wine from Germany in the United States? Not very often. So when the company asked us to make a return trip the next year, we jumped at the chance, but with a couple of differences: first, we decided to take Media and Zoë; second, we decided to stay in Assmanshausen, one of the few places in Germany actually best known for its red wines—specifically, Spätburgunder. Its Höllenberg vineyard is famous among wine lovers. How important is wine to this ancient region? Consider this: just as Hollywood has a giant sign announcing itself, as we drew closer to our destination we saw a giant sign high on a vine-covered hill:

ASSMANNSHAUSER HÖLLENBERG

Good thing it was a wide hill. In Germany, many people might own small plots of a large vineyard, which is why you might see so many wines labeled, say, Piesporter Goldtropfchen from different wineries. For the next several days, we just knocked on doors whenever we saw a place that looked like a winery. Sometimes they had bottles out front or signs with bottles on them. Most were someone's home. Think about it for a moment: a family of four, total strangers who don't speak the language, knocks on your door unannounced and asks to taste your wine. What kind of reception did we receive? Warm and welcoming at every stop. At one winery/home, we were greeted by a mother and her son. He was wearing Power Ranger socks, which Media and Zoë noticed right away. Our children had long ago outgrown their Power Ranger days, but it was nice to see that kids are kids the world over.

For lunch one day, we dropped into a market and picked up sandwiches, along with horseradish, mayonnaise, and mustard in toothpaste-like squeeze tubes (to the girls' horror). In our rented station wagon, we decided to drive to the top of the Höllenberg vineyard. Around and around we went on the narrow road, along the ancient stone terraces, encountering, every now and then, shallow, cavelike stone niches that housed religious statues. We were amazed at how steep the neatly planted vineyards became and how difficult it must be to tend the vines and harvest the fruit. Occasionally we'd see people doing just that, and we stared at them in awe. As our car climbed, we marveled at how wonderful the sunshine must be on those grapes while below us the Rhine and the charming villages got farther and farther away. Across the Rhine, we could see a magnificent castle, which we later learned was almost a thousand years old. We opened the sunroof, and the girls stood up and directed us, the wind in their faces. Finally, there we were, right next to the big sign. Even without wine—we did, after all, have to drive back down the steep hill—those were the best sandwiches we'd had in a long time.

When we came back down, we knocked on the door of a winemaker named August Kesseler, who we'd heard was an outstanding producer of Spätburgunder. In a minute, a man's head emerged from a window. We asked if we could buy some wine. He said he had no wine to sell, but we explained that we'd come all the way from New York to buy his wine. It was August Kesseler himself, and he said he was in the middle of a meeting and asked if we could come back in an hour. Because he was right next door to our hotel, we said sure. When we knocked later, a tall young man wearing a worker's apron answered the door with a smile, looked the girls over approvingly, and took us to see Mr. Kessler, who offered the girls juice and brought out several bottles of wine. "I have none to sell," he told us to our disappointment, "but I'd like you to leave with a good impression." He explained that he makes little wine and that only a tiny amount leaves Germany. He told us, as we knew, that German wine is a hard sell in America because Americans think of it as simple and sweet—the Blue Nun of their youth. Mr. Kesseler told us that a prestigious wine magazine had named him winemaker of the year twice and that he was hoping to win that honor again. Then, as if to prove his worthiness, he poured his 1999 Spätlese Trocken Spätburgunder, sat back, and smiled as he waited for us to taste it. It was far bigger and richer than the other wines we had tasted during the week, with the same hints of earth and pepper, but a deep, almost chocolate smoothness. This was a wine that we will always remember, well worth the entire trip.

Months later, we were at a restaurant in Sonoma during a trip to America's own wine country, and there on the wine list—we couldn't believe it— was a wine from August Kesseler. We'd never seen one in the States before. We ordered it, of course, and, of course, we loved it. It was one of those moments that reminded us that wine is universal.

Châteauneuf-du-Pape, France

Glen Cheney, Albuquerque, New Mexico

My wife, Jo, and I just returned after a month in France. Since we read your column about Châteauneuf-du-Pape just before going to France, we thought it would be great fun to taste some of the wines you mentioned at the wineries where they were produced. This decision led to some of the most delightful experiences we had in France, those totally unplanned and unpredictable interactions with the French.

One rainy, windy day in late September, we set out to find the winery, Domaine Charvin, that produced your top pick. We couldn't find Domaine Charvin on the local tourist map, but a very helpful young woman in the Châteauneuf-du-Pape Office of Tourism sketched in its location. It was on the north side of the village out past the ruin of the fourteenth-century Château des Papes, and off the road, D68, to Orange. After what seemed to be a long journey, but really wasn't, up D68, we turned left onto D72, a narrow but paved road that led to Château Maucoil, one of several landmarks recommended by the young woman. Another even narrower paved road to the left followed and led to the only sign for Domaine Charvin and to a dirt road that finally took us to our destination.

Domaine Charvin turned out to be a very small, family-run business. Except during the harvest, it was operated by a couple in their late sixties and their son, who seemed to be about forty. We learned later that they make only about twelve thousand bottles of Châteauneuf-du-Pape yearly. They also produce about twice that amount of Côtes-du-Rhône and some rosé. When I got out of the car to see if we could taste their wine and perhaps buy some, I found father and son in the winery in dirty work clothes, hands stained with grease, arms purple to the elbows, repairing some machinery. They asked us to wait fifteen or twenty minutes until the son, Laurent Charvin, completed some essential business. While we waited, Laurent's mother invited us into their "tasting room," actually a small cluttered workroom featuring a great tank for storing this year's vintage of their Châteauneuf-du-Pape and a small table set up with sample bottles of their wines. She gave us each a glass of their rosé, and we "talked." She spoke no English. We spoke only a little French. Nonetheless, the welcome we received was warm and friendly. We did learn that her grandparents had come to that part of France from Tuscany around the turn of the last century. We were all very excited to have communicated that much.

    In due course, Laurent returned and spent the next forty-five minutes or so describing, in English, his wines, the nature of the wine business, his philosophy of winemaking, the outlook for that year's vintage, and so on. When we got to wine tasting, we found his 1997 Châteauneuf every bit as good as you said it was. His 1998 was not released yet, but, if anything, it was even better. I wanted to buy a case of the Châteauneuf, but he would sell us only two bottles. He said he was almost sold out and was saving a few cases for family and friends who liked to come there for wine.

We are asked all the time for names of specific wineries to visit all over the world, but the world of wine is way too big to do that. In Italy alone, "more than a million grape-growers have some form of commercial production and, according to one source, some fifty thousand wineries produce wine countrywide," according to *Vino Italiano: The Regional Wines of Italy,* by Joseph Bastianich and David Lynch. Here is some general advice we'd give you. First, we'd offer you the same suggestions we included in the previous chapter about visiting United States wineries, with special emphasis on the designated driver. Remember that you'll be on rural, unfamiliar roads in regions that are new to you, so be very careful.

    ℭ **Use the Internet.** For instance, we simply went to the Google search engine and typed in *New Zealand wine tourism.* The very first hit was Hawkes Bay New Zealand Official Tourism Site. There's great wine-tourism information there, even including a map of the "wine trail." You can do that with just about every wine region in the world.

    ℭ **Get a guidebook.** Similarly, there are tourism guidebooks of just about every region. Go to amazon.com or bn.com and plug in *travel* and *wine* and *Loire,* for instance, and you'll be amazed at what you'll find.

    ℭ **Get a wine book.** Don't just look at tourism guidebooks. We have found that some of the most useful travel books are simply wine books that, in fact, will tell you more about where to go and what to do than supposed guidebooks. If we were going to Italy, for instance, we would first spend a great deal of time with *Vino Italiano* and wouldn't leave home without it, even though it is hefty.

⚬ **Talk to your merchant.** If you have a good wine merchant who travels abroad regularly to various wine regions—and many do—ask advice. The merchant may even offer to make some calls for you.

⚬ **Look for "wine trails,"** using your guidebook and a map. Almost every region has one that's well marked (and often well marketed) for tourists. Using that information, try to find a hotel on the wine road that's situated close to a critical mass of wineries. Remember that a winery is a farm, which means they're not generally located in the middle of big cities. Think about it: if you wanted to spend a week visiting wineries in Napa, it would be better to stay in St. Helena than San Francisco, and if you were going to spend a few days visiting the wineries of Long Island, it would be better to stay in Riverhead than New York City. Same thing overseas.

⚬ **Look for regional tasting rooms** that offer a variety of wines from the area. Many wine regions, from Germany to Italy to France, feature these places, often sponsored by the area's wine association, that offer many local wines. These outlets don't have the same charm as the wineries themselves, of course, but they tend to be a good place to start. For instance, the Manchesters, who wrote earlier about Rioja, also visited the Loire Valley of France and highly recommend dropping in when you find a *maison du vin,* where you can taste the wines of several wineries in the area and get more information about others. "Nearly every appellation along the Loire has one, and we visited most of them," they wrote. "It's a good place to start by getting a feel for the wines and grape varieties of the region."

⚬ **Look for the little places.** Even in foreign countries, you will often see a big winery whose name you recognize. If you are partial to that winery's products, great; drop in. However, the very best experiences will be at the tiny wineries whose wines you will never see back home because they're too small to export. These are special wines, special wineries, and special experiences—and all the more special because you found them yourself.

ℚ **Don't be shy.** If you see a place that looks like a winery—and we haven't been wrong yet—drop in. They will generally be flattered that you're there. If you don't speak the language, speak wine: smile when you taste, be demonstrative. Dottie has been known to pat her stomach in a broad gesture of satisfaction. You can always ask about the grape types, which are generally universal. Is this made from Riesling? From Chardonnay? We once dropped into a winery in Tuscany and were tasting wines with someone who didn't speak a word of English. When we tasted one, John took a pen and wrote "85% Sangiovese?" guessing that it was made primarily from the great grape of Tuscany. He figured that phrase was the same in English and Italian. Incredibly, and utterly by chance, the wine was indeed 85 percent Sangiovese and, as you can imagine, our host then became particularly enthusiastic about our enjoyment of his wines. It was the one time that Dottie didn't mind John's showing off.

ℚ **Avoid being in a hurry.** This is advice from Mr. Cheney, who told us about his visit to Châteauneuf-du-Pape earlier. He adds: "Not every winery owner or operator will want to engage visitors in conversation, of course. But they will frequently spend an amazing amount of time with you if you show interest in their wine, their grapes, the recent harvest, the business, etc. And discussing what you are tasting is most of the fun anyway." He also adds about language problems: "I find people of good will never have any real difficulty communicating at a basic level."

ℚ **The only essentials you need are an open mind and good manners.** This is the most important point of all: remember, you are a guest—often actually in someone's home. At the very least, you're a guest in their part of the world. This is true whether you're touring wineries in Virginia or in New Zealand.

Switzerland
Kenneth A. Rubin, Bethesda, Maryland

You will love walking along the Lavaux region through spectacularly terraced vineyards, perched on steep slopes, overlooking Switzerland's largest lake, surrounded by towering snow-covered peaks. Located between Montreux and Lausanne, in the French-speaking canton of Vaud, Switzerland, it is easily reached from Geneva by any combination of lake paddle steamers, trains, and cars. A narrow road, which looks like it was featured in a James Bond film, carves through immaculate vineyards. An adjacent walking path offers easy access to several small hamlets, with quaint cobblestone streets leading to dozens of picturesque caves or wineries, where visitors are greeted with genuine warmth and invited to try the local wines. Many are small, family-owned businesses managed with great pride and with characteristic Swiss thoroughness. While almost all the white wines are made from the Chasselas grape, they can be remarkably different, depending on the soil, the angle of the slope, and to what extent the grapes capture and retain the warmth of the sun reflected off Lac Leman (Lake Geneva) and retained in the ancient stones that form the terraces constructed by monks nine hundred years ago.

Thanks to the perfect synchronization of the Swiss travel system, I was able to make a complete loop of the most spectacular segment of the vineyards in just one day. I began high above the lake in Glion, looking down at Chillon Castle. After a steep funicular ride down to Montreux, I boarded a small Train des Vignes (Wine Train), which took me uphill from Vevey to the village of Puidoux. From there, the walk is all downhill. Signs along the well-marked trails provide helpful information about nearby vineyards and wineries. It's easy to detour into geranium-covered cafés and fine restaurants, especially in the ancient picturesque hillside hamlets of Epesses and Riex, where I sampled their eponymous wines. Eventually I made it down to the lake at the pleasant town of Cully, perfectly situated at a bend in the lake with long views in all directions. My first stop was the simple and very pleasant Café Major Daval, which serves many local wines by the glass and charges nothing for looking across the lake at some of France's highest snow-capped alps. While I walked the entire trail in one day, including a twelve-mile lakeside return to Montreux, most people taking this route might prefer to return by paddle steamer or train. Cully is a good overnight stop, and the Michelin two-star Auberge du Raisin, adjacent to the Major Daval, offers elegant fine dining. This is the culinary heart of Switzerland, and you can travel easily to another lakeside village by boat or take a comfortable, fast train to sample the local wines and cuisine at many restaurants.

A final tip: Start your walking tour in the morning and head east to west so that the sun is behind you. The angle of the light reflecting off the lake makes for superb photos. Then, at the end of the day, the setting sun will be behind you as you return to the eastern end of the lake, creating a wonderful alpine glow on the distant Dents du Midi, the enormous mountain range that frames the eastern end of Lac Leman.

Alsace, France

Jim Stewart and Benjamin Weil, New York City

At a restaurant called Au Valet de Coeur, a young but wise sommelier poured us a slightly chilled Pinot Noir—surprising, because Alsace is known for its white wines. I took one sip and gasped [Benjamin told us]. The sommelier said, "It's a 1997 Pinot Noir from Jean-Jacques Muller. They're very close by, in Bergheim." The sommelier gave us the address of Jean-Jacques Muller, as well as recommending several other local wineries to visit. After looking around Ribeauvillé we backtracked to Bergheim, milling through the tiny town until we found the address. The simple house was barely identified as belonging to Jean-Jacques Muller, and at any rate no amount of ringing or knocking produced any inhabitants. Disappointed, we left Bergheim and continued our tour of the wine route. A couple of days later, having spent the day in Colmar, we left the route des vins and were speeding back up to Strasbourg on the autoroute. Suddenly, like an omen, a sign for Bergheim appeared in the distance. Jim tore off of the highway and onto a small road leading to Bergheim, and the elusive viticulteur. Jim parked the car while I dashed around to the back entrance of the house.

A youngish woman answered the door. "Hello," I said, my speech already prepared. "We had your 1997 Pinot Noir at Au Valet de Coeur the other night and were hoping to buy a few bottles." "Oh, yes," she replied. "Please come in. How many bottles do you want?" "Just three," I said, knowing we could carry only four bottles back to the States with no trouble and already had one. "And I'm afraid we're in an awful hurry. We have a rental car we have to return in Strasbourg by five." "Of course," she said. Jim appeared while she was making out the receipt. Then, suddenly, a pair of double doors opened and a tall, elegant lady appeared. It was difficult to know how old she was, but the respect she immediately commanded made me think she was over sixty. "Bonjour. Je suis Madame Muller," she said. Somehow it was clear to all of us that there could be no more hustling to finish the transaction and sprint back to the autoroute. The conversation turned genteel and leisurely. Madame Muller could not have been more gracious.

"Is Jean-Jacques Muller your husband, Madame?" I ventured cautiously. "No. My husband was Jules Muller. Jean-Jacques was my son. He is also deceased." She did not seem perturbed by my query, but a thousand additional questions began to churn around in my head. How did her son die? He must have been awfully young. Was the younger woman his widow? She referred to her with timid deference as "Madame Muller." And why was this incredible wine not being shipped all over the world at exorbitant prices? After a further twenty minutes of conversation, we left with only one bottle of the treasured Pinot Noir, but also with a bottle of Gewürztraminer and a Tokay Pinot Gris, which, when finally tasted over a year later, turned out to be equally stupefying.

Bringing It Back

I f you visit the wine regions of the world, you're going to want to bring home some wine. For years, Dottie simply wrapped the bottles in clothes in our suitcase. The clothes became the padding, and she tried to space them comfortably throughout each piece of luggage. We never lost a bottle. Then we began to travel with two of those Styrofoam wine carriers that you can buy at packaging stores. Yes, various airline personnel and security officials looked at us warily as we traveled overseas with empty boxes. But as we visited wineries, we could put bottles into the box, making carrying them around the country much easier. When it came time to go home, we'd just check them with the luggage. Now we've heard from some people that this is a terrible idea, that for various reasons concerning the air pressure in the cargo hold, the bottles are in danger, so you might want to be careful here. We certainly don't want to be responsible for damaging your wine. Still, we have never lost a bottle.

How much wine can you legally bring back? That's virtually impossible to answer, because customs regulations are so confusing and also because the laws of your own state might come into play. Here is what Customs says about this:

One liter (33.8 fl. oz.) of alcoholic beverages may be included in your duty exemption if: you are 21 years old; it is for your own use or as a gift; it does not violate the laws of the state in which you arrive. Federal regulations allow you to bring back more than one liter of alcoholic beverage for personal use, but you will have to pay duty and Internal Revenue Service tax.

While federal regulations do not specify a limit on the amount of alcohol you may bring back for personal use, unusual quantities are liable to raise suspicions that you are importing the alcohol for other purposes, such as for resale. Customs officers are authorized by Alcohol Tobacco and Firearms to make on-the-spot determinations that an importation is for commercial purposes, and may require you to obtain a permit to import the alcohol before releasing it to you. If you intend to bring back a substantial quantity of alcohol for your personal use you should contact the Customs port you will be re-entering the country through, and make prior arrangements for entering the alcohol into the U.S.

Having said that, you should be aware that state laws may limit the amount of alcohol you can bring in without a license. If you arrive in a state that has limitations on the amount of alcohol you may bring in without a license, that state law will be enforced by Customs, even though it may be more restrictive then Federal regulations. We recommend that you check with the state government before you go abroad about their limitations on quantities allowed for personal importation and additional state taxes that might apply.

One time, John had a brainstorm. It was during our second trip to Germany. We had bought a bottle or two from each winemaker—we had them sign the labels, of course—and thus found ourselves with fifteen bottles of wine. We probably paid an average of about $6 each for them. While we have lugged wine around from vacations all over the world, we both have a bad disk in our necks—the very same disk; we always do everything together—and our neurosurgeon specifically told us to stop carrying wine around. So John asked the concierge at our hotel in Frankfurt to pack up the wine and send it to us at our New York apartment. She said it would be no problem. It cost more than $100, but, as John told Dottie at the time, "It's a lot cheaper than a visit to the neurosurgeon." Our trip home was so much more pleasant without having to worry about the wine. We kept congratulating ourselves on being so darn clever, but day after day the wine didn't arrive. Finally, we received a notice from British Airways World Cargo that our wine was being held at its warehouse at Kennedy airport. "Please contact your broker or advise us of alternative disposal instructions immediately," the letter said. Naively, we'd thought the wine would come directly to our apartment (and, indeed, many people have told us that they've sent wine directly home from overseas). We called British Airways, which said we had to come get it ourselves so we could clear Customs. There didn't seem to be much choice. We didn't have a car then, so John hired a car to take him to JFK and back. How long could it take?

You can't imagine how big Kennedy is when you're looking for Cargo Building 66. It was a fascinating tour of the bowels of the airport and, it was clear from the reaction of the driver, an expensive one, too. When John finally discovered British Airways, he found himself standing in line with burly truck drivers picking up tons of goods. "Yup," he told them, in a deep voice, "I'm here to pick up a shipment of wine." When he got to the front of the line, the clerk processed about two dozen pieces of paper for our wine and then said, "Now you have to go to Customs. Then come back." JFK is so big that he then gave John a map with directions to Customs, where John once again found himself in line with very large truckers. The pleasant but bemused Customs agent—"fifteen bottles of wine?"—took about fifteen minutes to process the growing pile of papers. Then he began to add up the amount of duty we owed. John panicked. He had forgotten to put extra cash in his pocket. "Do you think this will be more than $17?" he asked. "We'll see," said the agent.

The agent took out a calculator and seemed to punch in numbers forever. He took out a little chart and consulted it. He spent a while on his computer. Then he gave John the bill: *nineteen cents*. He told John to go over to the cashier to pay the duty and then come back to his window. All that done, John went back to British Airways, where the clerk stamped all of the dozens of papers with an old-fashioned rubber stamp and handed them to someone else, who got the wine from a huge warehouse. Then John had to go to security, where they photographed him and his driver's license. Finally, the wine was in the trunk and he was on his way home. The driver had a stopwatch. There was seventy minutes of waiting time. Total bill for the car: $125.

We have returned to carrying wine in our suitcases.

So how did it go with Sergey and Klara Iskoz, the Cambridge couple at the beginning of this chapter who were nervous about visiting France? We told them that wine people are really nice and they'd be fine. Were they?

We had absolutely no problems—many people spoke English, and we used our hands and bodies and smiled a lot when talking to those who didn't. The most memorable visit was in Sauternes, where after a very serious tour of Château de Malle we stopped by a smaller winery, Château Sahuc Lestour. There we saw a beautiful old house with a tower, flowers everywhere, and vineyards right behind the house. We parked our car, and then a dog appeared from nowhere and started to bark. Some time later, a man walked out of the house, and we told him that we wanted to visit the winery.

He spoke just a couple of words of English, but he took us inside the house and explained that this house was where he and his brother-in-law lived with their families and made their wine. He said his brother-in-law spoke English, but he was a little busy at the moment and would join us in a few minutes. Then the man showed us the fermentation vat and other equipment sitting in his garage, and then in the next room we met his brother-in-law, who was working a small machine to put labels on the bottles. The brother-in-law was very happy to see us because we were interested in their wines, and because he really loved speaking English but didn't have enough practice (his first wife had been English, and that's how he learned English). Then they took a bottle of 1999 Sauternes out of the fridge, and we all sat around the big table in the yard drinking the wine and talking about all sorts of things, from Botrytis cinerea *to last year's harvest to the world economy to Australian and South African wines to why Americans work so much. Then they brought in a few bottles of their wine to show us how the color of Sauternes changes with age—light yellow for the 1999 vintage, amber for the 1973 vintage, and dark ochre-orange for the 1947 vintage. We bought a bottle of their 1999 Sauternes, which was young and light and crisp and appley and just plain lovely. As they didn't have change, they gave us an extra half-bottle. So now we are proud owners of two bottles of 1999 and 1998 Château Sahuc Lestour Sauternes, whose labels show the house and the flowers and the trees under which we sat with the people who made the wine. We left their place almost pinching ourselves—we couldn't believe this was for real. The only problem is that we forgot to ask them to sign the bottles.*

Wine Shopping

How to Have Fun... or at Least Survive It

"What would I tell my wine merchant? In a word, 'Thanks.' Kameel Chamelly of Martha's Vineyard is knowledgeable, generous, trustworthy, fair, and interested in having his customers taste new and different wines. His wines run the gamut from $6 (or less) to the $1,000s. For me, wine is more than an adult beverage or a product to be bought and sold; it's one of the threads of life that ties together conversation, food, and friendship and provides the springboard for discussions of geography, culture, history, and ideas. I think Kameel agrees." —**BOB HENDRICKS, GRAND RAPIDS, MICHIGAN**

We know that this book is about enjoying wine and that most people see wine shopping as a chore at best and something truly dreadful at worst. But stick with us here, because you're never going to be able to fully enjoy wine until you find a wine shop that feels comfortable to you and a wine merchant who makes you feel welcome and special. Trust us: there are plenty of excellent wine stores all over America and not just in big cities. Maybe you don't think of Tallahassee, Florida, as a mecca for wine, but there are several fine wine shops there, and every time we visit Grandma Dot we find something interesting. We were in one shop there recently and saw something truly unusual: a Gewürztraminer from a winery called Enate in Spain. Gewürztraminer is a distinctive, peppery grape that's a specialty of the Alsatian region of France, but we'd never seen one from Spain. It was $13.99 and quite good: "crisp and a bit peppery, with some melon tastes. Absolutely lovely, and easy to drink, with character," as we wrote in our notes. When we called the importer later to ask about it, we discovered that only 350 cases of this wine were imported, and they were spread among twenty states. We'd never seen it in New York, but there it was in Tallahassee. Good wine is everywhere—and so are good wine shops.

Remember: we were regular wine consumers for twenty-five years before we ever wrote a word about wine. We know there are many bad wine stores out there, with overpriced wines and others that have sat on shelves forever. We know there are snobbish wine merchants who seem more interested in making fun of you than selling you wine. It's amazing how many people we've heard from over the years who have been snickered at in wine stores because they mispronounced the name of a wine. Unfortunately, the jerks have given all of the good merchants a bad name.

We were very lucky. When we were first learning about wine, we happened into a little store in the Coconut Grove section of Miami where "The Wine Lady"—we never knew her name—carefully showed us around the store and helped us choose reasonably priced wine from around the world. Before long, we really did enjoy wine shopping, and we still do. When John worked at *Newsweek* in the early 1980s, he had some difficult days and always consoled himself by walking over to the little wine shop across the street, where he chilled out by looking at the wines, touching labels, and thinking about similar wines that we'd shared.

These days we brake for wine shops. Just recently, we visited Atlanta for a family reunion and saw a little store called Peachtree Wine Merchants in a strip mall. We ran inside—Media and Zoë really hate this, so they stayed in the car, listening to music—and had an all-too-brief but fine time. The store had all sorts of wines we never see in New York, including some very unusual wines from Australia. There were enthusiastic handwritten signs all over the store (a good sign), and it was clear the people who worked there were having fun. When we later called the owner, Fred Bradshaw, he told us: "It would help if people looked at wine professionals like a sommelier. We can ask 'What have you had? What do you like?' I make the point to people who say they don't know anything about wine by saying I don't know about law. If I need legal advice, I talk to a lawyer. If people want advice about wine, they should talk to a wine professional, someone who is familiar with what they like. Too much wine is sold self-service, and people just pick a wine based on the label. That doesn't work well all of the time."

Many wine merchants, like Mr. Bradshaw, got into the business because they like wine and enjoy helping people with it. But, unfortunately, many got into it because—well—darn if we know why. They're the kind of merchants who make people avoid wine stores like dentists' offices. When we asked readers what one thing they'd tell their merchants, hoo boy, did we get an earful. We received far more positive notes like the preceding one than we would have guessed, but most of the notes weren't positive—far from it. Given a chance, here is a mixed case of things that customers would tell their wine merchants, leading up to the number-one thing. Do these sound familiar?

Tips to My Wine Merchant

12. Keep track of what I like and reward my loyalty. At a time when the video store and the pizza shop keep information about customers in their computers, readers wonder why wine shops can't do the same.

11. Play matchmaker. Readers pointed out that they usually drink wine with food, and they wish retailers were more willing and able to recommend pairings. As Frank Peterson of Herndon, Virginia, put it simply: "I buy wine to drink with food. I would like to be better at the pairings."

10. Offer more bargains. "Help me find cheap, great, but different wines from Chile, Spain, and perhaps France and Italy that I'll want to buy by the case just for drinking," wrote David Kuenzi of Downers Grove, Illinois.

9. Introduce me to new things. Wrote Josh Thomas of Greensboro, North Carolina: "Here's what I have to say to my wine merchant (the Wine Warehouse). Thank you. A few years ago I drank only California Chardonnays and an occasional California Merlot or Pinot Noir. However, as a direct result of my beginning to visit the Wine Warehouse, participating in its free tastings, and picking the mind of its owner, Mark

Lile-King, my wine appreciation and knowledge (I hope!) have grown exponentially. So, thanks!"

8. Hire better people. Readers feel that most store employees are either clueless or snobbish (or sometimes, in our experience, both). "I don't like snobbish clerks with an attitude and will avoid them at all costs. If I refuse assistance, I expect a reply such as 'I'll be over here if you need anything' or something similar. Snobbishness seems to be cultivated at a couple of local retail establishments here," wrote Ray Yurick of Akron, Ohio.

7. Speak English. Merchants who speak in wine-ese drive shoppers to distraction. "Keep it simple! Don't try to impress everyone with $25 language. No one likes to ask advice from a doctor and walk away more confused and embarrassed than they were before posing their question," said Gayle Wilson of Jacksonville, Florida. Describe wines in simple, plain terms. What we've often found over the years is that merchants who use the biggest, most impenetrable words are those who know least about wine.

6. Don't upsell me and don't hype. Wrote Josh Agrons of Houston: "Please don't lie or puff your wares; it insults my intelligence and destroys my store loyalty. All wines in your store are not universally excellent, and some are always going to be overpriced. In short, put less effort into selling and more into customer satisfaction, and you'll keep me coming back. When you recommend a wine, make sure it is something you've tasted and really do think is worthwhile, as opposed to something that the store owners are running a bottle bounty on to unload your excess supply."

5. Treat me with respect whatever my price range. "When I ask for a good, affordable everyday drinking wine, don't lead me to the $25 bottles. When I say it's out of my range, don't stick your nose in the air as if no wine under $25 is worth drinking," wrote Tim Hartigan of Bass Lake, Wisconsin.

4. Learn three little words. "Don't be afraid to say 'I don't know' instead of making up answers," wrote Shaun Breidbart of Pelham, New York. This rang many bells with us. We were recently in a wine store when a young man tried to sell us a bottle of Cabernet Franc. We talked to him about it a little, and finally he said, "Actually, I've never tasted a Cabernet Franc." We told him that it often smells a little like pencil shavings. "It does?" he replied incredulously. (It really does.)

3. Post more information, but make it accurate. Readers wanted more information from wine writers and publications posted, partly so they could shop without having to talk to store employees, who intimidate them. Many people complained, though, about posted reviews that feature a different vintage than the one the store is selling.

2. Don't treat me like a girl. There are a lot of angry female wine drinkers out there. Wrote Sara Brown of Palo Alto, California: "Don't ignore the midtwenties blonde woman walking into your store in shorts and running shoes. If you treat me right, you'll have a customer for life. Just because I'm not wearing a golf-ball-sized diamond and $300 shoes doesn't mean I don't have the interest or the money to buy wine. This is coming from lots of experience! I often get flat-out ignored in wine stores in my neighborhood." And this from Julie Tikekar of Ann Arbor, Michigan: "Wine merchants should not be turned off, intimidated, or offended by pretty young things that know something about wine, ask intelligent questions, and expect honest answers. I can't tell you how many times I've gotten answers that are either filled with tones of annoyance and intimidation or clearly wrong, which doesn't particularly help the cause. Next question: how to deal with French waiters when a PYT sends a bottle back?"

1. Tell me what *you* think. This was the biggie. Readers are hungry for both handwritten signs and personal advice from merchants. Said James E. Holtzman of Chicago: "If he really tastes all of his wines, he should set his own rating scale and mark the wines accordingly. With his rating scale out there for all to see, I can get a better feel for his tastes and then really learn to trust his ratings or move elsewhere." Added Jim Herbeck of Columbus, Ohio: "Tell me a couple of wines that *you* like, not what wines you think I would like. When I ask most wine merchants what they like, I get a barrage of questions in return about what I like. Dry? Sweet? White? Red? Smooth? Lots of bite? It's as if they are afraid to tell me what *they* like in case it doesn't meet my exacting wine specifications. I find that I enjoy a wine recommended *by* someone much more than a wine recommended *for* someone." Dan Riley of Seattle was more heated. "You snicker and act condescending when I ask for wines the *Wine Spectator* or *Wall Street Journal* recommends. Fine. If you say you taste all the wines in your shop, then write up your own paragraph for each wine and come up with your own store rating system and post them. You can write, can't you?"

Mr. Riley added this, which pretty much sums up so many of the concerns voiced by our readers: "In general, I think wine marketing in this country is dreadful. It's like they *want* people to be intimidated by it all. The moment everyone in the wine business realizes the point of wine is to have fun with the experience and enjoy the great variety of choice and give people a reason to try stuff, then maybe something will change. As it is, I don't see it. And it's too bad, because wine is a healthy beverage, not just nutritionally but emotionally, too."

Our Advice to Shoppers

One day recently, when Media had to visit the dentist, John dropped everyone off and went looking for a parking space. He made a right turn into a new development on Manhattan's West Side and immediately spotted a wine store that he knew he had to visit. How could he tell that from the car? The shop was well lighted, it had a sign outside announcing a wine tasting, it seemed open and inviting, and there was a man by the door with two bottles of open wine on a table. Sounds simple, doesn't it? Here are tips for how to spot a good wine shop. Sure, every shop is different and some stores might not fit these tips and still be excellent, but these are the ten things we look for to get a quick first impression.

1. The Gap test. You shouldn't ask less of a wine store than you do of a clothing store. It should be clean and appear to be carefully cared for. Of course, sometimes there are great bargains in stores that are dusty and seem neglected, but you need to be an expert shopper to excavate the gems. Dottie loves thrift shops, but she knows clothes. It's frightening to imagine what John might come home with from one.

2. Organization. There are many ways a wine store can be organized: by country, by grape type, even by price. Some chichi stores these days even organize wines by adjectives like *juicy* or *full-bodied*. What's important is that it's organized in some way that makes it easy for you to find your way around. This not only makes shopping easier but also shows that the management cares.

3. The temperature. Is it really hot in the store? It's a bad sign if it is. The wines are suffering, and they might have been suffering for some time. Cooked wines are not a treat.

4. The sales help. The staff at a store is critical, of course, but even before you get to know them, you can pretty well judge a store by that first contact. Do they ask if they can help you? After you say, "Not right now," do they leave you alone? We don't like Velcro merchants who won't let us simply peruse the store. As Arturo Ciompi of Durham, North Carolina, wrote us: "Please allow me two or three minutes to browse before you pierce the moment with 'Can I help with anything today?' Customers deserve that 'get into the mood' time before help should descend." John was recently chased out of a store by a merchant who refused to leave him alone after he made it clear three times that he enjoyed looking around. Since John was there to buy a couple of cases, that store lost a substantial chunk of business. It will be a long time before he goes back.

5. Handwritten signs. This is a sign of enthusiasm, and enthusiasm is good. As our readers pointed out, they want to know what the merchant genuinely thinks of the wines in the store. That's how to build trust. The merchant says, "I like this. You try it and tell me what you think." Enthusiasm can be contagious, and when it's well founded, it's good for the customer and the merchant.

6. Visible prices. It's incredible, but we have visited some wine stores where all the price tags are on the backs of the bottles. What are they hiding?

7. Price check. Look at a wine you know and see how the price compares. Charging $13 for a specific bottle of wine you usually spend about $10 on might be cause for worry. This is an important point, though: price isn't everything. A wine merchant who points you to good things and away from bad things is worth something.

8. Tastings. More and more wine stores offer in-store tastings. This is a good thing to look for. You can taste without having to buy a bottle, and that will help you and the merchant learn what you like.

9. New stuff. This one's really easy—and important. As you are looking around, do you see a whole bunch of stuff you've never seen before? If you do, it means that you can spend some serious time there and always find something new and interesting to try.

10. Case discounts. Many stores have big signs that announce, say, a 15 percent discount on any case, whether a solid case or a mixed case. That's a great way to reward your business and loyalty.

Now, notice that every one of these ten tips is something you can accomplish in just minutes and without speaking to anyone. If you decide to stay in the store and give it a try, you'll soon learn whether you want to deal with the people there. And once you start taking bottles home, you will discover whether you trust their opinions. Here's the most important point of all: don't suffer a bad wine merchant. There are too many good ones out there.

Advice from Some Good Merchants

W e called dozens of wine merchants around the country who have been recommended by readers as people who make wine interesting and enjoyable. We asked them this: if consumers could do one thing to make wine more fun, what would it be? We figured everyone would say "try new things," so we told them that was a given. What else? Here are some of their responses:

The Grapevine Cottage in Zionsville, Indiana. "Don't take it so seriously," said Doug Pendleton, the owner. His store provides "cellar cards" with each bottle, listing the price and information from reviews of the wine. That way people can remember what they bought.

Wine Warehouse in Greensboro, North Carolina. "Visiting wineries is helpful," said Mark Lile-King, the owner, who is also a minister. "You get a chance to see that making wine is not in most places just cranking out a product. It's performance art. You get a better sense of the mystery of what wine is about." He added: "It's important to try wines with other people to make a community. Wine lends itself to community building and enhances relationships, and that's a good way for people to experience wine."

Suburban Wine & Liquor in Yorktown Heights, New York. "Don't be embarrassed to ask the proverbial stupid question," said owner Henry Ponzio. His store has the Fifties Club. After customers buy fifty different wines over a two-year period, they get an extra discount. He said three thousand five hundred customers have joined the club and enjoy trying new things.

McCarthy & Schiering in Seattle, Washington. "Taste wines blind," said James Fessler, the manager. "Too many people are still biased toward labels."

Sherry-Lehmann in New York City. "You shouldn't forget that wine is meant to be enjoyed," said Michael Aaron, the chairman. "When you drink a bottle of wine at dinner, it's not as though you're having a final exam. You should sit down at the table and open up the bottle with the main intention being to have fun."

The WineSellar in San Diego. "The way to learn is to drink," said Gary Parker, the owner.

Binny's in Chicago. Don't expect to go into a wine store and pick up that unusual bottle of wine you drank at a restaurant last night, said Ray Denton, general manager/wine manager. "Some have restaurant-only labels, some have allocated wines and older vintages. People will tell me, 'I had a wine at a restaurant. Can you get it?' It's the single biggest source of frustration that I see on a consumer level. It's also difficult trying to explain to people that you can't replicate the experience of that great meal every time you open that bottle. It's hard to burst that bubble."

Zachy's in Scarsdale, New York. "Drink wine every night, whether you're having pizza or filet mignon," said Jeff Zacharia, president.

Table and Vine in Northampton, Massachusetts. "Try a noble grape that you've been avoiding: Riesling," said Paul Provost, the general manager. "Try it because we've had now a number of years of spectacular vintages in most parts of Germany as well as in Austria, and the prices are somewhat depressed. Get a producer you like, at whatever sweetness level you like, and follow that producer."

Off the Vine in Grapevine, Texas. "Don't cave in to any of the stereotypical snobbery," said Wayne Turner, part owner. "Drink what you like. Wine is fun. It's not supposed to be snooty."

Spec's Liquor Warehouse in Houston. "Drink wine at the right temperature," said Joseph Kemble, a manager of the wine department. "People generally drink red wines too warm." And use nice glasses, he added.

Century Liquors in Rochester, New York. "The best way to really enjoy wine is by trying one wine against another of the same type," said Sherwood Deutsch, the owner. "People can find a wine course in their area taught by someone who's reliable and trustworthy that will help them do that. Joining a wine-tasting group is also a good idea."

The Wine Shop in Charlotte, North Carolina. "Rather than go to a grocery store or a discount store where you can't get any help, find a local retail merchant whom you can get to know and who can get to know you and your taste. If I don't give people that personal attention, then what do I have to offer?" said Frank Redd, the owner.

And, as it happens, that brings us to . . .

Navigating the Aisles of Your Supermarket

W e've been talking about wine stores all this time, but we know that many people buy wine at supermarkets in states that allow it. That's what we did, too, when we were first learning about wine and living in Florida. We'd go into the Grand Union to pick up something for dinner and then wheel over to the wine aisle to look for something new. We remember the first time we saw Federico Paternina "Banda Azul" Rioja from Spain, for $2.99, and it became our house red for years. It isn't possible to do this everywhere—state laws forbid supermarkets in some places to sell wine, for instance—but, still, almost half the wine bought in stores is purchased at groceries and "supercenters," those huge stores that also sell food, according to ACNielsen Homescan. Warehouse club stores account for an additional 12 percent. We get tons of notes from readers telling us about the great buys they get at Costco or Trader Joe's or about the outstanding wine they bought at a Harris Teeter supermarket. The $1.99 Charles Shaw wines—"Two-Buck Chuck"—sold only at Trader Joe's were a sensation in 2003, and you never know what you'll find there: we once bought a 1997 Barbaresco—a fine Italian red from an excellent year— at Trader Joe's in San Diego. It wasn't as fruity as we expected it to be, but it was still good, and fun to try at just $7.99.

Selling wine and food at the same place makes such good sense. Wine is a beverage to serve with food, and having an aisle of wine next to the macaroni and cheese not only makes wine shopping easier but also makes an important statement about wine's place on the table. Some supermarkets take their wine seriously and offer excellent selections and expert service, and, of course, large stores such as Costco are offering more and better wines all the time. For now, let's talk about the plain old garden-variety chain-supermarket aisle. We've shopped for wine in supermarkets in several states for decades and we have some long-held thoughts about decoding the aisle, but we figured we could use an immersion course, so we spent a few days haunting the supermarkets of Florida—from Tampa to Orlando to Tallahasee, in stores like Publix, Winn-Dixie, and Albertsons. We chose this area because we're familiar with Florida stores and because we thought these would be midrange examples. We weren't comparing different chains or chains to wine stores. We wanted to come up with advice to make the wine aisle smaller and friendlier. Based on that visit and our many years of experience, here's our advice:

1. Take your time. If you're like us—and especially like John—you go to the grocery store with a list of foods and try to get finished as quickly as possible. This can hurt you in the wine aisles, because they're often organized strangely—or not at all. Sometimes wines are grouped by producer, sometimes by type, and sometimes by both. For instance, you might see one shelf with all of the Woodbridge wines, including the Sauvignon Blanc. Then there will be another shelf with Sauvignon Blanc, but not the Woodbridge. And maybe the Sauvignon Blanc shelf includes international Sauvignon Blanc, too, such as those from New Zealand— and maybe it doesn't. Some stores have sections for "fine wine," separated from other wines, but don't take their word for it. Sometimes it seems that wine is organized randomly. The industry giants—Gallo, Constellation, the Wine Group, Bronco, and such—tend to overwhelm the shelves with wines under many labels. Distribution is key in the wine industry, and the big guys control the shelves. You often won't know it from the labels, but, for instance, Rancho Zabaco, Frei Brothers, and MacMurray are all Gallo brands.

2. Eliminate the larger bottles, the boxed wines, and the frat-boy stuff such as MD 20/20 and Wild Irish Rose. Sure, some fine wines come in big bottles, but most of these are mass-produced jug wines that, in tastings, we haven't enjoyed much. This will immediately make the aisle much smaller.

3. Eliminate all the Chardonnay. We know most people really like Chardonnay, and so do we. But Chardonnay's popularity means the aisles are flooded with it. If you simply pass over that part of the aisle, you've once again narrowed your choices considerably. (If you want a Chardonnay, at least get one you've never tried before.)

4. Eliminate the familiar. You will be punished—price-wise—for refusing to leave your comfort zone. The wines that many Americans are most comfortable with—from Santa Margherita Pinot Grigio to Kendall-Jackson

Chardonnay—tend to be overpriced because supermarkets know that people in a hurry will grab the familiar. Don't. Consider this: at a Publix in Tallahassee, Santa Margherita Pinot Grigio was $22.49 and Kendall-Jackson was $12.69. For just $7 more than the K-J—which may be perfectly lovely, but, really, isn't something different going to make dinner a little more special?—and for $3 less than the Pinot Grigio you could get a Joseph Drouhin Premier Cru Chablis, a world-class wine that would make any meal more of an occasion.

5. Think outside California. There are some excellent California wines on shelves, of course, but you'll probably get better deals on wines from elsewhere. For some reason supermarkets always seem to have a few kinds of Châteauneuf-du-Pape, the earthy red wine from the Rhône Valley of France, and Vouvray, the white wine from France with a taste of just-picked green apples. The Châteauneuf-du-Pape would be great with stew and the Vouvray with pork—and they tend to be much better buys than more familiar wines.

6. Think Beaujolais and Pinot Noir. Almost every store has at least one Beaujolais, the lively, fruity red from France that's good with just about all food and costs about $8. And every store has some American Pinot Noir. These are extremely versatile with food, and they tend to be better buys than Cabernet Sauvignon or Chardonnay because they aren't as popular. At the Publix in Tallahassee, there was a Pinot Noir from Domaine Chandon. This producer of fine sparkling wine in Napa Valley makes a small amount of still wine, and finding this wine was a real treat. Yes, it cost $27.59, and that seems like a lot, but it is, after all, not much more than the Santa Margherita Pinot Grigio that many people put into their carts with little thought.

7. Look closely at vintages. Most wines in supermarkets are for immediate enjoyment. You want them young and fresh, from the most recent vintage available. Unfortunately, at many supermarkets, wines stand on the shelves until they're sold, and, like milk, the older stuff is moved to the front. On our Florida tour, we saw three-year-old white Zinfandels and Pinot Grigios and a 1996 Pouilly-Fuissé. Yech! We saw several vintages of the same wine standing right next to each other. At one store, a 2002 Jadot Beaujolais-Villages was behind the 2001, identical except for the vintage. Sometimes, however, you can find fine old bottles from great years that are real bargains because the store never raised the price. That's how we once bought a few bottles of 1974 Robert Mondavi Cabernet Sauvignon, a classic wine. Even at that, you have to wonder what kind of shape these older wines are in, since they've been standing up, under lights, for heaven knows how long.

8. Look for orphans. Some of our best supermarket deals over the years have come because there's one bottle of something left and there's no place for it on the shelves. That happened during our foray into stores in Florida, too. At one store on our tour, there was one bottle of Mumm's Cordon Rosé Champagne. We'd never seen this pink bubbly, and, when available, it's usually about $36. Well, this bottle was $16.99—marked down from $18.99. Think about your significant other coming home for dinner and finding that waiting at the table. There are good buys like that if you'll search (often behind other bottles).

9. Bigger isn't necessarily better. Some supermarkets that have more space devoted to wine actually have thinner selections. They display bottle after bottle of the exact same mass-produced wine, like a valley of the clones that swallows up space for the good stuff.

10. Check prices. That might seem obvious, considering that some of us note whether Winn-Dixie charges more for a can of peas than Publix. But too many people assume that wine prices are fairly stable, and they aren't. Stores compete on wine prices just like anything else. At the stores we visited, Sutter Home white Zinfandel ranged from $3.89 to $5.49, a 41 percent difference. The same is true for many other wines. And while this might also seem obvious, be sure to join the store's frequent-shopper club or whatever they call it. It seems like all big chains offer this now, giving discounts to regular customers who sign up for a card. There is always tremendous price competition on wine, and we found in Florida that the frequent-shopper cards saved even more on wine than on other products. Some stores even had "wine clubs" with special discounts for people who signed up.

Now, having decoded the shelves, how many bottles are left to choose from? Probably not many. If you're looking for a wine in a specific price range or if you're looking just for a red or for a white, there will be even fewer. Among those that are left, close your eyes and pick one. Something new will make dinner tonight more fun.

Football

"Real Men Do Drink Wine"

"John Fina, who was a tackle, and I were sitting together at a restaurant swirling and sipping when the rest of the team looked at us, and you could tell they were wondering, 'What has gone wrong with the NFL?'" —GLENN PARKER, **WHO PLAYED IN THE NATIONAL FOOTBALL LEAGUE FOR ELEVEN YEARS**

We're in the parking lot of Giants Stadium in New Jersey, hanging out before a National Football League game between the New York Giants and the Philadelphia Eagles. Our mission: find someone among the tailgaters who's drinking wine, not beer or liquor. We've arrived an hour before kickoff, but even before we get out of the car we can see that the parking lots are filled with very serious tailgaters, with tables, chairs, coolers, barbecue equipment, and even tents. We can already smell something cooking. The aroma of gas grills has filled the air. We park in a corner and walk by dozens of happy tailgaters. We're surprised to see that sausage is just about as popular on the grills as hamburgers and hot dogs, but we're not surprised by the amount of beer we see: light beer, dark beer, nonalcohol beer, foreign beer, domestic beer. We wonder if our quest has been in vain. Then, suddenly, a light shines down. "Look over there," John tells Dottie as he grabs her shoulder. "It's a bottle of wine—and it looks like a good bottle." As we get closer, we see that it's very good indeed: a 1998 Château Phélan-Ségur from Bordeaux. David Sanzalone, director of marketing for an industrial chemical company, has brought the Phélan-Ségur, along with a 1998 Puligny-Montrachet, which is a great white Burgundy, and a 1999 Rodney Strong Reserve Pinot Noir from California. He explains that his tailgating parties with wine began in 1990 as client events (the four people joining him and his wife, Carol, and their daughter Lilia originally were clients), but as these clients have become friends, the Giants games are just another excuse for them to have fun together. They've taken cooking classes together, and they eat out together often, too. "Wine is what we have in common," Mr. Sanzalone said, adding that it's perfect with the foods they enjoy. Today's fare features club steaks they grilled, penne pasta salad, marinated vegetables, Jersey tomatoes, horseradish sauce, Italian pastries, and coffee. Mr. Sanzalone said he brings wines from his seven-hundred-bottle cellar in New Jersey to the games "because it's what we enjoy. Wine celebrates and enhances life and friendships." When we leave, we leave with plastic glasses of the Bordeaux.

They are not alone. As we continue to walk, we see that tailgating isn't only for beer drinkers anymore. A few cars away, Winston Thompson, his son Robert, and two of their friends see us. "You're carrying wine and aren't giving us any?" he says. "Phélan-Ségur 1998," John says. Mr. Thompson raises his beer, points to it, and says, "Bass—last Thursday." It turns out, though, that Mr. Thompson and his friends are drinking beer today only because of the cuisine. Last week these Giants fans from Connecticut had a Sauvignon Blanc with shrimp on skewers and a big brawny Zinfandel with steaks and baked potatoes. "You can't get good wine inside the stadium," says a member of the party, Clint Howson, who builds elevators. Why do most people drink beer at tailgating parties? we ask them. "It's easier," Mr. Thompson muses philosophically. "With beer, you don't need glasses; you can drink from the bottle. It's not so good to drink wine out of the bottle." Right!

And so it went. Sure, there is more beer than wine, but there is plenty of wine, too—not to mention a cornucopia of dishes that we never would have imagined. Edward Zimbalatti, who works in clinical finance, and three friends arrived at 9:00 A.M., began the day with Bloody Marys, and then went through shrimp, Port-wine pâté, smoked ham, pork chops, and Brie. We're pleased to see a large bottle of Santa Carolina Cabernet-Merlot blend from Chile. "Wine is the essence of fine dining," explains his friend Todd Frasca. Even though Mr. Frasca says that with a glint in his eye, he's right.

We know most people think of beer when they think of football and other manly sports, but that's changing, albeit slowly, and even the wine industry is beginning to notice. A few weeks before our visit to the Giants Stadium parking lot, we were listening to a Giants game on the radio and, lo and behold, among the clutter of beer and car ads was one for Korbel sparkling wine. We were surprised enough to call Charlie White, divisional marketing director for Korbel in the Northeast, and ask what was up. The audience for the Giants, he told us, "is very upscale, with a longstanding, strong season ticket base. Football is so celebratory when your team scores, when your team wins, when there's a winning field goal, that I thought Korbel was just a perfect fit. It's about celebratory moments and memories, turning moments into memories. You can equate it to anything and any sport." The radio spot "was just a way to reach out to a new audience that we had left to beer companies." He added, by the way: "Tailgating has evolved. It's not just hot dogs and beer anymore."

Part of the reason for beer's longtime sports predominance probably has to do with the foods served at sporting events and around television sets tuned to sports: hot dogs, peanuts, salty pretzels. As arenas around the country have begun expanding their food offerings—to sushi, even—some are dabbling in wine, but selling fans on this will still be tough. Consider Louisiana State University's Tiger Stadium, a true football shrine. Jean and Harold Settle of Cropwell, Alabama, are die-hard LSU fans. One late November they traveled to Baton Rouge to do some tailgating and then watch LSU battle its rival, the Alabama Crimson Tide. Their own drink of choice: Piper-Heidsieck Brut Champagne. We asked them for an on-the-scene report. "The tailgating is amazing," Dr. Settle, a cardiologist, told us. "Tents are everywhere on campus. Tables are set up, grills are glowing, and coolers are full of soft drinks and beer, and the liquor is flowing. There are gas-powered generators and propane gas grills everywhere. These guys are unreal. There are ribs and ribs—smoked, barbecued, grilled—and the usual hot dogs and hamburgers. Some tailgaters have catered picnics with chilled shrimp, cold cuts, and elaborate sandwich fixings. And, of course, there are vendors galore hawking red beans and rice, shrimp Creole, and jambalaya. It's spicy hot. It's unreal. But there's no wine." The Settles themselves drank their bubbly before the game—and that was a good call. The final score was

Alabama 31, LSU 0. Said Dr. Settle: "I'm glad that we enjoyed it ahead of time, because after the thrashing Alabama put on LSU, I would not have been in any mood to pop a cork at midnight." Fortunately for the Settles, they had plenty reason to pop the cork after the 2003 season, when their beloved LSU team was the Bowl Championship Series national champion.

But wait. The Settles do have some company. Thomas and Yvonne Tryon of Sarasota, Florida, have been tailgating since 1994, when their daughter Julie enrolled at the University of Central Florida to study music. They "turned a few heads," Mr. Tryon told us, because they consistently brought wine to their pregame meals when Julie played in the university's band. They would drive for two hours to get to the stadium, arrive three hours before the game, and wait for the band to start warming up. "Now that she's graduated, she and other friends join us, and the event has become sacrosanct as a time when family and friends get together for fun and frivolity," said Mr. Tryon, editorial page editor for the *Sarasota Times Herald.* "Beer is terrific for a starter, but a bubbly or a nice wine with some cheese and beef makes the event a special occasion."

The Tryons have had fun deciding which foods work best at tailgating parties and discovering which wines go well with those foods. They started out taking "everyday whites" but soon decided to "make things nicer" with more special wines and foods. For one of their first tailgate dinners, they asked a favorite restaurant to prepare a picnic for them. Talk about being nice: the restaurant packed them a meal of sliced tenderloin and tucked in a bottle of Champagne and a light red wine. "Gosh, this is nice," Mr. Tryon said they decided, so they started experimenting in earnest to find other things that traveled well. They found that if they grilled a beef tenderloin in the morning and then sliced it outside the stadium, it tasted best; that chicken salad with curry and apples tastes great on pita bread; and that roast beef is good with pesto. A favorite pairing is shish kebab with Beaujolais. Rosés, light Italian whites such as Pinot Grigio, and Sauvignon Blancs are major hits. They also mark their anniversaries outside the game with Champagne. "We're not the only ones drinking wine," Mr. Tryon told us, "but we are in the minority." He added that there is a bonus for him: the attention of attractive young women. "Now the college girls think I'm romantic and cool," he said. "They walk by us and say 'Oh, that's so sweet.' Of course, it's twenty-five years too late." At one big game, when Julie and her husband, Shane Habert, couldn't make it, the Tryons went solo, and it was "a lot more romantic," Mr. Tryon said. "We found a good spot under a tree, and we were sitting there having some wine, and we looked over at another couple. It was clear that this couple had had a tiff. So the woman says to the guy, 'Look at them,' pointing at us. 'They're having a good time, and here you are drinking beer and looking at television.'"

Some wine is even beginning to appear at Super Bowl parties in front of television sets. Robin Dozier of San Francisco and her husband, Dion, have been having parties on Super Bowl day for IV years. Her husband, an accountant, drinks beer and wine, but she drinks only wine—"I haven't developed a taste for beer"—so she makes sure that their guests have a choice. The wine is usually Merlot. She serves it with confidence because it's a popular varietal and it's usually "absolutely wonderful." For Super Bowl XXXVII, the food and the wine had to be special. Mr. Dozier was born and raised in Oakland, and his beloved Raiders were in it. With about fifteen people expected—both sets of parents and lots of siblings and friends—the word went out early, she joked: "Don't come in the house rooting for anybody else." As expected, most of her guests were beer drinkers, but she steered a few people to the wines when her spicy red bean and pork chili was served. "The Beaujolais was a great match, and our guests enjoyed it," she said. "It didn't compete with the spiciness of the chili. It was light and fruity and provided a nice balance." She also opened a Malbec from Argentina that her wine shop had recommended. "I thought it was also a good pairing with chili, although I liked the Beaujolais better. It was fun to compare the two." Alas, the Raiders were as flat as a can of beer that had been left open for a week. They went down, 48 to 21. "Halftime was fairly quiet in our house. I could tell that my husband was in a funky mood, but he tried to appear upbeat, remembering that we had guests. Poor guy," Ms. Dozier told us. "Needless to say, we were all disappointed with the outcome. Thank God the food and the wine were good."

Look, if you don't think wine and football go together, don't argue with us. Argue with Glenn Parker, who is much bigger than we are—six-foot-five, to be exact. Mr. Parker retired from football in 2002 after playing for eleven years as an offensive lineman and left guard for the Buffalo Bills, the Kansas

City Chiefs, and the New York Giants. Mr. Parker, who then became an announcer for NBC's Arena Football League, loves wine and owns about four thousand bottles, mostly California Cabernet Sauvignon, Bordeaux, some Italian wines, and "a lot of Pinot Noir." For years he was the guy other players went to for wine advice in the locker room. He used to host tailgate parties after games for his teammates and their families at Giants Stadium. Since retiring, he has continued serving wine at tailgate parties he throws after Arizona college games (he was a third-round pick in 1990 out of Arizona) and at football parties at his home when there's an important game on television. "Of course, people who come to my house know that generally there will be wine on the table," he told us. "If it's early in the season, I'll have Pinot Grigio or Sauvignon Blanc, Chenin Blanc, Riesling. Anything else is too much" for the warm weather. He likes to pair Chenin Blanc and Riesling with "fruit salads and brats on the grill." As the season proceeds into autumn, he prefers to serve "heavy soups and chilis," and he tends to pair those with Pinot Noir, "which everybody loves," or Zinfandel, which is a great match with tailgate food like hotdogs and chili.

For Mr. Parker, football was in many ways a means to an end. He kept his eyes on broadcasting possibilities for his second act and dreamed of owning a vineyard. Twice, during off-season downtime, he interned at Robert Mondavi Winery. Once, when he was on the field facing Chris Doleman, a Minnesota Vikings defender and a fellow wine lover, Mr. Doleman asked him if he really was into wine. He said yes, and for the next few plays they chatted about wine until "the guys in the huddle asked, 'Will you just shut up?'"

It's a shame Chris Hinton wasn't in the same huddle. Mr. Hinton was an offensive lineman for thirteen years in the NFL (seven times All-Pro). Then he retired and acted on his passion. He and his wife, Mya, now own an outstanding wine shop in Alpharetta, Georgia, called the Wine Store. He doesn't go to many games now that he's not playing anymore, but he does host a Super Bowl party every year at which he barbecues ribs and serves wine. "Typically, we do reds. They're always a big hit," he said. "Some of the big Zins especially." Added Mr. Hinton, who is six-foot-five and weighs 305 pounds: "Real men do drink wine."

So, what to serve? We like the idea of muscular reds: wines from the Rhône Valley of France, brawny Zinfandels, Argentine Malbecs. We also appreciate that this is a time for big, informal jugs of red wine. We conducted a tasting of fifty red wines that cost $7.99 or less for 1.5 liters. Here are some recommendations. Overall, we found red jug wines from Italy to be most satisfying, and we'd suggest that you look for one.

Some Jug Reds

Belmondo Merlot (Delle Venezie). Italy. Easy to drink and pleasant. Great with barbecue because it's easy and round. (2000)

Blossom Hill Winery Merlot. California. Very soft, with some blackberry-cream tastes and a hint of grapefruit acidity. (1999)

Citra (Montepulciano d'Abruzzo). Italy. Chilled, it's charming—a bit grapey, but soft and easy to drink. If you're having anything Italian—a giant lasagne, pizza, or grilled sausages—this would be perfect. (2001)

Dario D'Angelo (Montepulciano d'Abruzzo). Italy. Fruity, fun, and very pleasant. Pretty dry and even a hint of earth. A fine party wine. (2000)

Ernest & Julio Gallo Winery "Twin Valley" Cabernet Sauvignon. California. Crisp and clean and almost Beaujolais-like. Soft and easy to drink. (Nonvintage)

Foxhorn Vineyards Merlot. California. Quite pleasant. Real wine, with a little bit of depth and a little bit of structure. Slightly herbaceous. Drier than most. (Nonvintage)

"[Dick Vermeil, the coach of the NFL's Kansas City Chiefs] has a quieter approach to productivity. In a game against Oakland earlier this season, Mr. Vermeil, a wine aficionado, casually approached his kicker Morten Andersen, a fellow oenophile, and said, 'You make this kick and you've got one of my Bryant Family Vineyards, and they're impossible to get.' Andersen made the game-winning field goal."

From the Wall Street Journal, Dec. 12, 2003

Saving the Memories

Why Germans Are Unlike Australians

"We were dining a few years ago at a lovely restaurant in Scottsdale with a large group. As it was on an expense account, someone ordered a magnum of Champagne. It had a perfectly beautiful label, and after the bottle was emptied I asked the waiter if he would please take it back to the kitchen and soak the label off for me. Off he trotted and later returned with...a clean and empty bottle! He had indeed soaked off the label—and thrown it away! Aaargh! I have since given up labels—they don't come off the box very easily anyway." —**JOYCE BISHOP, WINNETKA, ILLINOIS**

As you know by now, this book isn't really about wine but about occasions and memories. Everyone saves memories in different ways—with photographs, with diaries, sometimes with matchbook covers. We have saved ours with wine labels. That's how we know we had a Grignolino in 1978 at the now-shuttered, delightfully garish Mamma Leone's restaurant in New York; an inky Amarone at a wine bar in Venice in 1987 while staring at but not touching a plate of tripe; and a Tomasello Winery Cabernet Sauvignon from New Jersey the last time we ate at our beloved Windows on the World on September 6, 2001, five days before the World Trade Center was destroyed.

Over the past thirty years, we have saved more than eight thousand labels, and it often hasn't been easy. We never knew, though, that we weren't alone. We've discovered that many people save labels—or at least try to. When we wrote a column about label removing, we received hundreds of letters from all over the world from readers telling us stories about labels, sometimes bemoaning their label-removing incompetence and other times offering suggestions on how to remove them. We learned things about glue that we really didn't want to know. Wrote Jeff Ashby of Dallas: "I thought I was the only person who did not know how to properly remove a label. Having lost my expense account, I guess it really doesn't matter." And we received this, from Roger L. Amidon, a distinguished professor at the Norman J. Arnold School of Public Health at the University of South Carolina: "This is one of the more frustrating wine-related problems I've had in recent years. I've given up, believing the matter hopeless."

So it struck us that if you're going to follow even a little of our advice in this book, there might come a time when you'll need to tackle this sticky problem. After hearing from readers, we tried several of their suggestions, but first, let's just run through how we've done it for all these years.

1. Remember to save the bottle, whether you're in a restaurant or at home. You'd be surprised by how many people overlook this all-important first step, especially at a restaurant. Don't be shy about asking the waiter to pack up your bottle. The restaurant will probably be flattered (and might just take the label off for you—and give it to you).

2. Save the bottles in a prominent place until you have a few to attack at once. Why a prominent place? Because if you put them in the basement, you'll forget about them. Then every time you go down to the basement, you'll say, "Oh, yeah, I've got to get to those bottles," and then you'll forget about them again until there are so many that you'll just throw them out.

3. Fill your kitchen sink with hot water. Also, get a large pot, fill it with water, and heat to boiling. Be careful; burns hurt.

4. Lay a piece of plastic wrap or wax paper across your kitchen counter.

5. Immerse the empty bottles, with their corks removed, in the sink. After the bottles have been in for a while, some labels might float right off. This always makes our heart skip a beat. If the label hasn't floated off, lift and empty the bottle very carefully, place it on a towel, and try to get your fingernail under a corner of the label. At that point it might lift right off. When you get a label off, lay it flat on the plastic wrap.

6. If a label won't budge, put that bottle—very, very carefully—into the boiling water. This will often cause stubborn labels to give up and float off. Have a long spoon or fork ready to fish the label out of the water.

7. For labels that still will not come off, it's time to get serious with your fingernails or even a knife. This is best to do when the label is still wet, but it's difficult, because the bottle is still hot. Start at one end and carefully begin to work under the label. Take your time. If the label begins to fall apart, stop. At this point we often put the bottle back where it was for a while to cool, then put it back into the sink. With the bottle much cooler, it's easier to take it out later and work with it even more slowly.

8. Now, if everything fails, there's a commercial solution: label removers, which are essentially big strips of clear adhesive tape. Lay them over the label, press, and peel off. The labels usually come off with them (sometimes it's necessary to help them out by pulling up a corner). These are available in many wine stores and on-line wine-accessory retailers such as wineenthusiast.com and iwawine.com. Even in bulk, though, they often cost about fifty cents each, so we use them sparingly.

9. Once you have gotten the labels off and dried them on the plastic wrap, put them in a book. We use those photo albums with the sticky pages (they're not as elegant as leather-bound label books, but they cost about $9.99 for a hundred pages). If you don't put them in some sort of book, you'll just stack them up, intending to organize them someday, but you'll probably get less inclined to tackle that job as the pile builds up (as with the bottles in the basement).

We've made the organization of our labels into a kind of New Year's tradition. Throughout the year we put the labels into the photo book in random order as we drink the wines. Then, on New Year's Day, we lay out all of the labels on the floor and organize them by country and type. This is a great way for us to revisit our memories of the previous year. After organizing them, we write the year on the spine of the photo book and add it to our collection. We have label books going back to the 1970s.

There are great national and regional distinctions among labels. Burgundy labels and German labels float right off. Australian labels are impossible. California labels are all over the map. We mused about this in our column and were unprepared for the passionate explanations for this. Consider this, from Bill Scherbak of Thomasville, North Carolina: "Being involved in label design and printing, I may be able to shed a little light on the issue. In the domestic market, the label is a key element in conveying an image and level of quality to the consumer. The simple answer is that the labels should stick under any conditions, from condensation on the bottle on the production line through an hour or so in an ice bucket at dinner. Technology has stepped up to the plate to meet this challenge.

"There are two basic types of label applications. The old conventional method is wet glue and is still widely used by both German and French producers and 40 to 50 percent of American wineries. In this process, glue is applied at the time the label is being put on the bottle. As you can imagine, wet glue being slopped around will leave a real mess to clean up. The newer technology rapidly gaining popularity here and in Australia is the use of pressure-sensitive papers for label production. Much like return address stickers, an adhesive is bonded to the back of the paper. The paper is then placed on a backing to keep it from sticking where you don't want it to. Labels are printed on this stock, cut to shape, and sent off to the winery. In application, the label is simply lifted off the backing and stuck to the bottle. The pressure-sensitive adhesives are generally more aggressive than the wet glue. The paper usually disintegrates in the ice bucket before the glue breaks down. This format offers many advantages in production, design, and durability. The upside to this technology is that it allows for much more freedom in design to meet the competitive demands of the market place. However, it does make the collector's life more challenging."

Who knew? Several readers offered far simpler and more colorful explanations, such as this one from Bob Kelley of Creve Coeur, Missouri: "Why are French and German labels easier to remove than American labels? I was told once that because the penchant in the U.S. is often to put wine bottles in coolers and tubs with ice and water, the labels are put on with non-water-soluble glue to prevent them from floating off in the water. The French and Germans would of course never think of dunking a wine—white, red, or rosé—in a tub of ice! Why are Australian wine labels also hard—maybe even harder—to remove? No idea—but maybe those frontiersmen are even worse than we when it comes to tossing the wine into a tub of ice. Pretty hot there in the outback, don't ya know, mate."

Anyway, the range of label-removal solutions offered to us was astonishing. Did they work? Hang on.

   ℭℯ " 'I use a substance called 'wallpaper remover.' I had a bottle of something that wasn't particularly good, but it had a really neat label. Soaking the bottle in water didn't work. As I was redoing the kitchen paper at the time and had some of this stuff, I gave it a shot. Worked like a charm on that one and on others since.' " Terry Allen, Saint Joseph, Michigan

   ℭℯ "Spray the label with WD-40, once usually, twice on tough ones." J.W. Kelly, Birmingham, Alabama

   ℭℯ "Simply boil about 2 cups of water and fill the empty wine bottle with the boiling water. The label will peel off easily within about ten seconds. Another method you can use is to apply direct heat on top of the labels using a cigarette lighter. As long as you keep moving the lighter constantly, it won't set the label on fire." Motoko Toba, San Jose, California

   ℭℯ "A regular hair dryer set on hot position loosens a label on an empty bottle in approximately ninety seconds, allowing the label to be peeled off, gingerly." Brooks Honeycutt, Cumberland, Maryland

   ℭℯ "Boil water in a long-spouted teakettle. As the steam escapes out the spout, hold the bottle over the steam. In a few minutes, the label will start to curl. You may have to steam the entire label, but usually just the edges (where the glue is applied). This has not failed yet for dozens of labels. For the record, my most difficult was a 1978 Lynch-Bages we drank to celebrate my niece's engagement to a Frenchman. Patience always pays off!" Tim Smith, Boeing Commercial Airplanes, Bonney Lake, Washington

℃ "Here is the method my husband and I swear by. Once we have amassed enough bottles (usually when I say there is no more room in the cellar–these bottles have to go!), we fill a rubber trash can with bottles and hot water. Then we dump in about a quart of ammonia. We leave this all to soak for a while–maybe even a day or so, depending upon our time schedule. Then we take each bottle and, using a scraper with a razor blade, we slip the labels off the bottles. This whole process can be done outside as well, as the sun will warm the water in the trash can. You just need to be careful as you reach into the bottom of the can that you keep from inhaling the ammonia fumes." Suzette Bois and John Schnell, South Portland, Maine

℃ "Fill a Tupperware or Rubbermaid container with about two cups water. Fill the bottle about two-thirds full of water. Place the bottle top side up in the container (it will sit in the container at a thirty-three-degree angle–the neck resting on the side of the container). Put this combo in the microwave on high for twenty seconds. Remove it immediately and slowly slide a razor blade or a window scraper that uses a razor blade under the label and glue. Work slowly and carefully and reheat the containers another twenty seconds if necessary . . . more again if necessary. I sometimes lay a damp cloth over the label while in the microwave." Fran Conn, Roswell, Georgia

℃ "I work in wine compliance and have to remove labels occasionally. As I have to remove the labels from sealed bottles without spoiling the wine with heat, I had to resort to regular lighter fluid and a razor blade. Placing the bottle on its side on paper towels, I soak the label well with the fluid and then work from one corner, slowly scraping under the label, moving back and forth for the length of the label. If the label thinks you are desperate, it will undoubtedly tear at a most inopportune moment. Additional lighter fluid poured along the inside edge as you're scraping helps, too. The label is then placed on waxed paper to dry out. This is not a good hobby for chain smokers." Nancy W. Miller, Compliance Officer, the Country Vintner, Inc., Oilville, Virginia

⊙ And finally, this, which arrived in our office anonymously: "Just put the bottle in a very low oven (150) for an hour or so. The glue softens so you can easily pull off the label. Works every time."

Filled to overflowing with a sense of experimentation and adventure, we spent a week trying out all of these suggestions that didn't sound too complicated or scary. (We skipped the heat gun and the lighter fluid, for instance.) We tried ammonia, the microwave, a hair dryer, and more. Here's the bad news: while most of them worked on the easy labels, the ones that would come off in the sink anyway, they did little for the stubborn labels. Oddly, only one method worked, and it was—cue the *Twilight Zone* music— the oven method, the only one that came to us anonymously. We put bottles in a warm oven for an hour, and we found that some labels—particularly the kind with strong glue and thick paper—would indeed peel right off.

So, all in all, we'll stick with our own old-fashioned method, which leaves some people downright perplexed. It is the twenty-first century after all, so we received tons of letters like this one, from Phil Beisel of San Jose, California: "I have a solution that worked brilliantly when I traveled throughout Italy last year: I simply used my digital camera to snap a photo of the bottle in question. A high-resolution camera will capture every detail. I also snapped a photo or two or three of my favorite dishes, but that's another story."

101 Things Worth Knowing | All in Twenty Words or Less

Y̶ou don't need to be an expert on wine before you can enjoy it. In any event, as far as we're concerned, the only way to really learn anything worth knowing about wine is to open a bottle and drink it. We also realize that one reason people avoid wine is that they're afraid they'll sound stupid. We hear all the time about people's angst concerning wine pronunciations, for instance. Relax. Even expert guides differ. But if you're worried, there are many excellent pronunciation guides on the Internet these days. In fact, at some sites, you can actually click on words and hear them spoken. Here are some good sites to check out:

> **wineloverspage.com/lexicon**
> **stratsplace.com/winepronon_dict.html**
> **louislatour.com (from the home page, go to "Terroirs," then "Sound Library")**
> **bbr.com (from the home page, go to "Wine Knowledge," then to "Wine School," and then to "Wine Pronunciation Guide")**

At the same time, you shouldn't feel it necessary to memorize the grand crus of Burgundy to speak knowledgeably about wine. Here are a hundred and one terms that you might want to know next time you're in the company of wine lovers. You'll probably look at these and say "Hmmm, I already know most of these." Ultimately, that's exactly our point. You know more about wine than you think you do. Ready? Here they are, each one in twenty words or less. By the way, if you want much more than this, a great reference book, presented in an easy-to-follow alphabetical format, is *The Oxford Companion to Wine,* by Jancis Robinson, but be forewarned that it's quite heavy—both literally and figuratively.

ACID. *In the right proportion, gives many wines balance and longevity. Wines without enough acids are often called* flabby *or* fat.

ALSACE. *French region bordering Germany best known for distinctive whites such as peppery Gewürztraminer.*

APPELLATION. *Where the grapes came from. Often, the more specific, the better.*

APPELLATION CONTRÔLÉE. *French system that sets rules for winemaking in geographic areas. A world standard, though some now argue it's too restrictive.*

AUSTRALIA. *After a decade-long surge, the second-biggest exporter of wines into the U.S. by volume after Italy.*

BEAUJOLAIS. *French region producing delightful red wine from Gamay grapes.*

BORDEAUX. *French region best known for classy reds made primarily from Cabernet Sauvignon and Merlot. Some fine whites, especially in Graves.*

BOTRYTIS CINEREA. *"Noble rot" fungus responsible for making some great dessert wines in Sauternes and elsewhere by shriveling grapes and concentrating juice.*

BURGUNDY. *French region best known for reds made from Pinot Noir and whites made from Chardonnay.*

CABERNET SAUVIGNON. *Red-wine grape responsible for famous Bordeaux wines and many California "cult wines."*

CALIFORNIA. *Produces 90 percent of wine made in U.S., 67 percent of wine drunk in U.S. Most important regions: Napa, Sonoma.*

CAVA. *Spanish sparkling wine.*

CHABLIS. *French region (part of Burgundy) making seafood-friendly wines from Chardonnay. Unfortunately, used in U.S. to mean cheap, generic white.*

CHAMPAGNE. *French region making the world's best sparkling wine from Pinot Noir, Pinot Meunier, and Chardonnay grapes.*

CHARDONNAY. *Great white grape of Burgundy. Number-one "varietal" wine in America.*

CHENIN BLANC. *Fine grape for dry and sweet wines. Classic example: Vouvray from France. Sometimes used to mean "cheap white" in U.S.*

CHIANTI. *Red wine from Tuscany in Italy, based on Sangiovese grape. Name used for cheap reds in U.S. for years.*

CHILE. *Up-and-coming wine exporter best known for value-priced Merlot and Cabernet Sauvignon.*

CLASSIFICATION OF 1855. *Famous ranking of Bordeaux wine by "growth"—based on quality, price, and politics—that's still important today.*

CONSTELLATION BRANDS. *World's biggest wine company (U.S. wine arm: Canandaigua). Among many brands: Almaden, Hardys, Alice White, Ravenswood, Simi, Paul Masson.*

CORKED. *Wine tainted by TCA, which contaminates corks, barrels, cellars. Wines smell moldy, like wet cardboard or a wet dog.*

CULT WINES. *Symbol of nineties bubble. Rare, excellent, very expensive, and generally red California wines more often bought and sold than drunk.*

CUVÉE. *A blend. Often used in reference to Champagne, where different lots of wine are combined for a consistent taste.*

DECANTING. *Pouring a wine into a decanter either to aerate it or to pour it off its sediment. We generally don't.*

DISGORGE. *Process in Champagne in which the sediment is popped out of the bottle before the final cork is inserted.*

DOCG (DENOMINAZIONE DI ORIGINE CONTROLLATA E GARANTITA). *Italian symbol of highest quality, though it can be hit-or-miss.*

DOM PÉRIGNON. *Monk important in early Champagne-making, though he didn't really "invent" Champagne. Also the name of a fine, expensive Champagne.*

DRY. *A wine with very little residual sugar.*

DUBOEUF, GEORGES. *French winemaker and brilliant marketer who did much to popularize Beaujolais Nouveau around the world.*

ESTATE BOTTLED. *In the U.S., a wine made from a winery's own vineyards.*

FINISH. *The lingering taste a wine leaves after you swallow it.*

FIRST GROWTH. *Top French Bordeaux wines as classified in 1855: Châteaux Lafite Rothschild, Latour, Margaux, Haut-Brion, Mouton Rothschild (elevated in 1973).*

FORTIFIED. *Wines, such as Port, with brandy or other spirits added.*

FUTURES. *Buying today—especially Bordeaux—for delivery when vintage is released, betting prices will rise and you'll look brilliant.*

FRENCH PARADOX. 60 Minutes *report on this (1991) hinted that red wine keeps French healthy. Led to surge in U.S. red-wine consumption.*

GAJA, ANGELO. *Great winemaker and trend setter in the Piedmont region of Italy.*

GALLO, E. & J. *World's second-biggest winemaker. Makes one of every four bottles sold domestically. Carlo Rossi, Rancho Zabaco, MacMurray among many labels.*

GEWÜRZTRAMINER. *Peppery white wine that's a specialty of the Alsace region of France.*

GOÛT DE TERROIR. *"Taste of the earth," the notion that grapes should pass on the natural aspects that are present where they're grown.*

GRAND CRU. *In France, generally means a top-notch wine. Elsewhere it can mean anything.*

ICE WINE (EISWEIN IN GERMANY). *Sweet wine made from frozen grapes. A specialty of Canada.*

ITALIANATE. *American wines made from traditionally Italian grapes, such as Sangiovese and Barbera. Big trend recently.*

ITALY. *Biggest source, by volume, of imported wine in America.*

KABINETT. *The lightest, and usually driest, fine German wine. Up the ladder of ripeness and usually sweetness: Spätlese, Auslese, Beerenauslese, Trockenbeerenauslese.*

LABRUSCA (OR VITIS LABRUSCA). *Not Lambrusco, the inexpensive Italian red, but the kind of vine that produces native American grapes, such as Concord.*

LATE HARVEST. *Grapes harvested late are generally more concentrated and sweeter. On a label, this usually indicates a sweet wine.*

LEGS. *Wine that drips down the inside of a glass. Means nothing. From interaction of alcohol, glycerol, and air.*

LOIRE. *French region best known for summery whites.*

LUXEMBOURG. *Biggest wine-drinking country per capita (15.6 gallons). U.S. is thirty-fourth (2.3 gallons).*

MAGNUM. *A 1.5-liter bottle that's twice as big as regular bottles. Bigger still: nebuchadnezzar, the equivalent of twenty regular bottles.*

MERITAGE. *Name for red and white blends in the U.S. made from classic Bordeaux varieties. Rhymes with* heritage.

MERLOT. *Bordeaux blending grape. First released as U.S. varietal in 1972 by Martini and Sterling. Top red varietal in America.*

MÉTHODE CHAMPENOISE. *The traditional, time-consuming method of making Champagne and, now, other sparkling wines, involving a second fermentation in the bottle.*

MONDAVI, ROBERT. *Visionary California winemaker greatly responsible for U.S. wine renaissance that started in late 1960s.*

MOSEL-SAAR-RUWER. *German area best known for flowery Rieslings.*

MUSCAT. *Honeylike grape grown all over the world to make slightly sweet to very sweet wines.*

NEBBIOLO. *Great grape of Barolo and Barbaresco in the Piedmont region of Italy.*

NEW ZEALAND. *Up-and-coming wine-producing country best known for its juicy Sauvignon Blancs. Most-talked-about winery: Cloudy Bay.*

NORTH DAKOTA. *Last state in the U.S. to have a commercial winery, which opened in 2002.*

NOSE. *How a wine smells. (Some use* aroma, *and some use* bouquet, *especially for older wines.)*

OAK. *Wood used in winemaking to add complexity and various flavors to wines often fermented and/or aged in oak barrels.*

OENOPHILE. *An expert on wine. Pronounced EN-o-file.*

OLD VINES (VIEILLES VIGNES). *Older vines produce fewer, often more concentrated, grapes, but this term on a label doesn't necessarily mean anything about quality.*

PARIS TASTING OF 1976. *In a head-to-head blind tasting, French judges preferred American wines, a turning point for U.S. wines.*

PARKER, ROBERT M., JR. *Publisher of* The Wine Advocate. *Most powerful wine critic in the world. His hundred-point scale widely replicated.*

PHYLLOXERA. *Plant louse that kills vines. Devastated French vineyards in the nineteenth century, hit California hard recently.*

PIEDMONT. *Italian region best known for lusty reds including Barolo and Barbaresco.*

PINOTAGE. *Spicy, unusual red wine of South Africa.*

PINOT GRIGIO. *Italian wine—same grape as Pinot Gris—that became the most popular imported wine in the U.S. in 2002.*

PINOT GRIS. *Specialty of Oregon and a trend in California. Though the same grape, often fuller than American wines called Pinot Grigio.*

PINOT NOIR. *Great red grape of Burgundy. Experts used to believe incorrectly that the U.S. couldn't make fine Pinot. Specialty of Oregon.*

PORT (OR PORTO). *Fortified wine from Portugal. Often incorrectly used to mean a fortified wine from elsewhere.*

PUNT. *Indentation in the base of a bottle, especially in Champagne, helps stabilize the bottle and shore up glass where vulnerable.*

QUALITATSWEIN MIT PRÄDIKAT. *Symbol of high quality on a German label.*

RACY. *Term often used by experts to indicate a wine with zingy acidity.*

RESERVE. *In some countries, indicates high quality and/or longer-aged wine. In U.S., it can mean that or nothing.*

RHEINGAU. *German region best known for Riesling wines.*

RHÔNE. *French region best known for its earthy reds. Most notable grape is Syrah.*

RIEDEL. *Stemware company that popularized the idea that there is a perfect glass for every wine. Rhymes with needle.*

RIESLING. *Great white-wine grape at its best in Germany. Also good in northern states such as New York and Washington.*

RIOJA. *Spanish district best known for woody red wine.*

SANGIOVESE. *Great grape of Chianti.*

SAUVIGNON BLANC. *White grape that makes grassy dry wines all over the world. Also used in dessert wines. Sometimes called Fumé Blanc.*

SAUTERNES. *Great dessert wine from Bordeaux. Most famous and best: Château d'Yquem.*

SEDIMENT. *Naturally occurring muddy stuff in the bottom of some bottles, especially old ones. It's harmless.*

SHIRAZ. *Australia's signature red-wine grape. Same as Syrah.*

STAINLESS STEEL. *Notation* all stainless steel *means wines were made in temperature-controlled steel tanks and meant to be fresh, fruity, aromatic.*

SULFITES. *Naturally occurring substance also added to preserve and stabilize wines. Present in virtually all wines. Often incorrectly blamed for headaches.*

SUR LIE. *Allowing a white wine to sit on its dead yeast for a while, often giving it extra complexity and mouthfeel.*

SWEET. *Not just a wine with residual sugar, but a taste that can be caused by lush fruit or even alcohol.*

TANNINS. *Naturally occurring substances that give red wines their backbone and often their longevity. Sometimes cause mouth to pucker.*

TERROIR. *The total environment in which grapes grow—the soil, the climate, etc.*

TURLEY, HELEN. *Great American winemaker responsible for many cult wines.*

TUSCANY. *Region of Italy best known for Chianti and Brunello di Montalcino.*

TWO-BUCK CHUCK. *Charles Shaw wine, a $1.99 Trader Joe's exclusive, was a 2003 sensation that dramatized wine glut, attracted new wine drinkers.*

UNFILTERED. *Wine that hasn't been rendered clear by filtering, which some believe strips wine of richness and character.*

VARIETAL. *Wine named for grape type. U.S. requires Chardonnay, for instance, to be made from at least 75 percent Chardonnay grapes.*

VINIFERA (OR *VITIS VINIFERA*). *Species of vine that produces classic European wine grapes such as Cabernet Sauvignon and most of the wines produced today.*

VINTAGE. *Year grapes were harvested. In U.S., 95 percent of wine must be from that year's grapes to be labeled that.*

YEAST. *Naturally occurring substance that creates fermentation in grape juice to make wine. Sometimes a commercial form is used.*

ZINFANDEL. *U.S. red grape (originally from Croatia). White Zinfandel, colored from the juice's brief contact with skins, outsells red seven-one.*

Acknowledgments

We love our jobs. That might seem obvious—we get paid for drinking wine, after all—but the real reason isn't so obvious. We love our jobs because, through them, we have met thousands of people who have enriched our lives. Readers often tell us how much our writing has meant to them; they don't realize we are the ones in debt to them, for their support, ideas, and good cheer. We are grateful to every one of the readers quoted in this book, and they are only representative of thousands of others who continually inform our writing.

Because of our jobs, we've also had an opportunity to meet some people professionally who have made a huge difference to us in so many ways. Harriet Bell, for instance. Harriet is a great editor. We met her when she edited our first book, *The Wall Street Journal Guide to Wine*. We came to trust her judgment and admire her quiet determination and remarkable wisdom. We were so pleased to be able to work with her again.

Amanda Urban, our agent at ICM, has become far more—a friend, a mentor, and a tough yet fair critic of our work. She's one of those rare, acutely wise people who makes your brain expand. We feel privileged to know Binky and very lucky to be one of "her" people.

None of this would be possible without Paul Steiger, the managing editor of the *Wall Street Journal* and the world's greatest boss. Paul is smart, kind, and a man of vision, and, hey, how many people, especially journalists, would say that about their boss? We are fortunate to have become friends of Paul and his wife, Wendy Brandes. We also owe so very much to Joanne Lipman, a friend and the creator of *Weekend Journal*. In 1998, she asked us to write a wine column for the new section, and then she beat us up until we got it right.

At the upper reaches of Dow Jones, which publishes the *Wall Street Journal,* we have received quiet, behind-the-scenes encouragement for years from a number of people, including Peter Kann, Karen House, Dick Tofel, and Gordon Crovitz. They will never know how much their support has meant to us. We also are indebted to Steve Adler, Walt Mossberg, Jim Stewart, Norm Pearlstine, and John Postley for a constant stream of good advice and kind words when we needed them.

We owe a big debt to Shallé McDonald-Bosman, our researcher on this book, who has the most amazing way of finding people and facts. Our assistant at work, Lyneka Little, helps us in a million ways. She has a very unusual—and often stressful—job, but she always keeps her smile.

Our families—Grandma Dot, Juarlyn, Karen and David, Jim and Judy, Kris and Beth—have always been very important to us, even if we don't call as often as we should. At home, our kids' longtime caregiver, Louise Williams, is an indispensable part of our lives.

It's very special for a married couple to be able to work together, but it can be hard on the children. Mommy and Daddy leave for work together, travel together, and talk endlessly about work—in our case, wine—together. If it seems to us that we're always working, imagine how it seems to our daughters. Fortunately, Media and Zoë deal with this with unnatural patience. They are the most wonderful people we know.

Index